MOST DANGEROUS MAN

A Personal Memoir

Emanuel Fried

"This is the hand that shook the hand
of the most dangerous man in
Western New York—Manny Fried."

Published by John Brown Press
P. O. Box 5224
Kansas City, Kansas 66119
Copyright 2010 Emanuel Fried

ISBN 978-0-9841937-0-7

A Few Notes by Manny

A Jesuit priest from Canisius College—for which school some years earlier I'd played quarterback on the freshman football team—raised his hand high above his head as he stridently addressed a St. Joseph's breakfast meeting of post office employees: "This is the hand that shook the hand of the most dangerous man in Western New York—Manny Fried."

*****

Buffalo Evening News Labor Reporter Ed Kelly deliberately warned me that the FBI had labeled me "the symbol of the Left who must be broken."

*****

The attorney for the Buffalo Sabres hockey team—he and his wife at the time were close friends of my wife and me—personally delivered to me and my wife the message that he said the FBI had asked him to give me: "You must publicly repudiate your Communist union and your Communist politics or you will end up in jail."

*****

The wife of a highly respected judge, who many years earlier had been the secretary that typed up the FBI agents' reports about me—now she was the mother of the set designer for a Chekhov play production in which I was acting—met with me in a tea room and told me that FBI Director J. Edgar Hoover had sent a team of FBI agents to Buffalo "to get me." She said they trailed me round the clock, opened my mail and bugged my phone. They then sought to have a federal grand jury indict me—arranging for the Steelworkers Union Regional Director, publicly a strong opponent of mine, to be named foreman of the grand jury. He secretly sent word to me not to worry, that while he differed with me inside the labor movement he was not going to help to send me to jail—he squashed the FBI effort to have the grand jury indict me—and we quietly became longtime friends.

Part One

"I want to be a star—of stage and screen!"

Chapter 1

I'm going to start you off on your movie career," Gadge said. "There's a good part for you in this film."

The movie was *Boomerang*, and the director proposing to re-start my acting career was Elia Kazan who had directed me some years earlier when I played the lead role in the Theatre of Action's production of *The Young Go First*. Gadge, as we called him then, had been one of several members of the Group Theatre who had "adopted" us in the younger and more radical Theatre of Action troupe and for several years conducted classes in acting for us.

It was November, 1946. The day before I met Gadge, I had been separated from active service in the army, at Fort Dix in New Jersey. A first lieutenant, I was still in uniform. My civilian clothes were back home in Buffalo, New York.

After the Japanese surrendered in 1945 I had been sent to Korea, assigned to headquarters of the 20th Infantry Regiment in Kwangju, where our immediate job was to move all Japanese soldiers and civilians back to their own country. For a short while I served as Public Relations Officer (PRO), a position I had requested because of my interest in developing as a writer. My immediate assignment was to write feature articles about soldiers in our outfit, to be printed in their hometown newspapers. Before being sent to Korea, I had been an instructor teaching use of weapons to infantry recruits at an army post in Macon, Georgia.

From the time I volunteered in April, 1944, to join the army to fight against the Nazis, my history of previous membership in the Communist Party and my employment since 1941 as a union organizer with the United Electrical, Radio & Machine Workers of America, generally known as the UE, had followed me to every post to which I had been assigned. I assume the commanding general in Korea finally got that information, which resulted in my being transferred out of the PRO job at regimental headquarters to head an infantry platoon with the regiment's Second Battalion in Pusan.

Depressed, I wrote a long letter to Kazan, unburdening my feelings, telling him how, by an unplanned set of circumstances—the candle in the wind—my life had shifted from being an actor in New York City to being a union organizer in western New York.

Gadge's wife, Molly Day Thatcher, who had treated me kindly when I was a young aspiring actor, responded to my letter, telling me that Gadge wanted me to get in touch with him as soon as I was discharged from army service. When I made the phone call to Gadge's home, Molly answered the phone, told me Gadge was waiting to hear from me and wanted me to come right away to see him on location in a town just north of the City, where he was shooting the *Boomerang* film.

Gadge introduced me to the screenwriter who agreed I could perform the role of the priest in the film. I told them I had a wife and child back in Buffalo whom I hadn't seen in over a year and before I did anything else I wanted to see them. Gadge told me to go, that it would be at least another week before they got to my scenes with Arthur Kennedy—he was playing the lead role—but I must get back by then.

Rhoda and our four-year old daughter Lorrie had been living with me off the post in Macon, Georgia. When I was shipped off to Korea they went back to Buffalo and moved in with Rhoda's parents in The Park Lane. We were still holding onto our apartment in The Gates Circle, an apartment house next door to The Park Lane. Rhoda's family, the Luries, owned The Park Lane, Buffalo's most prestigious apartment house, with its exclusive restaurant and cocktail lounge, the "saloon" where the city's rich and famous, its socialites, and its huckstering nouveau riche climbers, politicians, city officials, "respectable" union leaders, and well-heeled movers and shakers drank, dined, danced and used the place to meet across class and political divisions and make deals.

When Rhoda died of a stroke at age 71 in 1989 we had been married forty-eight years and along the way had intermittently agreed that with our very different backgrounds we never should have married. My friend George Poole—while we were still like brothers and before his experience with Russian soldiers while he was with the army in Europe led him to change his political affiliation and join the forces trying to drive me out of the labor movement—had warned me immediately after Rhoda and I got married in The Park Lane in 1941 that the marriage couldn't work.

"The Park Lane and the UE," he insisted, "can't sleep in the same bed."

"But we are," I said, "we are."

Rhoda and I first met when I returned home from New York City in 1939 to direct the Buffalo Contemporary Theatre, a worker-oriented theatre company that had advertised for a director through the left-wing New Theatre League.

Out of curiosity, Rhoda had let her manic-depressive (now termed bi-polar) sister Ruth, who was in a "high state," persuade her to come to our first performance. That was the candle in the wind, again, which unpredictably and drastically changed the lives of both of us.

When I told Rhoda about Kazan's offer to re-start my acting career by casting me in *Boomerang*, she was not impressed. Rhoda had the sultry kind of sexy face that had photographers repeatedly asking her to pose for photos for magazines like Vogue. She considered herself far above that. Continually sought after because of her connection to The Park Lane—her envious detractors calling her Miss Park Lane—she didn't need getting her picture on the cover of a fashionable magazine to make her feel superior and important. (The publicity I would get following the subpoena to appear before the House Committee on Un-American Activities would brutally haul her down off that height.)

Rhoda's interest was painting. She had her studio in a small room in the rear of The Park Lane, one of several small rooms usually occupied by tenants' live-in maids. She credited marrying me with changing her from what she called "a Sunday painter" to an artist who painted every day from early morning to three o'clock in the afternoon—when, if I was around, she would ignore my disapproving but tolerant look and reward her hard work of the day by literally running to get her previously prepared martinis out of the freezer, urging me to join her, which I usually did for the first drink.

"You can go move back to New York or go to Hollywood," she said. "But Lorrie and I are not going to move. We're staying here."

The next day I went to visit Charlie Cooper in the hospital to tell him about Kazan re-starting my acting career. I thought I owed that to "the old man," as many of us in the union fondly called him. Charlie had stuck his neck out to help me organize thousands of workers in the factories in Tonawanda and North Tonawanda, two small industrial cities bridging the Erie Canal, a few miles north of Buffalo.

Charlie was one of those old-time union guys who asked nothing for themselves, having refused to take a paid staff job with the union. Working in the Remington Rand plant in Tonawanda, he had led several successful strikes against notorious union buster Jim Rand —at that time the sole self-made owner of Remington Rand—whose home was in North Tonawanda and who publicly exulted about how he loved to fight his scrappy Tonawanda employees, actually taking a perverse pride in his neighbors being tough enough to be worthy opponents to fight with. He fired Charlie for trying to organize a union.

Charlie's case had gone all the way up to the U.S. Supreme court, which upheld the Wagner Act establishing the right of workers to organize, resulting in Charlie being reinstated to his job with back pay—and Charlie becoming the beloved hero of labor in the area.

Charlie had lost a leg while he had been a young sailor with the merchant marine. In the hospital now, surgeons had sliced off another piece of that leg, way up into his thigh.

Now in his late fifties and president of the local union representing Remington Rand workers in the Tonawanda and North Tonawanda plants, he continued to work in the machine shop and refused to take any pay for performing his union position.

He had been like a father to me when I started the union organizer job. I had never negotiated a contract, handled an arbitration or taken full charge of a union organizing campaign. I told this to Charlie and he told me not to worry. With his help we organized thousands of Tonawanda and Buffalo factory workers into local unions affiliated with our UE union, and I learned from him how to conduct strikes, negotiate contracts, handle labor-management arbitrations and argue on behalf of workers with on-the-job grievances.

"When you coming back to work, you redhead?" Charlie finally got around to ask me, with a gesture that wanted to know when I was discarding the soldier's uniform I was still wearing.

"Charlie," I began, and stopped, not knowing how to tell him. I began again. "Charlie, it's all an accident. I'm an actor, not a union organizer."

We talked a long while. I told him about Kazan's offer to re-start my acting career, how much I loved my life in the theatre, quickly adding that I also loved the union work and especially the people I was working with—but that it had had always been my ambition to be a great actor—and here's my chance. His hand gripped my arm, he wouldn't let go as he kept interrupting me with almost a teary desperation.

"Don't you abandon us, you redheaded son-of-a-bitch!—Don't you abandon us!"

He kept saying it, that same phrase, over and over, interjecting it between my emotional efforts to explain and justify, all the while he was squeezing my arm, making me feel guilty as all hell about thinking of myself and not concerned enough about all the men and women who'd stuck their necks out to support me in tough organizing campaigns and strikes we'd gone through— developing that kind of closeness like army veterans who've risked their lives together in fierce combat.

"Don't you abandon us!"

When I left him, my face tense and tight, I had promised him that whatever I decided I wouldn't just go off without coming back to talk to him.

"Don't you abandon us!" That was the last thing he ever said to me. He died that night. A blood clot broke loose and stopped his heart.

I stayed with the union, never called Kazan, and since I hadn't given Kazan my address or phone number, he couldn't call me even if he wanted to. Karl Malden got the part I was supposed to play in *Boomerang*, and with Kazan's help he went on to play important roles in *On The Waterfront* and a zillion other films, becoming a big movie star in Hollywood.

A few years ago I was visiting my younger daughter Mindy who was then 52 years old, in Boston, and we talked about the choice I made back in 1946. She wanted to know if I ever regretted it.

"No. I've thought about it, what might have happened if I'd become a Hollywood star. But I've had an unusually complex and exciting life, the kind of life I would never have had if I'd gone the other way."

"And you never would have had me," she reminded me, assuming that that choice would have ended the marriage before Rhoda was pregnant with her.

"True," I said. "That's true."

We both laughed in a warm kind of way at that thought and agreed that if it were even only that, it validated the choice I'd made. But then we spoke about the certainty that because of my previous association with the Communist Party back then I would have been called before the Committee on Un-American Activities, as Kazan was summoned before the committee about ten years after we talked about him giving me a role in *Boomerang*. And Kazan named names of theatre people he'd worked with who had been members of the Communist Party with him, condemning them to be blacklisted, ruining their careers. Would I have done that? Mindy didn't think so, citing my refusal to answer any questions when I, a union organizer, was called before the committee about the same time as Kazan and I sought to be indicted for contempt of Congress so the courts would have to decide whether the enabling resolution establishing the committee was unconstitutional, putting them out of business, or I would go to jail.

"But who knows what kind of person I might have become," I said to her, "if—when I was called before the committee—I had accepted the role of the priest in *Boomerang* and with Kazan's help was climbing up the ladder to be a movie star in Hollywood?"

Chapter 2

That conversation with Mindy prompted me to think about Robert Frost's poem with its "fork in the road" and the choice which "made all the difference" —and to think about what made me the person I became by the time I confronted that "fork in the road" and led to my making the choice that had "made all the difference."

If I recall correctly, it was *Moby Dick* author Herman Melville who wrote that the course of one's life is determined by heredity and environment—and the candle in the wind.

At age 95, looking back, I'd like to search out to what extent, despite heredity and environment, my life was determined by "the candle in the wind," and I'd like to dig out, relentlessly and honestly—and no matter what the cost to my ego—what were my true motivations beneath the surface of what I've done with my life. It must seem silly, even stupid, to younger people, but at my advanced age I need to find out why I have become who I am—*and who am I now?*—in order to decide what to try to do with the rest of my life.

I was 43 years old when I was forced out of my job as a union organizer and blacklisted. Both Lorrie and Mindy were unexpectedly and unfairly cut out of their professional jobs at a similar age. That I was able to withstand tremendous pressure and deal with the difficult situation that confronted me must have come from what I unconsciously imbibed from my parents by something akin to a process of osmosis. And I like to think that what I got from them, enabling me to bounce back and work my way through extremely difficult life-destroying situations, has been similarly imbibed by Lorrie and Mindy, enabling them to bounce back and work their way through several extremely difficult life-destroying situations they experienced as adults.

It's hard to believe that my mother was only 13 years old when she came over alone to this country from her home in what was then the Austria-Hungarian Empire. The village where she was born is today part of Slovakia. In New York

City she went to work for an uncle, operating a sewing machine in a sweatshop. She said he was good to her. When she complained that sewing under the bad lighting made her eyes hurt, her uncle had a gas light placed closer to her sewing machine. At age 17 she returned to the village in Europe to bring back her parents who were too fearful to try to make the trip to America by themselves.

My father was born in a village not far from where my mother was born. When his parents came to America they took along all their children except my father, leaving the young boy to keep his grandmother company. His grandmother placed him with some rabbinical scholar to study, where—he told us—his meals consisted of a roll and water. When his grandmother was on her deathbed she arranged for some family to bring my father over here to join his own family. Since some years had passed since seeing his mother and father and his brother and sister, he felt like a stranger with them.

My father never said it, but I don't think his family life could have been very happy. His father was a peddler, carrying a pack on his back, going out into the country to sell goods to farmers. An orthodox Jew, his physical appearance and clothes must have invited some hurtful insults. The story handed down is that he returned home one day, climbed into bed and never left the house again.

That was one of my grandfathers. I don't remember ever meeting him or his wife, my grandmother on that side. They might have died before I was born. I do remember, vaguely but with warmth, my grandfather who was my mother's father. His job was delivering milk. He was a giant of a man with a long beard, who smoked a long stem pipe. I remember that he took me to a service in a synagogue located in a small room, lifting me, a small child, to stand on top of the altar. And I remember him sitting on the top step in the back hall next to the open door to the kitchen, scraping horseradish for my mother. I don't remember his wife, that grandmother. She may have also died before I was born.

The story we were told is that my mother was supposed to marry a man who had been selected for her, an arranged marriage. Instead she married my father. Sounds romantic. But neither my mother nor my father would tell us more about it.

I believe it was my parents' great courage facing hardship that rubbed off on me and enabled me many years later to deal with the difficulty of being cut off in my early 40s from the job I'd held from 1941 to 1956 as a union organizer— leaving me blacklisted, with FBI agents visiting a series of U.S. employers who hired me, telling each one that I'm a dangerous communist, getting each one to fire me. (I finally got a job with a Canadian insurance company whose international corporate vice-president met with me and told me he was refusing the FBI effort to get him to fire me.)

My mother and father worked very hard, finally developing their own successful business, manufacturing children's dresses. My mother told us how she would walk down Fifth Avenue and sketch out patterns based on what she saw in windows of the finest stores. My father did the cutting of the dress material back at the factory. Employees did the sewing. According to my father, he was the first manufacturer to introduce the idea of sizes for children's dresses.

They were doing very well financially. We had servants in our house. Then came the disaster. The dress factory burned down. Here it's as if what happened was the basis for the very successful Hollywood movie, Barry Levinson's *Avalon*, which was made not too long ago. My parents' insurance agent was a relative. Instead of turning the premiums over to the insurance company, he had pocketed the money. When the factory, with all its contents, was destroyed by the fire, my parents' dreams were also destroyed. My father had to declare bankruptcy.

For many years following that disaster my father had to go out on the road as a salesman, traveling across the country for Butler Brothers Dry Goods. I can imagine how difficult that must have been for him, a strict orthodox Jew. During those years he was home only a few months each year. All the while he worked for Butler Brothers I distinctly remember that we used their catalogues for toilet paper.

Shortly after he started working for Butler Brothers we moved to Buffalo, a part of my father's territory. He and my mother had decided it would be a good place to raise their children and also establish their own business. That must have been a tough move for my mother, with nine children. I was five years old then and have only a misty recollection of that 1918 train ride from Manhattan to Buffalo where my father was waiting to meet us. The older children helped take care of the younger ones. Gerry, the baby, was only a few months old. The oldest, Sam, was fifteen.

My parents' plan was for my father to continue as a salesman on the road while my mother would open and tend the dry goods store. The goods for the store would be bought from the Butler Brothers salesman, my father.

Our first night in Buffalo we moved into a house on Division Street—South or North Division—that had been rented by my father. Our new home was an old wood frame structure. Quite small. It must have been a very difficult comedown for my parents. Until our furniture arrived we slept on piles of Oshkosh overalls. I can still recall the distinctive smell of those new denim garments. Years later I would joke that I never knew I grew up in a slum until long after I was out of it.

The store was opened on Genesee Street near Mortimer Street. (I now drive past there on the Route 33 expressway almost every day.) We moved there, living in rooms behind and above the store. For years my parents, being observant orthodox Jews, closed their store on Saturdays. A few years later my father bought a building on Genesee Street near Pratt Street. The dry goods store was in front on the first floor. The family kitchen was in the rear of the store and the bedrooms were upstairs on the second floor. My mother still ran the store with help from my older brothers and sisters.

My father stayed out on the road, selling for Butler Brothers, until finally he decided to stay home and take command. At that time I deeply resented him, wishing he'd stayed out on the road. I don't think I was alone in that respect. And he may have sensed this. I can recall how again and again he would berate us children—and our mother—angrily proclaiming, "I am boss in this house!" Since I—and one brother and one sister—had red hair, and neither he nor my mother had red hair, I often wished when I was a young boy that he wasn't my father.

Each of the children, as we grew old enough, put in our time working in the store. I hated it, and while still in my early teens swore I would never trap myself into permanently living that kind of life, dependent upon some customer buying a piece of goods about which I didn't really give a damn—except for the need to make a sale. If I didn't achieve the sale I would be nagged for days by my father about what I had done wrong. Only much later, thinking back, did I realize that for him each sale, no matter how small, meant the difference between having or not having enough to feed our large family.

During the Big Depression of the early '30s food was short in our house and I remember how after we had eaten what was our evening meal my father would say to us nine growing children: "If you're still hungry here's bread. Fill up on bread."

I don't think my father had received much love from his parents, which may explain why he apparently didn't know how to convey love to his children. I knew that my mother loved me and the rest of my brothers and sisters. I just felt it. But there wasn't much time or energy left for her to pay special attention to us. She worked from early morning till late at night, working in the store and also taking care of us children in all the necessary ways, including cooking and sewing—with some help from us children, especially the older ones. Thinking back, except for one short memory of my father holding me above the crib while I was still a baby and softly singing to me, I cannot remember my father or my mother ever kissing me while I was growing up. I was the seventh child, quickly replaced as the baby by Joel and then Gerry.

My father—before he got into the dress manufacturing business—had worked in a cigar making factory, where he became a follower of Daniel DeLeon, head of the Socialist Labor Party. Even after he became a dress manufacturer he still called himself a socialist and referred to our family as a socialist family, which in my youth meant nothing to me except that we were on the side of labor, and it was never more clearly defined than that.

The only positive thing my father seemed to retain from his cigar making trade was the ability to take a mouthful of wine and spray it over cheap cigars, making them "expensive cigars." He took great delight in showing us how he could do that with a whole box of cigars.

He was a strange kind of socialist because I remember him reading in the newspaper about some factory workers being out on strike, saying, "They should shoot them." Yet when I was subpoenaed to appear before the House Committee on UnAmerican Activities in 1954 he told me, "Tell those *momserim* to go to hell," (*Momserim:* Yiddish for bastards.) And when my mother, distraught because of redbaiting attacks leveled against me in the newspapers (accusing me of being a subversive trying to overthrow the government) burst out, "How would you like to have a son who's a traitor?"—my father defended me, saying, "He's a good boy, he's doing right." Boy? I was 41 years old, with a wife and two children. Traitor! Coming from her, that hurt. I've never forgotten that and it still hurts. Yet, even when my mother said that, I knew she still loved me. Her face creased with held-in emotion, she followed up, to my father, "I know he's a good boy and I worry what will happen to my boy."

My father was well into his 80s when—after he had been beaten badly twice by young thieves—several of us, his sons, combined finances to trick him into giving up the store by subsidizing a buyer to meet the high price he insisted upon getting for all the unsold goods he had there.

After he retired I dropped by to see him and my mother in their flat in North Buffalo every day on my way home late in the afternoon, and my father would pour a *schnappsel* for each of us, and my mother would bring out a plate loaded with chunks of sponge cake. My father insisted that only barbarians drank whiskey without the accompaniment of a piece of cake. And it was in the midst of one of these warm moments between us that he spat in my face when I defended the right of one of his grandchildren, my youngest brother Gerry's daughter, to marry a young man who wasn't Jewish. I wiped my face, stood up and left the house without saying a word, hearing my mother angrily berate my father for what he'd done. It was weeks before I dropped in again to see them— and my father quickly served me a *schnappsel*, his way of apologizing. Not long after that I heard him ask his granddaughter, now married to that young man, "When are you going to bring your husband so I can meet him?"

Now at my age of 95, I drive by that old brick building where we once lived behind and above the store. It's the only structure left on that block, part of the ghetto inhabited by poor black people. It's unoccupied and in complete disrepair in an area that looks like it's been hit by a bomb. I recall how my father and mother and the seven boys and two girls in our family, plus my widowed aunt and her two daughters, lived in this small two-story brick building, in the little room back of the store and several small rooms above the store, in total space less than I occupy now in my house where I live alone.

Balanced against some negative feelings about my father that I still seem to have difficulty forgetting, I believe now that back then I got from him—and yes, from my mother—the stubborn ability to pick myself up and go on after I was hit with economic disaster in my early 40s. I recall how at that time of my blacklisting I again and again reminded myself about hearing my father talk about his economic setbacks, including the burning down of his uninsured dress factory and several bankruptcies in connection with the Buffalo store, saying very simply, "I fall down, I pick myself up, and I go on."

My father had his own way to express his feelings for us. Once he brought home a bushel—actually a bushel—of books he'd bought in a second-hand store. He plopped the bushel of books down on the floor in front of us kids and said, "Here, books. Read." He didn't seem to know any other way to show affection.

I try to understand why he was such a terrible nagger. It was hard to do anything that would draw his approval. The hard life he had led probably caused him to push us all too hard. If I brought home a report card with a grade of 99 he'd loudly berate me, "If you got 99 you could have gotten 100 if you tried harder." When his children were all grown—all nine of us—and well established in whatever work we had ended up doing, I remember him angrily chastening a group of us, "You're all failures because none of you listened to me." By then we were apparently secure enough that our reaction to that, I recall, was that we all laughed.

But when I was cut out of my job as a labor leader in 1956, blacklisted, with no idea on what to fall back on to make a living for my family, I believe it was the remembrance of the courage and strength my father—and yes, my mother— evidenced in dealing with their tough situations that helped me pick myself up and go on. And I believe it was that conduct—theirs and mine—that years later helped my daughters Lorrie and Mindy quickly pick themselves up and go on when they, separately, got hit with devastating economic blows.

Chapter 3

I was 28 years old in 1941 when, a member of the Communist Party, I was asked to become a union organizer. I was newly married, about to become a father, and—by order of the Army Air Force colonel at the Curtiss Wright Aircraft plant—had been removed as "a subversive" from my job, a template maker in the mold loft department, just after I had completed laying out on sheet metal the master template for the entire instrument panel for the C-47 aircraft. Prior to that, my desperate aim in life was to become a successful writer. A Broadway playwright. And an actor. A star on Broadway. A star in Hollywood.

I had not yet chosen that as my goal when, a redheaded urchin maybe 8 or 9 years old, I ignored my father's objections and started my work history by hawking newspapers on a street corner. "Hey, get your pee-po-paper here." I vaguely remember the cold rainy day when, as it was getting dark, a man confronted me and gruffly asked how many papers I had left. Apprehensive, not knowing what this total stranger wanted from me, I counted the newspapers and told him how many I had. He took all my papers, slipped me several dollar bills, and gruffly said, "Go home, kid." It was a kindness I've never forgotten.

When I was 10 or 11, I stood on the curb in front of the entrance to the zoo in Buffalo's Delaware Park, selling balloons for a partially crippled boss, in his late twenties, who mercilessly exploited kids like myself, paying us pennies for working in the hot sun all day on Sundays during the summer months.

I was about 12 when I graduated to selling candy bars in the baseball park and advanced from that to selling hot dogs—"They're hot, they're red hot!"—for old man Jacobs, the Jewish grandfather and great-grandfather of the present Jacobs family members who developed his concessions business in one ball park into ownership of stadiums and racetracks and all kinds of concessions in cities all across the country and around the world. Now apparently wealthy and part of Western New York's upper crust, I've been told they presently are members of the Christian faith.

My brother Dave was 16 years old—and I was 14—when he got a job to stand in front of what was then the Ford Hotel on Delaware Avenue near Chippewa Street, directing tourists to park their cars overnight in the Huron Garage several blocks away. Dave worked there one week, hated the job, said he was quitting—so I took his official chauffeur cap and told the people at the garage I was taking my brother's place. They accepted that, asking no questions about my age. The job required working late seven nights a week. The pay was tips I got from tourists.

I liked the job. It got me out of the house that I found to be very depressing during the evening. I'm still not sure what produced that feeling, but I do remember thinking I would always want a job that required me to work evenings. Though I'm reluctant to blame it on my father's nagging—because I believe he meant well—there always seemed to be an underlying tension between him and my mother that may have stemmed from worries about not enough money. Dad was a sucker for salesmen. Since he had lived that hard life he insisted on buying some goods from every salesman who pitched his wares. I can hear Mother again and again accusing him, "Why? We don't need it!"

The job in front of the hotel introduced me to a world different from that I had known, and in retrospect I can see that it was the beginning of my separation from the boys I'd grown up with—children of lower middle class retail trades people whose parents hoped they would become doctors, lawyers or dentists—or if not that, then teachers or pharmacists—or if not that, then post-office workers or civil service employees. Working in front of the hotel I got to know the prostitutes who worked the area and also learned for the first time about homosexuals, who occasionally caused mayhem with wild parties they held in the hotel.

I remember standing in the open doorway of the apartment of two of the prostitutes, catching a brief exchange between them about the good time they had had at the beach.

This led to the first play I wrote, at age 15—about a young man who worked in front of a hotel directing tourists to the garage—he's in the apartment of two prostitutes, listening to them talk about having fun at the beach, realizing that "whores" are human beings just like other people. Seeking to be encouraged as a writer, I sent my only copy of the play to one of my older brothers, Marty. Recognized proudly by our whole family as our intellectual academic, he was studying for his Ph.D. in English Literature at Harvard.

"I've torn up your play," he wrote me. "It's bad enough you're a pimp without letting the whole world know."

I had never thought of it that way, but at that young age I suppose I was technically a pimp. One of the prostitutes had given me business cards to give to anyone at the hotel who asked for their services. For each man I sent them I was given one dollar. That's why I was in their apartment, to collect my "finder's fee."

I had expected praise from my brother. Encouragement. I think now that what I felt after reading his letter was betrayal. Betrayed by the brother I thought would help me find my way as a writer. And there was no one with whom I could share how I felt.

I don't want to leave what Marty did then without talking more about our relationship. Marty got his education the hard way. He did get a small amount— $100, I think—from some kind of scholarship when he graduated high school. He attended State Teachers College, which later became Buffalo State College, where he subsequently ended up teaching in the English department.

Marty worked nights and weekends at the post office to finance the rest of his university education. He selected Mark Twain to be the object of his research and writing, and was on his way to be recognized nationally for his writing on that subject when this was aborted because he was my brother. A student of his, a reporter for the Buffalo News, told him confidentially that—apparently because of my activity as an organizer for a union accused of being communist-dominated—his editor had declared that Marty and I from then on were to be treated as non-persons, never to be named in the newspaper. This was a case of Marty—a cautious liberal and in no way a left-winger—being found guilty by association with his younger brother, me.

For many years I think Marty, with his fine academic credentials, considered himself the writer in our family and saw me, who did not achieve a college education until I was approaching 60, as some kind of vulgar pretender. When he saw the opening production of my play *The Dead Hand*, winner of a Buffalo Junior Chamber of Commerce sponsored play contest, he dismissively remarked to our youngest brother Gerry, "It's only dialogue."

At one point, after my play *The Dodo Bird* was produced in New York City in 1967, he conceded that I was a writer, but said to me, "The difference between us is this. If we both were going to write about a pig pen, I'd research everything written about a pig pen. You'd go roll around in one." He did not intend it as a compliment.

But in 1972, despite my being already 59 years old, Marty successfully used every bit of the political muscle he had developed at Buffalo State College— and he had a great deal as the senior professor in the English department and as a close friend of the college president—to get me off the blacklist, hired to teach Creative Writing there.

And then came a devastating punch in our relationship, which I can see unfolding with my mind's eye. A few years after Marty had retired, the Buffalo

21

State College Alumni Association announced he would be honored at a special dinner. Marty invited his brothers and sisters, along with their families, to join his family—his wife and children—for the dinner and award ceremony. After we had all eaten, the master of ceremonies called Marty to the front of the room and shook his hand.

"Martin," he began, adopting a formal tone, "in recognition of the fine contribution you have made and are continuing to make with your writing—the plays you've written and have had produced—and the novels you've written and have had published—the Buffalo State College Alumni Association at this time takes great pleasure in publicly acknowledging and honoring you"—

He was interrupted by Marty. "No. Wait." After a moment of silence Marty went on. "I'm afraid you've made a mistake. You're talking about my brother Manny." With his wife and children and all our families there, watching and listening, I could think only about how he must feel.

It was in 1964 that *The Dead Hand*—my prize-winning play Marty described as only dialogue—was given its premiere production, the prize, in the second floor lounge of the Ford Hotel where I had worked years before.

The chief bellhop Old Bill, the other bellhops, the desk clerks, the house detective—all the people I'd come to know so well back then when I had moved up to become an elevator operator and then a bellhop inside the hotel—were all gone. But, crossing through the lobby, I could, with my mind's eye, see and hear Old Bill, having sized up a guest with luggage coming into the lobby and having determined how little tip that guest would give, yelling out to me, "Front boy." He saved the big tippers for himself. I was a teenager, a junior and then a senior in high school, and he must have been in his mid-forties when, to me, he was Old Bill.

And I still remember the young man my age who worked behind the soda counter in the drug store on the corner of Chippewa and Main Streets, where I stopped every night during my supper break for a sandwich and a chocolate milk shake. We seemed to recognize a sadness in each other, possibly connected with being shy teenagers who were working nights while the boys we grew up with were out playing. We never got to know each other's name. With my red hair, he called me, "Red," and I think I called him, "Pal." In what I think of now as some kind of instinctive act involving one working kid to another working kid, without either of us saying a word about it he started charging me for only a coke when I was having a sandwich and milk shake.

My work at the Ford Hotel was primarily a summer job, during the tourist season. While attending Hutchinson Central High School during the school year, I worked evenings and weekends as an usher at several movie houses on Main Street, first at Shea's Hippodrome, then at Shea's Buffalo, a magnificent movie palace which now houses touring musicals. The theaters' patrons back then were entertained by vaudeville performers at Shea's Hippodrome and by big bands at Shea's Buffalo, along with seeing a feature film.

Writing in the April 18, 2001 weekly Blue Dog newspaper about my stint at Shea's Buffalo, I described how *"night after night last year, waiting for my entrance cues during my performance as Lafew in the Irish Classical Theatre's production of All's Well That Ends Well at the Andrews Theatre, I would look through a window facing a deserted Main Street and see ... the changing electric signs appearing on the Shea's Buffalo marquee.*

"Pictures flash before my mind's eye. I see a redheaded high school kid proudly showing himself off in his usher's fancy uniform ... his hands encased in white gloves, he struts back and forth with other uniformed ushers in close order drill, not knowing that this is a rehearsal for the real thing he'll be doing in World War II ... and this scene brings to mind a fellow high school usher Harry Southard, back then an up-and-coming Golden Gloves boxer, who is talking me into entering the ring with him at a fund raiser for his church ... he promises we will just go through the motions for three rounds, he won't hurt me ... I could clearly see myself in that very first round, desperately trying to defend myself as Harry uses me for a punching bag ... My mind's eye sharply switches over to another fight that took place much later, in the '60s, in front of that same theatre ... a non-violent Gandhi-kind of response by myself and a half dozen others as we were bumped, shoved, tripped, pummeled by what I thought were government agents determined to break up the first outdoor public demonstration in Buffalo against the Vietnam War."

So far as I can recall, my only other job during my high school years was selling shoes at a cheap chain shoe store on Seneca Street, in a rundown area where there were pawn shops, second-hand clothing stores, panhandlers, druggies and drunks. Two of my older brothers worked there on Fridays after school and Saturdays, and they arranged for me to work with them on the big sale days preceding Easter Sunday and the like. The manager was an affable guy who had spent some time in Mexico and showed his limited knowledge of their language by frequently proclaiming with good humor, *"Entiendo-sted?"*—I still occasionally find the opportunity to talk about him and ape his jovial *"Entiendo-sted!"* I'm sure we both mispronounced what's supposed to mean: Do you understand?

But I think I got more than that from him and much more from the mechanics and other workers I got to know at the Huron Garage, where I directed the tourists to park their cars, and from all the other working people I got to know at the hotel and at the movie theatres —something I have difficulty describing exactly. I know I liked most of the people I worked with and I felt that they liked me. My red hair may have helped, enabling them to easily have a name for me: "Hey, Red." In retrospect, I think this may have been a further step toward my beginning to align myself with labor, with working people, "the working class," a process intensified when I graduated high school and worked for several years in the Dupont Rayon and Cellophane factory on River Road in the Town of Tonawanda, one of the many factories lining the Niagara River all the way from Buffalo through the city of Niagara Falls.

That row of factories along the Niagara River came to have a symbolic meaning for me. Shortly after I had been subpoenaed to appear before the House Committee on UnAmerican Activities for the first time in 1954, Rhoda said she was going to leave me, taking the kids with her, that she could no longer take the pressure being put on her because of my union and political activity. I left the house, got into my car and drove over to the road along the Niagara River. My hands tightly gripped the wheel of my speeding vehicle as I instinctively tried to find some source of solace there to choke off the gulping sobs which had finally broken through between my wild howls into the night as I drove past the Dupont plant where I had worked and past the factories in the cities of Tonawanda and North Tonawanda, whose workers I had helped organize into unions, and on along the Niagara River past the long string of chemical factories in Niagara Falls, whose workers had been organized into unions by my good friend Charlie Doyle who had openly been the head of the Communist Party in Western New York ... and speeding by all those factories where I could imagine the guys working in there ... the night shift workers at their machines ... and the cold wind rushing through where I'd fully opened the car's window ... my cheeks cooling off ... my face drying ... and with my mind and heart finally settling into a feeling of peace, a saddened and subdued peace, I rolled up the car window, turned the car around and drove home.

Chapter 4

In 1926, a freshman, I began attending Hutchinson Central High School on the corner of Chippewa Street and Elmwood Avenue, just one block from the Ford Hotel. Back then, although the school was highly rated academically, it was looked upon socially as being below Lafayette High School which had a high attendance of WASPS (White Anglo-Saxon Protestants). Hutch's student body included more of a mixture of children of Italian-American and Polish-American Catholics, and children of Jewish immigrants from Eastern Europe. There were some children of African-American families, and back then it was still acceptable to speak respectfully of them as Negroes.

Some years later, with our country heading into World War II, African-American families poured up from the South for jobs in defense plants, and the number of their children attending Hutch subsequently swelled to a point where the segregationist forces in the city, disturbed by the growing number of black students mixing with white students in Hutchinson Central, acted to change Hutchinson Central to Hutchinson Central Technical School, a high tech vocational school generally referred to as Hutch Tech. This was tied in with building a new school, Woodlawn Junior High, in the heart of the black ghetto, to drain black students away from Hutch, separating them from white students.

My opposition to that led to my involvement in a brouhaha where I was attacked in an editorial in one of the local newspapers, accused of trying to agitate a revolution in the city, cited as an example of how one subversive individual, if not checked, could single-handedly create chaos. By then I was a union organizer, the International Representative for the United Electrical, Radio and Machine Workers of America, known as the UE, which represented approximately 30,000 workers in 15 manufacturing plants in Western New York. To put it bluntly and without false modesty, despite being publicly and continuously attacked as a dangerous Communist, I had strong rank-and-file support, not only from our union members but also from other workers and some middle class progressives in the area, which gave me political clout.

I was in the 8ᵗʰ grade when the school principal had me deliver a Christmas basket of food to a black family who lived around the corner from where I lived. That is a scene I have always remembered—when I for the first time became aware of and was troubled about the condition of poor black families. Along with several of my brothers, I was attending vocational grammar school 47, around the corner from our family's mom-and-pop dry goods store. 7ᵗʰ, 8th and 9th grade students had to go to classes in machine shop, woodworking shop and sheet metal shop half of every school day and were expected to go on to a vocational high school and factory work. My parents had to do a great deal of arguing to get us admitted into the kind of high school that could prepare us to go to college.

But it was in the 7th and 8th grades at School 47 that I learned the trades of a machinist, a carpenter and a sheet metal worker, all of which came in very handy when I did become a factory worker in the control lab at the Dupont Cellophane and Rayon plant and again some time after that when I became a template maker in the mold loft at the Curtiss Wright Aircraft factory and unexpectedly—the candle in the wind—became a union organizer.

My oldest brother Sam had preceded me as a student at Hutchinson Central High. However, for some reason I can't remember, Martin went to South Park High in South Buffalo in the heart of the Irish neighborhood—an area heavily populated with families of steel plant workers—strong labor union territory, an area heavily seeded with gin mills, taverns, bars, saloons, pubs, drinking joints (whatever name you prefer) where union members drank beer and/or tossed down shots of whiskey with beer chasers and argued and got into fist fights over shop problems and union politics and differences regarding what was being done or not being done by those elected local, state or federal "sellout artists."

It was in the Twenties, while Martin was attending South Park High, that the street car workers became involved in a long bitter strike. Young as I was, I still remember seeing armed National Guardsmen in uniforms riding the street cars to protect the scab operators from grown-up strikers and young sympathizers who threw rocks to smash the street car windows.

My poor brother Martin, the innocent unaware of the consequences, took his usual street car ride one day to South Park High and when he emerged from the street car in South Buffalo he was badly beaten, bloodied, by other high school students who were strikers' sons and sympathizers. From then on, Martin rode the "nickel jitneys"—autos owned and operated by striking street car workers.

If I remember correctly, I felt sorry for Martin but I also had a friendly feeling for the striking street car workers, especially since their jitney drivers gave me free rides to wherever I wanted to go, not collecting the nickel fares from young kids.

My oldest brother Sam had graduated high school before I entered as a freshman. But many of my teachers had taught him and they expected me to match his high scholastic achievements. Also, he had preceded me on the school's football team. He filled one of the guard positions. The coach shifted me from one backfield position to another. Years later that high school football experience would open some doors for me.

Our coach had a serious problem. During practice the players were stealing the footballs as fast as he supplied them—the players taking advantage of the coach's attention being elsewhere to throw the ball over a small hill bordering the field, picking it up there later. The coach tried but could not get any of us to snitch on the thieves. So he came up with a brilliant idea. He gave me and several others our own footballs to keep, provided we agreed to bring them to practice during the rest of the season and loan them to the team each day to practice with. It was a good lesson in how to deal with a seemingly insoluble problem.

But the main thing I got out of high school—the candle in the wind, affecting the rest of my life—was my introduction to theatre by my favorite teacher, Miss Edith Haake, who surprised me by marrying the brother of one of the female students with whom she was most friendly in our drama club.

What reinforced my memory of her is that years later, when I was challenging the public school superintendent's decision to change Hutchinson Central to Hutch Tech and build Woodlawn Junior High in the black ghetto, Miss Haake came back into my life. I had not heard from her since my high school days, and when she phoned me, her frightened voice made me think she must be aware of how, because of my union battles, I was being demonized constantly in the newspapers as "that dangerous commie Manny Fried." She did not give her name, possibly fearing the phone was tapped, which it may have been. She said I might not remember her but that she had taught me in high school and she had been closely following my acting career in New York City and my subsequent work as director of the Buffalo Contemporary Theatre (all of which had preceded my becoming a union organizer). She asked if I knew who she was. I said I did. And then, her voice trembling with emotion, she said she wanted to thank me on behalf of herself and other teachers at Hutch Central for opposing the action of the school superintendent. Appreciating that for her this was an extremely brave act, telling "that dangerous commie Manny Fried" that she supported him for what some prominent community leaders were attacking him in the newspapers, I thanked her and asked about her sister-in-law, my former fellow student in the drama club. But, apparently too frightened to extend the conversation, she thanked me again, said, "God bless you," and hung up.

It was Miss Haake who introduced me to the work of Eugene O'Neill, his one act plays about sailors and also his full length plays—including *Anna Christie*, his play about a sailor and a prostitute. It was *Anna Christie* that encouraged me at age 15 to write my first play, about the prostitutes I met when I was working at the Ford Hotel. Reading O'Neill's plays in high school steered me later to write about the factory workers I worked with, those I met while working at Dupont and at Curtiss, and more so, those whom I came to know very well on a deeply personal level over the years I worked with them as their union representative during organizing campaigns, strikes, contract and grievance negotiations, arbitrations, picnics, union meetings, political and labor fights of all kinds, and so many other events and situations that included complicated mixtures of positives and negatives connected to the people I worked with. It finally led years later to my conscious decision to concentrate with my writing on trying to bring onstage working people, labor people, as fully rounded human beings with their full complexity—to try to be a voice for working people.

And for many years, actually continuing right up to the present, my writing about labor, about working people, has again and again, like a powerful magnet—though initially to my great surprise—drawn negative attention to me from the FBI. Much more about this later.

But sticking momentarily with my effort to be a voice in the theatre for working people, let's briefly jump ahead to 1967 and the New York City Off-Broadway opening of my play *The Dodo Bird*. The New York Times second-string drama critic Dan Sullivan began his review:

"Most plays smell like other plays; some plays smell like life. Emanuel Fried's 'The Dodo Bird,' which opened at the Martinique Theatre last night, falls into the welcome second category.

"It is a long one-actor about a long evening in a workingman's bar. The three chief characters work at the foundry across the street, and by the time the bar closes we know more about the foundry and the guys who work there than we ever thought we'd want to know, and it's fascinating.

"It's fascinating because Mr. Fried has been there ... These are not workmen seen through the rosy glasses of ideology, not noble primitives from the anti-capitalist 1930s but men you'd find any night at the local pub—as un-heroic, as tired, as shrewd, as funny."

Following immediately after this high praise for my play, critic Dan Sullivan was offered a deal he apparently found hard to refuse, to be first-string drama critic at the Los Angeles Times. Although I knew (and will later recount in detail) how the FBI tried to sabotage that production of *The Dodo Bird*, for the present let me add something that happened years later to a different drama critic, in Buffalo, that made me wonder if Dan Sullivan had been deliberately lured away to Los Angeles because he was "too strongly supportive" of my writing about labor people.

When my play *The Second Beginning* was presented at the Buffalo Ensemble Theatre a few years after the New York production of *The Dodo Bird*, critic Adolph Dupree wrote a very favorable review in the The Challenger, Buffalo's

African-American newspaper, with the bold heading: **"WHO'S AFRAID OF MANNY FRIED?"**

I phoned Mr. Dupree to thank him. During our conversation I learned that his day job was working for IRS—Internal Revenue Service—in the Buffalo office. We agreed to meet for lunch and talk further. But the next day Mr. Dupree phoned me and cancelled our lunch appointment. Without warning he, a Buffalo native, had been given an immediate permanent transfer away from Buffalo, told to report at once to the Rochester office of IRS. I assume that his phone— or more probable, my phone—may have been tapped by the FBI.

Meanwhile, Dan Sullivan at The Los Angeles Times encouraged me to keep in touch with him. He read my play *Drop Hammer*—much of which is based on my experience with the men working at the Blaw Knox foundry and machine shop in Buffalo. Two small presses, West End Press and my own press Labor Arts Books, were about to publish the play. I hoped that publishing the play would help get it a production. By this time I believed that the FBI was actively working to prevent production of my plays and I was angry enough about that to have founded my own small press, determined not to let them block me from getting my plays read and produced. I asked Dan Sullivan if he would give me a quote to use in connection with publication of *Drop Hammer*. What he gave me to use on the cover of the book encouraged me to keep going in the direction I was pursuing with my writing.

He said that though this was not yet part of a review of an actual production of the play, I could officially credit the following as coming from Dan Sullivan, Theatre Critic, Los Angeles Times:

"No playwright writes so knowledgeably and so sensitively of labor's rank and file as Emanuel Fried. He knows what drives workingmen and their families, their fears, their sense of honor. He knows the things they can say to each other and the things they somehow cannot bring themselves to say. And he never preaches. This is a people's playwright who can see the individual face."

Dan Sullivan then recommended the play to Bill Bushnell, artistic director of the Los Angeles Actors Theatre. By strange coincidence, the theatre's play reader turned out to be the son of Mike Jiminez who years earlier had been the district union representative above me when I was a union organizer. The play reader strongly recommended that the theatre produce the play. Incidentally, Mike Jiminez was the man on whom Ernest Hemingway based the male hero in his novel *For Whom the Bell Tolls*—Mike had blown up bridges during the Spanish Civil War to slow the advance of the oncoming Franco forces. In World War II, Mike became a favorite of General William Donovan who headed the Office of Strategic Services—the OSS, which later became the CIA. Mike parachuted down alone behind enemy lines to make contact with the partisans, many of whom had fought alongside him in Spain. Mike told me that Donovan sent word to members of the House Committee on UnAmerican Activities that if they tried to subpoena him, Mike, Donovan would blow the whistle on things he knew about them. Despite his personal political history, Mike was never called before the Committee. But his experience blowing up bridges in the Spanish Civil War was deliberately demonized by anti-labor columnist Victor Riesel who publicly attacked Mike again and again in his columns, labeling him "Mike Jiminez the dynamiter," trying to make it look like Mike used dynamite in his labor activities in this country.

Anyway, *Drop Hammer* got great reviews from all the Los Angeles drama critics, one critic actually calling it "a work of genius." For the first time in its history, with unions buying large blocks of seats for their members, the Los Angeles Actors Theatre sold out all seats for the entire run of the play. Several years after that, when I ran into artistic director Bill Bushnell, he told me he had been warned that if he ever produced another play of mine, it would be the end of his getting financial support for his theatre.

When Buffalo school superintendent Benjamin Willis proposed changing Hutch Central to Hutch Tech and to build Woodlawn Junior High in the black ghetto, I appeared at the school board's public hearing and was surprised to find that leaders of the black community who I expected would oppose his plan never showed up. They may have known that anyone who opposed the plan might be severely attacked by the media, as I was. One black community leader from the Urban League—I will not embarrass any of his living relatives by naming him—did show and supported Willis' plan.

When I rose and started to speak, I abruptly was interrupted by the president of the school board, Pascal "Pat" Rubino.

"Who do you represent?" he asked?"

I knew Pat well. He and his family owned several funeral homes and he was a familiar drinker at the exclusive Park Lane Restaurant and Cocktail Lounge that, along with the prestigious adjoining Park Lane Apartments building, was owned at that time by my wife's family, the Luries.—(My marriage to Rhoda: the candle in the wind.)—Pat's cold tone of voice signaled that there must be powerful forces in the community supporting the Willis plan. My union organizer assistant and close friend, Warren Brown, an African-American, was with me, and through his brother, a city councilman representing an essentially black district, I had a good background on what was going on.

"I am here," I responded, matching the antagonistic coldness of Pat's voice, "as the representative of the national office of the United Electrical, Radio & Machine Workers, also designated to speak on their behalf by our Local Union representing black and white workers at the Buffalo Foundry and Machine Division of Blaw Knox Corporation, and I'm also here as the father of two children attending public school in this city."

30

"You have the floor," Pat quickly conceded, forcing a polite smile.

I spoke at length about the Willis plan, charging that its deliberate purpose was to intensify segregation in the Buffalo school system. When I finished, a city councilman—not naming him now to avoid embarrassing any surviving relatives—rose and stridently attacked me, charging my ulterior motive was to agitate and create racial trouble. I knew this particular councilman playing the holier-than-thou concerned citizen was the front man for the taxicab mogul who had just been named Citizen of the Year by the Buffalo News and who was soon to be snared as he tried to jump over the fence and avoid being caught by state troopers raiding the Mafia's top level Appalachian meeting.

Pat adjourned the school board meeting to the next day, giving the newspapers time to feature the councilman's scathing charges against me and to editorialize about my supposedly subversive motives. When the school board met again, the meeting room swarmed with "suits' who I thought might be plainclothes cops and/or FBI agents. They tried to intimidate me and Warren Brown by steadily staring at us throughout the meeting, giving us what I call "the fisheye."

As expected, the school board ignored my accusation that the Willis plan was intended to intensify segregation in the public school system. They voted unanimously to go ahead with it. And as Willis left the room, he directed a sneering remark about "ten little Indians" in the direction of Warren Brown and myself. Following behind Willis, but seeming to hold back until Willis left the room, was Assistant School Superintendent Joe Manch. He had not spoken during the meetings. Joe had grown up with me and my brothers on the East Side of Buffalo. As he walked out of the room, Joe momentarily hesitated beside me and then, so no one else would hear what he said, whispered, "Manny, you're right."

That's not the end of it. Conservative forces in Chicago hired Willis to do there what he had done in Buffalo. But the black community there had learned from the mistake of Buffalo's black community. Massive demonstrations in Chicago thwarted Willis' effort to introduce his segregation plans there; he was fired— and I've been told, by an officer of the NAACP (National Association for the Advancement of Colored People) Willis then became a Catholic priest. Some years later, in 1972, HOME (Housing Opportunities Made Equal) under the leadership of two volunteers, black Frank Mesiah and white Norm Goldfarb, filed suit against the new school superintendent Joe Manch and the school board, charging that students in the public school system had been deliberately segregated. Goldfarb phoned me. I had just started teaching Creative Writing at Buffalo State College. Goldfarb asked if I would testify in court, telling what I had told the school board when I expressed opposition to Willis' plan. I said I'd do that. But a few days later he phoned to say there was no need for me to testify because school superintendent Joe Manch and the school board had agreed to stipulate that what I had said back then was true. Judge John Curtin in 1976 ordered the desegregation of the Buffalo public schools, resulting in the integration of black and white students, including students in the very same junior high school that Willis had built in the black ghetto to promote segregation—it became an integrated magnet school.

Not long after that, unfortunately, Norm Goldfarb died at a relatively young age. Frank Mesiah was elected president of the Buffalo Branch of the NAACP.

Chapter 5

It was my high school science teacher Mr. Hopkins who got me hired at the Dupont Cellophane and Rayon plant after I graduated at age 17 from Hutch Central in 1930. Jobs were scarce. The 1929 stock market crash had ushered in the Big Depression, which I believe truly ended only when World War Two created a strong need for workers in war plants, while young men were being siphoned off to become soldiers.

The 1930 edition of the CALENDAR, the Hutchinson Central year book, carries my photo along with those of other graduates, and states: "Emanuel J. Fried— Undecided (this related to what I'd do after graduation)—'Even Jollies Fate' (I'm not sure what that meant)—Lunchroom Monitor '29,'30, Football '29, Track '27–'30, Cross-country Squad '27, School Play '30; CALENDAR '30; Chairman Student Social Committee '30." And then my motto: *"There are better things in life than just financial success."*

At the graduation ceremony I was given an award as the best all-around student and athlete, which meant that my name would be added on the bronze plaque posted in the school's hall. And it was announced that Charles Scheeler had been granted the University of Michigan Award, which would provide him four years free tuition at that university. We had similar records in studies and after school activities, but he was a skinny boy who did not participate in athletics.

Charles Scheeler belonged to a small WASP social group at Hutch Central. I was the only Jew invited to participate in the group, and I'm ashamed to admit that I was flattered that I had been brought into their after-school social gatherings. This included being invited by Mr. Hopkins several times to come with Charles Scheeler and others from that select group to his very nice home. At that time, politically, I was a blank. The plaques and framed certificates hanging on the walls in Mr. Hopkins' home, identifying him as an ardent member of the American Legion, did not affect me in any way. In retrospect, I think Mr. Hopkins might have been politically leaning to the right, but I admired him very much and—though the prospect seemed very unlikely—I wished I could someday become like him and live his kind of life. Mr. Hopkins may have sensed my admiration, which could be why—when he learned that unlike Charles Scheeler I had no plans to go to college—he offered to get me the job at the Dupont plant.

Later I learned that Charles Scheeler came from a well-to-do family who owned the Buffalo Wire Works, which—remembering that when we graduated I got my name on a plaque and he got four years of free university tuition—prompted a rueful laugh on my part. I had been told by other Jewish students, but didn't want to believe it, that being a Jew disqualified me with the local University of Michigan alumni for their free tuition award. Ironically, Charles Scheeler and I ended up sitting across from each other at the bargaining table at Buffalo Wire Works, Charles having become president of the family-owned company and I having become the union organizer representing the workers in his plant. Buffalo Wire Works was a relatively small outfit with less than a hundred employees and we got along fairly well, working out contract agreements without our union ever being forced to strike the plant. And, possibly because of our past history, Charles was one employer who never directly red-baited me, though occasionally he would slyly needle me about the way some of the big corporations with whom I was negotiating were publicly playing the red-baiting card .

I try to recall why, when I graduated from Hutch Central, I had no plans to go to college.

None of us, the children, could expect financial help from our parents. The money simply wasn't there. To go to college, each had to earn his/her own way. All my older brothers, as each graduated from high school, took a test that won them some kind of financial aid based on scholarship. I didn't apply to take that test because—having been convinced I was the "dumb one" in the family—I assumed I would not win a scholarship and would never hear the end of that from my father. When I graduated from high school in 1930, Martin and Maury and Dave and my sister Sadie were already attending college. Martin and Sadie were students at Buffalo State Teachers College where tuition was free for New York State residents. Dave and Maury had won scholarships to Cornell University. Dave was studying to become an architect, a goal he successfully achieved. Maury graduated with a Bachelor of Arts degree and—during the Big Depression— worked for only a short while as a bank teller before being laid off. Our older sister Gert graduated high school and went to work as a bookkeeper for Star Ring Corporation, one of the leading jewelry manufacturers of expensive rings in the United States. When Gert got married she quit the job and arranged for Maury to take her place. He climbed the ladder from there to the top position, running the company for the children of the deceased founding owners.

If I remember correctly, after graduating from Hutch Tech, our oldest brother, Sam, got a job sewing fur coats for a retail furrier. The owner of the firm was a buxom woman somewhat older than Sam. I remember her being somewhat matronly, and I was very much in awe of her when she several times dropped into our home, sitting briefly with us in the kitchen in the rear of the store on Genesee Street. She dressed and conducted herself in a way that made me think of her as "a rich lady." That was underlined by how my mother and father acted toward her. They were very respectful, too respectful. She brought us all kinds of gifts. I believe—sort of sensed it even back then— that she had adopted my good-looking and athletically built older brother Sam as her young lover. With the money Sam earned working for her, he enrolled at Cornell University. When he was completing his second year there he spoke to his advisor about entering their Engineering School and was advised that since he was Jewish it would be a waste of time to choose engineering as a career since no engineering firm would hire a Jew—which may have been true back then. That may have been why he quit Cornell and, while working full time at the post office, studied dentistry at the University of Buffalo and became a dentist. (But there were some hushed whispers in the house, hinting that the real reason for Sam quitting Cornell was that a young woman from a prominent well-to-do family, whom he had expected to marry, dumped him for someone more socially acceptable.)

Through the effort of my high school teacher, Mr. Hopkins, I was the first Jew ever hired to work at the Dupont Cellophane and Rayon factory on River Road in the Town of Tonawanda, just north of Buffalo. I became their "token Jew," which caused some hard feelings a few years later when I quit the job at the Dupont factory to become a freshman at the University of Iowa in Iowa City, Iowa.

I don't know if I can adequately describe what it was like for me to go to work at the Dupont factory. Physically, the factory was a combination of several very large buildings occupying a great deal of open space bordering the Niagara River. I was seventeen years old and had never before been inside this factory world. It was strange to me. It scared me. When I first walked through the building where rows of women, young and middle-aged, were packaging cellophane sheets, I was caught off guard, embarrassed, when some of them whistled at me. Years later, I read a short story by a Russian writer about his venture into the society of the Cossacks and particularly his experience for the first time getting to meet on a personal level the Cossack women who were different from the women he knew in the society from which he came. I thought my experience at Dupont was similar in some way to his with the Cossacks. True, my contact with the women working at Dupont was superficial. I never spoke to them, nor they to me. But it was the beginning of what developed in full force—an entirely different perspective on my part regarding women who are factory workers—when I became a union organizer meeting and speaking and planning with thousands of women and men in heavy industry factories.

My job in the control lab at Dupont was somewhat repetitive. Every hour I gathered samples of chemical solutions and raw materials from tanks and other places in several buildings, tested the solutions and materials, and reported results back to operators who made any necessary adjustments to meet required specifications.

The building where cellophane was made was awesome. There were rows of machines, each the length of a long city block. At the front end of each machine a reddish-brown jelly-like mixture made from wood pulp and caustic (viscose) was shot out of a wide thin slit, up through a sulphuric acid bath, producing a continuous wide thin sheet of coagulated material which was then threaded without a break over rollers down into and out of heated chemical solutions contained in a long series of tanks, some of the liquids heated so hot that their surfaces heaved and tossed and sent up clouds of steam. After being threaded through the tanks of hot liquids, the unbroken cellophane sheet passed over large metal heated rolls which dried it by the time it came to the end of the block-long machine, where the finished product wound continuously into big rolls, some to be shipped as they were, others to be hauled to the building where other workers, predominantly women, cut the rolls of cellophane to create the packaged sheets to be sold to customers.

There were elevated wooden catwalks running along both sides of each of those block-long machines. Taking samples from the series of connected tanks of boiling chemicals, I hurriedly walked, sometimes even ran on these catwalks— and after I was sufficiently familiar with the machines to ape the bravado that characterized some of the operators working on them, I would occasionally, while holding the handle of the wooden case with its bottles of samples of different chemical solutions I'd taken from the tanks, cockily leap back and forth from the catwalk on one machine to the catwalk on the next machine, though that was forbidden by management as being too dangerous.

Inevitably there were times when there would be a break in the long continuous sheet of material winding into and out of the solutions in the tanks. At the point of the break the sheet would keep winding around one roller. That was emergency time. Operators would shout. A loud horn would sound. The operator assigned to that machine would have already raced to pull the rope hanging in front of the machine—the rope tied to some mechanism that slowed down the speed of material passing over the rollers. Operators from all the other machines would come running to converge on the affected machine—with their knives (like hunting knives) out and ready to cut away the material piling up on the roller at the point of break. Sometimes, while they were working to repair the break in the continuous sheet on the first machine, there would be a break in the continuous sheet on another machine. Again, there would be the warning shouts and the blasting of the horn. An operator would peel off to the second trouble spot to cut the sheet in front of the area where it was winding on one roller and then he'd keep pulling the slimy sheet off to one side into a gooky pile on the catwalk until other operators were freed from repairing the first trouble spot and could come over to help him clear the material off the roller where the break had occurred. Then the operator would again feed the sheet of material into and out of the tanks and over the heated metal rolls.

Sometimes, despite the operators washing down the catwalks with a hose after repairing this kind of break, there would be some slippery residue left on the boards, which I'd step on as I moved quickly back and forth between catwalks. I've had my feet slip out from under me and I've fallen down onto the catwalk or down to the floor between and below the catwalks. Though I did get badly scraped and bruised several times, I was aware of the company's constant campaign to keep down the number of reported injuries and fortunately was never hurt enough to feel compelled to report it.

While over seventy years have intervened since I started to work at Dupont and I worked there for only a little more than two and a half years, there are a few people I worked with there whom I remember well, mainly because thinking about them later affected my life.

Howie Valyear kept coming back into my life every fifteen or twenty or twenty-five years. We had worked together in the control lab and we both had wanted to be recognized as writers. Howie had more realistic goals than I had. He was happy writing short pieces for the company bulletin. We both belonged to the so-called "independent union," but while I worked there we never had anything to do with it. Years later when I did become aware of what a union is, or should be, I thought that what had existed back then had been a "company union" formed and controlled by the company in order to keep the employees from creating a real union. When I met Howie shortly before he retired he was still working at Dupont and he was writing the union's newsletter. He believed that the union— though still not affiliated with the main body of the labor movement in the AFL-CIO—was now truly independent, no longer controlled and dominated by the company. Howie was a very quiet man, introverted, never confrontational. Every so often when I was under attack politically—especially when I was being crucified in the newspapers as a dangerous subversive—Howie would somehow surface into my life again and with a shy smile he'd hesitantly offer support and agreement with my views. As far as I could tell from our brief meetings and conversations spread over seventy years, I assumed he was a loner since he never mentioned anything indicating he had a wife or children. I could have asked him, but I've always worried too much about invading people's privacy.

Several others contributed parts of themselves to the characters in my plays. "Dusty" Rhodes, a skinny blonde-haired operator on the cellophane making machines always greeted me in a very friendly way when I came out to take samples from the tanks where he was working. "Hiya, ya redhead," he'd shout over the loud noise of the machines. And there was the slow moving pot-bellied

Welshman, also a machine operator, who kept telling me, jokingly, he had a daughter he wanted me to meet. He always had a smile for me, even when I gave him some very negative readings on the chemicals in the tanks on his machine. And there was the young man in the control lab, only a few years older than I was, who had built his own little propeller airplane. On his days off he would noisily circle his plane over our building until he drew us outside and then he'd daringly fly it low enough to wave to us as he buzzed over our heads. It was his way, I thought, to establish that he was *somebody*, not just an ordinary factory worker like the rest of us.

I tested the heated chemical solutions in the tanks every hour and wrote the results on charts at the head of each machine, to be seen not only by the operators but also by the supervisor on the shift. These chemical solutions had to be kept within fixed ranges, and the machine operators made corrections as needed. (Incidentally, these machines operated 24 hours a day, seven days a week. Operators and control lab employees, including me, worked all three shifts, rotating each week to the next shift, with a 16-hour shift at the end of the week on one shift to effect the turnaround to the next shift for the following week.) If the operators failed to adjust the strength of the chemical solutions to keep them within prescribed ranges, the resulting product could fail inspection and become scrap. An operator who, despite my reporting to him the results of my hourly tests, failed to make the adjustments to keep the chemical solutions within prescribed ranges, could draw a strong reprimand and/or written warning from his supervisor.

The truth is I didn't know the exact limits of these ranges. I did the testing and wrote results on charts posted on work stands in front of each block-long machine. Operators, knowing the exact limits permitted, checked my figures on the charts and quickly made adjustments in the flow of chemicals into the tanks. Sometimes, when what I wrote on the chart indicated to the operator that a chemical solution had descended below or risen above permitted limits, the operator on that machine would angrily challenge the accuracy of my test results, trying to intimidate me into revising the figures. I considered it important that I not establish any precedent that I would give in to this kind of pressure.

A clash about this with one machine operator brought elements of him later into several of my plays. Though I don't remember his name I can clearly see him with my mind's eye. He was at least one head taller than my 5 feet and 9 ½ inches, at least a good foot wider than my size 42 shoulders, and weighed about twice my 155 pounds. With his bulging bare arms and shoulders and chest covered with colorful tattoos, he was a formidable figure as he came roaring into the control lab, demanding, "Who's the sonofabitch who wrote those lying figures on my chart?"—I said it was me.—He bellowed a long tirade of obscenities directly into my face as he charged over and over that I had marked down the wrong results. Shouting down my efforts to justify my figures, he kept yelling that he wanted me to go out there and change them.—"Right now!" I knew that he wanted me to change the figures before his supervisor saw them. He ordered me over and over that he wanted me to go out there and change those figures, "Right now!—Right now!"

Feeling humiliated by his tone of voice, I hesitantly interrupted, "You go to hell."

He stopped yelling, glared at me in disbelief, then quietly demanded, *"What— did—you—say?"*

I looked up at this formidable giant ready to destroy me, I swallowed, and I squeaked out: —"I said you go to hell."

He glared down at me while I waited for the punch that would destroy me. Then he threw his head back and he let out a roaring laugh and then he reached out and grabbed me in those tremendous bare arms and hugged me to his chest as he lifted me high up above the floor.

"You're okay, kid," he shouted, laughing. "You're okay, kid." He put me down and patted me on the head like I was a little boy. "You're okay, kid." He shook his head and was still chuckling as he left the control lab.

Those are some of the good memories about working at Dupont. But most of the time I was not happy about working there, since I still cradled the ambition to be an actor and playwright. Also, my mood was very much affected by the lousy economic situation, the Big Depression revealing itself early each morning as I came off the graveyard shift—the long sad lines of unemployed men waiting for the personnel office to open, hoping to get hired, when those of us working there knew it was more probable that there'd be more layoffs, not new hires. I was a lucky one, laid off for a only few months, then called back.

Working rotating shifts at Dupont, I saw less and less of the young crowd I'd grown up with, the members of our Emanon Club at the Jewish Community Center—Emanon is No-name spelled backward)—and the members of our high school fraternity—and the guys from the neighborhood.

I was the only one in the whole bunch who had ended up working in a factory, but it wasn't until many years later that, looking back, I defined and recognized the importance of this different direction developing between my life and the lives of those who had been my boyhood friends. By then Carl Frey had become the successful owner of a used car business, Isaiah Zisser had his own jewelry store, Harry Perlmuter owned several taverns in the black ghetto, including Buffalo's famous Little Harlem night club, and "Sonny" Benderson headed one of the biggest real estate development firms in Western New York and beyond.

All of us had grown up in an integrated East Side neighborhood, playing baseball, basketball and even tackle football (wearing no protective equipment) in the graveled playground with teams made up of black and white players. That may partly explain why, as we grew older, we got along very well on a personal basis with black people.

Years after our lives had parted and I'd rarely seen any of the old gang, during my worst period of being red-baited and blacklisted, Carl Frey and Harry Perlmuter—when I did see them—still were loyal friends, expressing support. Zisser had moved out of town. I saw him only once more when—during that same tough period in my life—I foolishly accepted his invitation to attend a reunion of the old gang and found it hard to talk to him, and even to Carl Frey and Harry Perlmuter. One reason I attended the reunion is because it was held in a private room in The Park Lane Restaurant which, as I've already mentioned, was owned at that time by my wife's family, a fact that I reluctantly recognized seemed to impress the old gang, adding to the rift developing between us.

My relationship with Sonny Benderson shifted back and forth over a period of many decades. When I was getting my plays produced in New York City's Off-Broadway theatres, he did put $1,000 into a play of mine, and through the years, though he had become rich and influential, he'd exchange a friendly but brief greeting with me when we occasionally ran into each other in restaurants and other public places. But when his firm, under the leadership of his son, formed and headed up a coalition of developers and contractors to fight against using union labor, Sonny stopped saying hello to me.

Contributing to my depression while working at Dupont was that my face—which I superficially counted on to get me recognized as an actor—was becoming faintly lined with caustic burns caused by spattering and dripping of hot chemical solutions on my face when I reached over to take samples from the boiling liquids in the tanks. It took years for those faint lines in my face to heal and disappear, but remaining from those caustic burns I still have a slight hollow across the right side of my nose.

My dejection caused by lack of hope that I'd ever create a career as an actor was unexpectedly dispelled—*The candle in the wind*—.A young chemist, who frequently came into the control lab to have material tested, somehow mentioned that he had done some acting. That led to my telling him about my interest in acting and playwriting. He told me the University of Iowa, his alma mater, had a nationally recognized Theatre department. He suggested that I might get a scholarship if I wrote to the department chairman, Professor E. C. Mabie, telling him about my interest in theatre, my working background, and the play I'd written about prostitutes. He also suggested that I include news clippings about my playing quarterback on my high school football team. This resulted in an offer of a one-year football scholarship providing free tuition. Fortunately I'd saved enough money from my work at Dupont to be able to handle the cost of a room at the dormitory—and the university arranged a job for me, washing dishes at a *Jewish* fraternity house in return for my meals.

When I gave notice that I was leaving Dupont, the head of personnel came to the control lab and told me that if I stayed at Dupont I would have a good future there. The only explanation for his concern that I can come up with is that he didn't want to lose his "token Jew," and I wonder if this related to something developing higher up in the corporation, since some years later I read that a newly named president of the Dupont corporation was Jewish. But I stuck with my decision to quit Dupont and go to the University of Iowa to advance my theatrical career.

Chapter 6

Leaving Buffalo to go to the University of Iowa in Iowa City was another step away from my previous growing-up world. My trunk containing clothes and other things was sent ahead. Included in the trunk was a velvet bag containing the black straps and phylacteries—small leather boxes containing Hebrew scriptures—which, under the watchful eye of my father, I'd bound around my left arm and my forehead as I said prayers every morning. I never again took those black straps and phylacteries out of the velvet bag to bind them around my arm and forehead, never again said those morning prayers. By then, when I had recited prayers at home or in the synagogue—where my brothers and I went every Saturday and on High Holidays with my father—the praying had become meaningless. Rocking my head back and forth the same way the old-timers did while they prayed, I mumbled the Hebrew words and never thought about what the words meant. That's not something I'm proud of or ashamed about. It's simply that those prayer rituals had lost their meaning.

Though it's been a long time since my father made me go straight from public school to Hebrew school every day, I still can read Hebrew but don't remember what the words mean. For me and for my brothers, the way Hebrew school was conducted did not contribute to serious study. Old bearded Rabbi Diamond sneaked around the classroom with a ruler poised to smack us over the head or on the hands to prop up our attention. (Rabbi Diamond's son David later became a highly respected New York State supreme court justice and an ardent supporter of Franklin D. Roosevelt's New Deal.) Several of my brothers and I were in the same classroom on the first floor, and during the warm days when the windows were open, if we saw old man Diamond heading for one of us with his ruler upraised, we'd shout a warning and then throw folding chairs directly in front of the old man to block him as we all scrambled out through the open windows. It became a game, the brothers versus the bearded rabbi with his ruler. Years later, as a union organizer, I learned from my Catholic friends that they had similar problems with nuns wielding rulers. Anyway, we didn't gain much respect for religion from attending Hebrew School. So, when I headed for the university, it was sort of a declaration of "free at last," breaking away from that superimposed regimen that no longer had any real meaning for me. This in no way detracted from my developing belief in and dedication to the social philosophy of Judaism. Our father had repeatedly warned us, his children, to accept our responsibility to deal with our problems, saying, "God helps those who help themselves." Gradually over the years I have dropped God out of that equation and without knowing it when I began my journey to the university—and with many deviations in the years ahead—I was on my way to becoming a humanist, a secular Jew.

After I took a bus to the end of the line and stepped out onto the highway to begin thumbing rides to Iowa City, I did something about which I still feel some guilt, but which dramatically, metaphorically, says something about my state of mind. Worrying that I would get hungry, my mother had given me a brown paper bag filled with sandwiches wrapped in wax paper. Standing on the side of the highway, about to step out to hold up my hand and jerk my thumb back and forth to ask drivers of passing vehicles for a ride, I tossed the paper bag into a grassy field. At the age of 19 I was breaking with my past, starting a new life.

A young redhead wearing sneakers, white pants and a sweatshirt sporting a large brown and blue H, a football letter, I must have been an appealing character as I asked for rides with my jerking thumb. I averaged over 400 miles a day. Two times I was given rides by male drivers looking for a young boy for sex. One of the drivers was a chauffeur pimping for his boss. When I, hiding my fright, abruptly rebuffed these approaches I was summarily kicked out of the cars.

In Wayne County, Indiana, I got a ride from a salesman, a member of the Wayne family on his way to a family reunion back deep in the hills. Did I want to go to the reunion with him? It was a new experience for me, meeting these poorly dressed gaunt backwoods people who treated me like family. I remember especially the bent old man (probably younger than I am now) who had no teeth left. He proudly showed me the platters of plums he had baked dry over the wood stove in his little shack, so he'd have food ready to eat during the coming winter.

And then, unexpectedly, *the candle in the wind* again. A large automobile driven by a uniformed chauffeur passed by me, its occupants ignoring my gesturing thumb. But about a hundred yards down the road the car pulled over and the chauffeur got out and beckoned to me. I ran to the car. It looked like a Cadillac. The chauffeur opened the door for me to step into the rear of the car where a well dressed middle-aged woman greeted me with a warm smile. She asked where I was going. I told her I was on my way to Iowa City to go to the university. She said they would give me a lift in that direction since they were going to Los Angeles. She apologized for having first passed me by, said that she never gives a hitchhiker a ride but that my red hair reminded her of her redheaded son. As we drove west we talked, for hours. She bought meals for me along the way and as we approached the spot where I would have to leave to take the road going north to Iowa City, she suggested I ride with them to California. I had told her I wanted to be an actor. She said Los Angeles was the place to be and she might be able to help me.

We came to the crucial "fork in the road" and the chauffeur parked the car. I had to make my decision. Go west to Los Angeles with this friendly lady and try to break into the movies? Or get out of the car and hitchhike north to go to the University of Iowa with its outstanding Theatre department?

With my trunk on the way to the university, with the football scholarship all set, and with my dorm arrangements made and everything else tied to my going to the university, I reluctantly thanked the woman and said that I better go to school. She wished me good luck and we shook hands, saying goodbye. I got out of the car and continued hitchhiking to Iowa City.

Just for the hell of it, I sometimes wonder what my life would have been like if I'd gone on with that nice lady to Los Angeles instead of Iowa City and the university.

One thing I remember well about my time at the University of Iowa is that back then, in 1932, students like me who were Jewish were treated differently from the way other students were treated—both by some of the other students and by some faculty and staff. When I was interviewed at the university's personnel office and was offered the dish washing job, the interviewer emphasized that the job was at a *Jewish* fraternity house and made a big point, intended as praise, telling me that I was "different from other New York Jews on campus." I'm ashamed to say that I let that pass unchallenged when I knew the difference was only that I was from Buffalo, possibly the only student from that city at the western end of New York State, and did not speak with the interviewer's conception of a downstate New York City/Brooklyn accent. A fraternity member where I washed dishes shared with me that he had a non-Jewish girlfriend on campus and they had to meet secretly because if her relationship with a Jew became known she would be expelled from her sorority and be shunned by her friends. A student who stopped his car every day to offer me a ride as I was walking to my dish washing job, and who was impressed when, in response to his questions, he learned that I was one of the quarterbacks on the university's freshman football team, asked me to join his fraternity, at the same time making a derogatory remark about my washing dishes for those *Jews* at the *Jewish* fraternity house where he was dropping me off. When I, after a moment's hesitation, let him know that "I'm Jewish," he mumbled a brief apology, and from then on he looked the other way as he drove past me.

Then I was 19, now I'm 95. My University of Iowa experience took place so long ago that it's difficult for me to characterize exactly what it was like. I didn't quite fit in. I don't think it was that I was Jewish, though I must say that up until then I had not been made aware of that difference as much as I was made aware of it then. But I think the main reason why I felt different was that I had worked in the Dupont factory. Back then factory workers and children of factory workers generally did not go to college. At that point in my life, having come directly from working at Dupont to the university, I thought of myself as a factory worker. (It was the right of World War II veterans to get a college education with tuition paid by the federal government that years later brought working class kids in full force onto college campuses.) In any case, the fact is that I did not make a single close friend at the University of Iowa that entire year. The closest to it that I did achieve was a warm relationship with Professor E.C. Mabie, chairman of the Theatre department. I auditioned for him and was cast in the role of the German accented director in *Once in a Lifetime*, a play authored by Moss Hart and George Kaufman. I had no idea then that a few years later I would act in New York in one of their plays and talk to Moss Hart.

I'm sure I was not a great actor in *Once in a Lifetime*, but I did well enough to attract the attention of the chairman of the department. Professor Mabie was a very friendly, somewhat overweight, easygoing gentleman who did his best to encourage me and the other actors. His favorite actor, who played the lead in a number of plays that year, was Richard Maibaum, an upper-class student, possibly a senior or post-graduate, who had a large physical build and a powerful deep voice. I guess I was jealous of the attention he got. He was the star of the Theatre Department, expected by everyone there, including himself and me, to be the student who would become a highly successful professional actor. A few years later I did see his name mentioned in a news column about Hollywood—as a screenwriter on some film—and that was the last I heard of him. The theatre and movie businesses are cruel that way to actors and writers.

What I remember of that year at the University of Iowa that now gives me some insight into why I did what I did in the future is that in my freshman composition class I wrote something that says a lot about what my father had hammered into my mind. I wrote that no matter what it is that any person attempts to do, he or she, with only one exception, is doomed to be a failure—because only one person can be the best. Fortunately in the years ahead I learned how destructive that belief is—it produces impotence—and I told my daughters, "You do as good as you can do, and that's fine." And then there was my experience with training in ROTC (Reserve Officer Training Corps), a requirement for all students because, I believe, this university got a land grant or something like that from the federal government. An army colonel was in charge of ROTC. I remember him being arrogant and insulting, much different from most of my fellow officers during World War II. His idea about how to train us to be reserve army officers was to shout at us as if we were stupid idiots. When I had done close order drill as an usher at Shea's Buffalo, I thought I did very well. But when I was marching in close order drill in the armory at the university, trying hard to be the best man at close order drill in our squad, the colonel apparently did not think my marching was up to his standard. Maybe I was trying too hard. He grabbed me by the shoulder, pulling me out of the formation and, accusing me of being out of step with the other men in our squad, literally screamed at me, "What are you, a communist?"—"NO-O-O!" I exploded back to him, out of a deep sense of having been accused of something horrible. Thinking about that now—specifically that only a few years later, when I had become a member of Actors Equity, the actors union, in New York City, I was recruited into the Communist Party by another actor—the change in my thinking in such a short period of time startles me.

How and why did this change really come about? Never mind the surface causes. What was it beneath those surface causes that made me stand fast when I was subpoenaed to appear before the House UnAmerican Activities Committee in 1954 and again in 1964, when I was labeled "the most dangerous man in Western New York," blacklisted from 1956 to 1972, unable to hold onto jobs with a number of U.S. companies who had hired me, the FBI visiting those employers, getting them to fire me, punishing and pressuring me because I refused their demand, conveyed to me by a close friend, to publicly condemn my union which was accused of being communist-dominated, and refused to publicly repudiate my political beliefs and name names of "communists and communist sympathizers"—a refusal which prompted that close friend, a prominent lawyer in Western New York, to become my active enemy who cooperated with the FBI to increase the punishment and pressure by getting all the middle and upper-middle class friends of my wife Rhoda and myself to cut off ever again being with us—and later, as an officer of Studio Arena's executive board, to block production of my plays and my appearance as an actor on the stage of Buffalo's leading professional theatre.

Years later, in 1945, I recalled the screaming of the University of Iowa ROTC colonel after I drew a similar angry attack from the colonel in charge of a court martial proceeding in Korea. An article I wrote about it appeared in The Buffalo News on March 14, 2002. The point I made was its relevance to what might happen with the military tribunals President George W. Bush established by executive order following the September 11, 2001 terrorist attack which destroyed the World Trade Center Twin Towers in lower Manhattan.

Because someone in the Advocate General's office may have known I had been a militant union representative in civilian life, that office had appointed me Defending Officer for a private accused of raping a young Korean woman. I was an infantry second lieutenant and our battalion, with the 20th Infantry Regiment, was stationed in Pusan following the Japanese surrender ending World War II.

A court martial board of officers had been appointed to decide the fate of the soldier whom I—not a lawyer—had been appointed to defend. Only one member of the board, another infantry second lieutenant whom I knew very well, was from our battalion. I first saw the accused, a white soldier probably in his early twenties, when he was brought into the room under armed guard. I had no chance to speak to him, could only wonder if he was guilty as charged. A middle-aged Korean man, the first witness, pointed at the accused and then, through a translator, identified himself as the father of the young woman who had said that the accused was the soldier who had assaulted her. When the colonel indicated that the witness could return to his seat I stood up and said I'd like to question the witness.

"Lieutenant!" The colonel slapped his hand on the table and with a peremptory gesture ordered me to sit down.

Startled, I said, "Sir, I respectfully—"

"Lieutenant!" the colonel literally screamed at me as he pounded his fist on the table. His face flushed red and he leaned forward to glare at me, his body language ordering me to sit down.

Though frightened, I stood there, refusing to sit. There was a moment of frozen silence. Then the colonel abruptly adjourned the hearing to the following morning. As my second lieutenant friend and I headed back to officers quarters, he passed on a warning from the colonel. "The General"—that was General Hodge, commander of all U.S. armed forces in Korea—"has sent down word that he wants a conviction." The gist of the message from the colonel was that I'd better keep my mouth shut or I'd be in big trouble.

I immediately contacted the Advocate General's Office, stating that since I was not being permitted to defend the accused I did not wish to participate any further in this court martial proceeding. The Advocate General's Office rescinded my appointment as Defending Officer.

Since then—I'm glad to add—the rights of our accused soldiers have been much liberalized. But when I wrote the Buffalo News article, President George W. Bush had ordered that military tribunals may secretly convict and sentence non-citizens accused of terrorism, not allowing such non-citizens legal representation and other rights guaranteed to American citizens. I warned that if non-citizens were deprived of these rights, some politicians were certain to demonize U.S. citizens—as I had been demonized during the Cold War—and, charging them with "obstructing the war against terror," would try to take away from such U.S. citizens the rights taken away from non-citizens. And of course that is exactly what the George W. Bush administration then went on to do. Fortunately, unlike judges under Dictator Franco in Spain and Dictator Pinochet in Chile, some judges in our courts made strong, though not completely successful, efforts to resist this attempt to deprive such U.S. citizens of their legal rights.

Unfortunately at the University of Iowa I did not perform well enough as quarterback on the freshman football team to be asked to return the following year with continuation of the football scholarship providing free tuition. But even with free tuition I would not have been able to return because I did not have enough money left from what I'd earned at Dupont to pay for the dorm and other fees. My brother Dave, studying at Cornell University to become an architect, was being helped by my parents. They did not have the money to also help me. Since Dave was already into his second or third year I agreed that he should come first. While the people at the fraternity house told me I could come back the second year to wash dishes in return for my meals, the truth is that I did not have a strong desire to continue at the University of Iowa. It's hard for me to explain why, but despite my acting role in *Once in a Lifetime* I felt out of place there, that I was getting nowhere with my life. Thinking about it now, I believe that if I had really wanted to continue at the University of Iowa, I would have picked up some kind of extracurricular job that would have enabled me to scrape together enough money for tuition and some place to stay. I also might have been able to get a student loan.

Now I'll tell something I've never before revealed. One of my reasons for not doing well at the quarterback position is that I was nearsighted. I had difficulty accurately seeing players to whom I tried to throw the football. To see well off the football field I wore glasses. But back then we did not have contact lenses or special helmets for nearsighted football players. That's my excuse. So far as the coaches were concerned I wasn't good enough to be asked to come back. But that was not the end of my football career. A few years later I played freshman football again, illegally, at Canisius College, a Jesuit school in Buffalo, and quit school when the football season ended. It was a temporary interruption between appearances on New York's Broadway and Off-Broadway stages. The Buffalo sports writers had fun with it, calling me "the matinee idol quarterback."

Chapter 7

But before getting to New York City as an actor, I returned to Buffalo from my freshman year at the University of Iowa and at age 20 got a job as a clerk at an A & P grocery store. Working there, frustrated and angry because I still yearned for a career as an actor, I responded to an item in the newspaper and was accepted to appear onstage as a non-speaking 'extra" with a professional theatre company (known in the theatre business as a "a stock company") who staged a series of play productions at Buffalo's Teck Theatre on Main Street. There was no pay for my acting with them, except the experience, which was fine with me. That was so long ago that I don't remember what plays I appeared in, but I do remember two members of the acting company: the leading man, Lawrence Fletcher, and the leading woman, Rosalind Russell. I got to talk quite a lot to Larry Fletcher since I was allowed to use his dressing room. He encouraged me to come to New York City, gave me his phone number and address there, and said he would give me information about whom to see and how "to make the rounds." When I did get to New York City he did meet me one afternoon and gave me that information. Since he and Rosalind Russell had been a hot item back in Buffalo, I asked about her. He said she was fine. Period. I said to say hello. His relationship with her may have already ended. In the immediate years ahead he appeared in minor roles in several plays, never connected to rising movie star Rosalind Russell—and then I never heard of him again. I learned later, from my own experience, that that's not unusual with personal relationships in the theatre business.

Meanwhile I kept on working at the A&P store as an assistant to the head of the produce section. I remember that I was busily stacking the produce out in front of the store when I heard that President Franklin Delano Roosevelt had ordered a national bank holiday to halt the run on the banks during the Big Depression. Back then the store, on Jefferson Avenue, was in the center of a white working class neighborhood. Years later the neighborhood became part of the black ghetto.

I was promoted to head the produce section and did a very good job of figuring out ways to present the produce in an inviting manner, doing such things as wrapping bushel baskets with white wrapping paper to set off the fruit and vegetables. The man in charge of all A&P stores in the city, a genial Irishman, seemed to take a special interest in me, possibly because of my red hair, my Irish-looking mug, and my eager beaver approach to the work. Again—this time overhearing him talk to the manager about me and my future with A&P—I heard that disturbing remark which I cowardly did not contradict but accepted as a compliment: "He's different from the other Jews." Subsequently he told me that I was going to be upgraded to the post of Assistant Supervisor in Charge of Produce for all their stores in the area. I was given the impressive title with the promise that sometime in the future there would be an increase in pay. And strange though it may seem now, back then I temporarily thought it was possible that moving up the ladder within the A&P organization might lead to a satisfying life.

I learned that that was not how my brother Maury felt. During those Depression days he had lost his job as a bank teller and, though he tried, he had been unable to find work. While I was not being paid very much I did receive a paycheck every week and I gave

him an allowance of, I think, about $3 a week. At that time I was still in charge of produce at the Jefferson Avenue store. My helper quit and I hired Maury to work with me. Each morning when the weather permitted we would place planks of wood across apple crates in front of the store and then we'd set out bushels and boxes of fruits and vegetables on this makeshift stand. At the end of the workday we'd take everything back into the store. When I think about the comic routine Maury created each time we did this, I still laugh. I was gung-ho as I'd enthusiastically lead him to the crates of oranges inside the store, saying, "Maury, let's get out our oranges." He'd stop me, putting his hand on my shoulder, and he'd dryly say, "Not ours." He'd repeat this each time I led him to put out things like bags of potatoes or bushels of apples until finally I started beating him to the punch line. I'd say, "Let's get out our crates of strawberries," and before he could say anything, I'd say, "Not ours!" Fortunately Maury did not have to stay there very long. When our sister Gert got married he took over her job as bookkeeper at Star Ring Corporation—and in a few years moved up the ladder to become the CEO in charge of the entire corporation.

As Assistant Supervisor in Charge of Produce, I was sent from one store to another throughout the entire area. My job at age 20 was to teach the store managers the proper way to display their fruits and vegetables and the best way to price them. I did not have the sense to be tactful in giving orders to men who were more than twice my age. Let's put it bluntly: I was a miserable boss, arrogant in my belief that I knew more than the store managers, insulting in the way I ordered them around. Fortunately for my future, some store managers complained to my boss and after a few months I was bounced back to my previous job, handling produce at the Jefferson Avenue store.

Back then that demotion was hard to accept. The anger, the resentment, the frustration I felt led me to do what it took to put me back on course to develop my career as an actor. I came in early one morning, boiling inside about the state of my life as I started to set up the stand in front of the store. I brought out the apple crates and placed them on the sidewalk next to the plate glass store windows. I carried out a heavy plank of wood. But instead of carefully laying it down in place, I angrily tossed it at the tops of the crates. The heavy board bounced off the tops of the crates and noisily crashed through one of the large plate glass windows. I stormed into the store and met the manager as he rushed toward me.

Before he could say anything, my frustration spoke from my gut, beating him to the punch. I angrily shouted, "I quit!"

"You don't quit!" he shouted back. "You're fired!"

And that was how I escaped from my promising career with A&P.

Chapter 8

Still living at home with my parents and brothers and sisters in our always crowded house, I was determined to get back on track to an acting career. I made no effort to find another job. Instead I somehow got a list of summer theatres, probably from the New York Times, and wrote to several who had advertised for apprentices. I cited my acting experience in *Once in a Lifetime* at the University of Iowa and my appearances with the stock company at the Teck Theatre, and also mentioned that I had performed in Shakespeare's *A Midsummer Night's Dream* at Buffalo's leading amateur community theatre, The Studio Theatre.

I don't remember when I squeezed in that performance in the Shakespeare play. My brother Martin, through his connection with Buffalo State College, knew Jane Keeler who headed the Studio Theatre. He arranged for me to have an audition with her for a role in the Shakespeare play. She cast me as one of the crude workmen who performed to entertain the queen, and I thought I was extremely clever when, acting the part of the lion, I let my red hair grow so very long that I was able to use it as the lion's mane.

The Studio Theatre subsequently became the Studio Arena Theatre, a professional theatre, a member of the League of Regional Theatres (LORT). Most of its actors are brought in from New York City, with some local actors occasionally used. Years later—after I had acted On-Broadway and Off-Broadway and had several of my plays produced Off- Broadway in New York City—I would be blacklisted at Studio Arena: the chairman and vice chairman of its board of directors would be bitter opponents of mine because of my political and union activity, and its artistic director Neal Dubrock would apologetically tell me that no play of mine could be performed on its stage and I would never be permitted to act there. He was wrong. Recently, many years later, I did perform there.

A bottle tossed into the ocean, my letters to summer theatres, drew an offer of a non-paying apprenticeship, except for room and board, with The Rip Van Winkle Theatre in Haines Falls in the Catskills resort area, north of New York City. On a tattered page in my crumbling theatre scrapbook I am listed as assistant to the stage manager, but I did a lot more: helped build sets, worked with lighting and did kitchen duty. But I also was given the opportunity to act in several plays there.

What I still remember very well about this major step towards my acting career is the scene it prompted with my father the morning I was to leave home. Since I was going to hitchhike to Haines Falls, I was traveling light, having mailed my clothes and other things ahead. It was early in the morning, just beginning to get light outside. I'd said goodbye the night before to my father and mother and my brothers and sisters. I was in the kitchen, getting ready to leave. My father appeared, still in his long underwear.

"Why are you going?" he asked me, and before I could respond he said what since then I've often thought about, not only in connection with my acting career but also in connection with my career as a playwright. "Acting," he said, trying hard to establish emotional contact when he must have known that by now there was little he could do to break down the wall that had developed between us and influence me. "Acting," he said. "is for rich men's sons, not for you."

"I'm going," is all I said, quickly thinking that this was very late for him to be talking to me for the very first time about my choice for my future and also that my mother had probably pushed him to talk to me. "I'm going," I said, flatly, and turned away and walked out of the house—to begin my hitchhiking trip to Haines Falls.

I remember my experience with The Rip Van Winkle Theatre with great fondness, probably because for the first time I was fully engaged in the theatrical life for which I'd always yearned. As part of launching my new life I adopted a stage name, derived from my first name, Emanuel. I broke that in half: *Eman* and *uel*, and then *Eman* became *E. Man* and that became *Edward Mann*, my stage name, with friends calling me Eddie Mann or "Red" Mann—and that was the name I used from 1933 until I returned permanently to Buffalo in 1939 and rejoined my given name Emanuel "Manny" Fried, sticking with that from then on, even when—after my years as a union organizer—I returned to acting and also playwriting.

Years later, as a union organizer, I was in charge of a strike of Columbus McKinnon Chain Company workers in Tonawanda and North Tonawanda, the twin industrial cities just north of Buffalo. The publisher of the Tonawanda News, Mrs. Hewitt, sent me a message that she was going to drive "the outside agitator from Buffalo" out of town. She had a reporter write a list of "embarrassing questions" that strikers should ask Manny Fried. "Will he deny that for years he used a name entirely different from the one he uses now?" I publicly replied, telling about my acting career and my stage name, Edward Mann. This response actually helped me gain greater acceptance in the Tonawandas. The reporter who, on orders from Mrs. Hewitt, had urged the strikers to question me was so disturbed when he read my response that he quit his job with the Tonawanda News, apologized to me, and shortly after that he went to work for a Buffalo newspaper. He and his wife invited me and my wife to dinner at their house. We became friends. Incidentally, Mrs. Hewitt's son Charles—he'd been a foreign correspondent in Europe for some news service and had become my brother Gerry's bridge partner—dropped in unexpectedly at the Gates Circle apartment where I was living with my wife Rhoda and daughter Lorrie (before my other daughter Mindy was born). He said he disagreed with his mother, approved of what I was doing. Then his mother died and he inherited the newspaper. But very shortly after that it was reported that, while standing with his wife on a cliff overlooking the sandy beach of Lake Erie far below, Charles Hewitt slipped and fell to his death. His wife became the publisher of the newspaper and she continued her mother-in-law's effort to drive out of town "that outside agitator from Buffalo."

It was the summer of 1933 and I was still only twenty years old—that's so long ago—when I got my chance to act in several plays with the Rip Van Winkle Players, advertised as "A Company of New York Actors." I had minor roles in *The Gold Watch*, *Latchstrings*, *Co-operative Husband* and *Ten Nights in a Barroom*. I'm not aware that I learned much about the craft of acting there, except what I might have unconsciously imbibed from performing with other actors before an audience. But most of the actors there seemed to be primarily concerned only with remembering their lines.

Thinking back, I must have been a very naïve young man then, fascinated as I was by what I was experiencing there. Two plays were being tried out with the thought of possibly being taken into New York. *The Gold Watch* was a Hungarian play that had been translated into English by R.C. Sherriff, author of a hit war play *Journey's End*. All I remember of *The Gold Watch* is that the central character was the watch and how it played a role in different people's lives. Even unschooled as I was about playwriting back then, I thought it was essentially flat and lacking in getting anyone to deeply care about what was happening. The other play being tried out was *Latchstrings*, written by the producer and the woman who directed that play. What fascinated naïve me who, as yet, had little experience with the complicated relationships that develop with adult life, complications maybe more evident between people involved in the arts, was the triangle that—I sensed—involved the producer and his aging musical comedy actress wife and the woman with whom he had collaborated in writing the play, which seemed to embody something of their experience. All three seemed to be comfortable with their apparent triangular relationship, and that—something new to my experience—is one thing I remember very well about that summer. But I also warmly remember the producer's older brother, Harry Chapman Ford. He had directed plays for David Belasco, the theatre producer who believed in using the real thing on stage. Harry and I got along well, and he told me a lot of theatre anecdotes, including how Belasco had him bring over Arabs and their horses for "the desert play" and the wonderful time he had when he went back to visit the Arabian riders who had been paid enough by Belasco to enable them to go home and live without working the rest of their lives. Listening to him, I had no idea that a only few years later I'd be performing onstage in the Belasco Theatre.

While at that time, working with the Rip Van Winkle Theatre, I truly loved what I was learning about life, my mind was not in the slightest way concerned with what was happening with politics and unions. To be recognized as an actor—and hopefully as a playwright—was the all-consuming goal to which I dedicated all my thoughts.

Yet currently, when I talked to an actress friend about this, she disagreed. "Seeking approval," she said, "was your goal—to get the applause you needed because you were the seventh of nine children, quickly replaced by your two younger brothers, quickly ignored, lost in the crowd."

But I think it's more complicated than that, and I'm trying to dig out what it really is, why I've made the choices that led to my becoming the person who went on to do what I did.

When I became a union organizer and was writing a story a week for The Union Leader, the Buffalo CIO (Congress of Industrial Organizations) newspaper, Angus Cameron—who had been a senior editor with publisher Little Brown and was starting his own book club—asked me to write a novel about my experience, always keeping in mind the following: "What is really happening here and why?"—That question, written on a 3 x 5 index card many years ago, now yellowed and scratched, is still pasted above where I write.

"What was really happening?—and why?—from the time I left Buffalo in 1933, wanting to become an actor on New York City's Broadway stages, to the time in 1939 when I returned to Buffalo and two years later, in 1941, chose to become an organizer for a union accused of being communist-dominated?"

In those years between 1933 and 1939 I was politicized, becoming a member of the Communist Party. Prior to that, though my father—a holdover from his early work in a cigar making factory—spoke of himself as being pro-labor and a follower of Socialist Labor Party founder Daniel DeLeon, I don't remember him engaging in any overt political activity. I don't remember the name of Karl Marx or the Communist Party ever being mentioned in our house. My father often did say we were a "pro-labor socialist family." But that never meant anything to me except that we were favorable to labor, without any clear understanding as to exactly what *that* meant. Nor do I remember ever seeing a political pamphlet or political book or political newspaper in our home. All of us children were readers, taking many books out of the public library, but I was never aware of any social or political content they might have contained.

My younger brother Joel did develop into a lifelong member of the Socialist Labor Party, becoming part of the family of that party's local leader, marrying his daughter, dropping out of our Fried family so completely that he changed his name to J. Brenn Morgan, taking the name of a noted anthropologist who specialized in the study of Native American culture. It wasn't until many decades later, at a Fried family reunion in San Francisco in the summer of 2000, that the Morgan family came together again with the Fried family.

But I don't yet understand—on a deep level—why I turned to theatre and later became a union leader. David Caro, author of *The Years of Lyndon Johnson*, says that the compulsion driving LBJ was that he had to be somebody—to stand out from the crowd. That's what my actress friend said about me. It's true that wanting to become somebody and stand out from the crowd was a strong part of whatever was driving me. From the time I read Eugene O'Neill's plays in high school I yearned to become a playwright like him and get the recognition he was getting, and from the time I played a character in a reading of one of his plays in high school I wanted to become a professional actor who would get the kind of attention that movie stars were getting.

But even before that I decided I did not want to become a businessman, in part because of my experience working in our family's mom-and-pop dry goods store and in part possibly because of many anti-Semitic remarks I heard, accusing Jews of being obsessed with making money and cheating people to make money. Strongly affecting me, I still vividly remember the scene that I, a young boy, witnessed in our family's mom-and-pop dry goods store, a scene I recently included in an article I wrote for The Buffalo News.

"Again I see the frightened red-haired grammar school boy I was, helplessly listening to a heavyset woman screaming at my father, calling him a dirty Jew, ignoring his anguished denials as she accuses him of stealing her purse. People crowd into the store.

Two policemen arrive. The woman demands that they arrest my father. She describes in detail exactly how she placed her purse down on the counter and when she looked away 'the dirty Jew' grabbed her purse and hid it from her. My mother pleads with the policemen: my father is an honest man; he would never steal a penny.

"The red-haired boy's throat is clogged as he watches his mother fighting back her tears and his father desperately denying the woman's screaming accusations.

"At last the manager of the A&P grocery store pushes his way into the store, holding high a purse that was left on the counter in his place across the street. The woman angrily grabs the purse and runs out of the store."

Chapter 9

I arrived in New York City, still a very naïve twenty-year old, with only a few dollars in my pocket. Fortunately, I was able to stay with the family of my father's brother in Brooklyn until I got my first acting job. I don't remember ever having met my uncle before that. He spoke only Yiddish, which I did not understand. When he talked about me to his sons, my cousins, who were older than me and whom I'd also never met before, I could tell—from the way in which they, with embarrassment, gave revised translations of what he had said—that he didn't think very highly of my ambition to become an actor.

They did not seem to disagree with him, and as long as I lived with their family I felt as if I was mired in the same discouraging atmosphere my father pushed on me when I was leaving home in Buffalo.

But all that was about to change. In the immediate years ahead—through the plays I would appear in and through the life I would lead as I tried to achieve my ambition as an actor—my growing belief in the hidden class nature of our society, along with developments in my personal relationships, would so change my thinking that I would make the choice which turned me away from striving to achieve that ambition as an actor, choosing instead a role in life that my uncle and my cousins would find even less to their liking—a committed left-oriented union organizer.

Fortunately, my red hair shortened my stay with my uncle's family. Because of it, I got picked to play a sailor in the road company of *Sailor Beware*, the color of my hair setting me apart from the rest of the young sailors in the cast. Completely devoid of any serious social content, the play had been a fluke hit on Broadway. The week before it opened, the producers were so sure the play would be a flop that they offered to sell the production to any buyer for $5000. There were no takers. The play centered around a bet on whether the leading man, a sailor with a reputation for getting young ladies into bed, could succeed in doing that with the leading lady, a bar girl known for her cool resistance to all attempts to board her. I was part of the comedy relief, a much too serious young sailor who will not go near the bar girls because "I'm promised to a girl back home."

On November 13, 1933 our road company of *Sailor Beware* opened at the Hanna Theatre in Cleveland, then moved on to open November 19, 1933 at the Selwyn Theatre in Chicago. In both cities the critics' reviews of the play were not great, most probably because there wasn't much in the play to wax great about. But living out of a trunk in a room in a cheap hotel in both cities and getting my first deep taste of raunchy bohemian life late at night after performances in Chicago—it was a fascinating experience for the naïve twenty-year old kid I was. As yet there was no hint in my mind of the dedicated labor and political activist I was to become. I drank in the experience, relishing every bit of it, including several unexpected sexual adventures. At age twenty it was exhilarating to feel that I was breaking free from what I thought was my humdrum and oh so very uninteresting and ordinary life.

In the Creative Writing: Narrative classes I started teaching at Buffalo State College in 1972, I would ask my students: "What are the two most important things that determine the direction of people's lives?" In response I got all kinds of answers with only a few students coming close to what I had in mind.

"Money and sex!" I'd finally blurt out. "Money and sex! Karl Marx and Sigmund Freud!" This usually prompted heated discussion, some students agreeing, others disagreeing.

The role that lack of money played in much of my early life is clearly there for me to explore. The role that sex played from early on in my life is something I still have difficulty digging out and dealing with in its naked and at times embarrassing truth. But if I don't dare to risk probing into that I will be leaving out what may be—what undoubtedly is—an important part of what's determined the direction of my life, what has profoundly affected the choices I've made when the candle in the wind confronted me with situations where I had to make a choice.

I must have been about eight or nine years old when, rigid with fear, I lay awake night after night, waiting to hear the suppressed crying sounds of my mother who was in bed with my father. Three double beds were squeezed together in a large room above the Genesee Street store. With one of my brothers, I was in one bed. Two more brothers were in the second bed. My mother and father were in the third bed. I don't remember how many nights of fearful listening it took before I realized what was happening. But that they were engaged in something sexual did not alleviate the rigid terror with which I waited night after night to hear those frightening sounds my mother made. I thought my father was hurting my mother.

When I was fourteen or fifteen and, after working late into the night at the Ford Hotel, I came home to a silent house, undressed and went to bed—this is hard for me to think about—I was the target of "sexual abuse." Feigning sleep, I vigorously repulsed the attempt. Night after night after that, frozen in terror, I'd lie stiffly in bed, waiting, gearing myself up to resist. Needing to escape from that, I told the rest of the family that I wanted more room to stretch out. I retreated to the living room above the store and slept on the couch there, fully dressed, until over a year later our family moved away from the store into a house where I slept alone on a folding cot in the enclosed rear sun porch.

Earlier, something happened that became entangled in a peculiar way in my mind with sex. A bloodied rat, terrified, was cornered in our yard inside a circle of adults and kids—I was one of the kids—all armed with brooms, shovels and sticks, hitting the terrified animal again and again as it frantically darted back and forth, becoming a bloody mess as it tried to escape, finally scooting out of the circle to disappear under the house. I don't remember if I physically participated in bloodying that rat. I hope not. But years later, at times when I had sexual difficulty, that scene—the bloodying of that rat—came clearly into my mind, its terror connecting with the terror of those nights I listened to hear what my father was doing to my mother and those nights that I tensely waited, gearing up to repel a possible repeat of the attempt to sexually use me.

I mention these experiences now because my struggle with them—though relatively successful—did affect my sexual life. And my sexual life did strongly influence the choices I made in connection with my involvement in theatre and union and politics.

Reluctantly I admit that at the outset my sexual relations with the opposite sex were definitely in no way connected with love and affection. My first experience with sexual intercourse was a tawdry one in a cheap whorehouse in Niagara Falls. I was in my early teens, still too young to drive. A group of us teenagers, boys and girls, had been at a party at the home of one of the girls. We, the boys, thought of the girls as "nice girls." One of the boys, Stewie, had borrowed a big limousine from his uncle who owned and operated The Palace, Buffalo's only burlesque theatre. We, the boys, kissed and fondled the "nice girls" in the car as we drove to the whorehouse. The "nice girls" waited in the car, parked in front of the whorehouse, until we, the boys, returned. Not a word was spoken about what had happened in the whorehouse. What we, the boys, had done in the whorehouse was something done with "bad girls," something at that point in my life I did not do with "nice girls"—something I did not associate in any way with love and affection. It actually had been a cold and somewhat mechanical act ending with orgasm as quickly as it began. Yet, as some glimmer of a change about to develop in my thinking, it was about this time that I wrote my play about a teenager discovering that the prostitutes he met while working at the Ford Hotel were human beings like other people.

I would for the first time in my life—a few years after my appearance in the road company of *Sailor Beware*—become seriously involved sexually, along with being intensely in love, with a young woman who was the granddaughter of a former governor of the state of New Jersey. The relationship with Dolly was another instance of *the candle in the wind*. It resulted in a choice to be made, a choice I did make, a choice that contributed to changing the entire direction of my life. It was then, when I discovered sexual intercourse as an expression of love, that I also struggled with that terrified bloodied rat bursting into bloom in my head. Add to it that at that time I was already a member of the Communist Party. And I'm still searching, probing, to dig out how all that affected what happened with Dolly—because I'm quite certain it did.

It was a few years *before* that change in my outlook on sex and politics that, on my way to the hotel in Cleveland after a performance of *Sailor Beware*, I was approached by a young woman—but somewhat older than my twenty years— who asked me where Euclid Avenue was. We were standing on Euclid Avenue, the city's main street. Without answering, I took her by the arm and she willingly went with me to the hotel and spent the night with me. Next morning she said she wanted to go to Chicago with me. I said, "No," and she readily accepted that. Thinking about it later, I wondered if she was a prostitute who had decided to forego charging the young redheaded actor her usual fee.

But my experience with Mona Lita in Chicago was different. Mona Lita was much older than me and told me several times, "Don't you fall in love with me." We met at the cheap hotel where we both were staying. One of the other "Sailor Beware" actors, Byron Shores, who had struck up a conversation with Mona Lita in the hotel's coffee shop, introduced me to her. She was also a performer, a stripper, billed as "Mona Lita in the Dance of the Seven Veils," doing her act in Chicago's nightclubs. A few years later, when I was performing in *Having Wonderful Time* on Broadway, I learned that Mona Lita was being featured by famed burlesque producer Minsky in a theatre just a few blocks away. The show was titled something like *Burlesque Comes to Broadway*, and it consisted of a series of burlesque acts topped by "Mona Lita in the Dance of the Seven Veils."—In Chicago Mona Lita fulfilled for me what I've read is many a young man's fantasy: an older woman, experienced in matters of sex, seducing the young man and educating him. She seemed to enjoy, to get a real kick, laughing out loud, having fun, teaching different positions in bed to this naïve redheaded twenty year old, to whom all this was an unexpected and delightful surprise dropped out of the sky. "But don't you fall in love with me."—To fall in love with her never occurred to me.

Mona Lita preferred that we be together in my hotel room rather than hers. This led to a scene that demonstrates that at that time I still separated "good girls" from women with whom I had sexual relations. Laura—sadly, I can't remember her real name—was the daughter of one of the stagehands at the Selwyn

Theatre. She was about my age, maybe a little younger. We became sort of pals, doing things together before or after the evening performances, like seeing a movie or having a soda—and in a very platonic way we held hands, briefly kissed and hugged. One morning she surprised me by dropping in to see me at the hotel. We were sitting in my room, talking, when there was a knock on the door. I asked who it was. It was Mona Lita. I shooed Laura into the bathroom, opened the door, telling Mona Lita that I was just getting ready to leave, and we left together. When I came back to the room a little later, "good girl" Laura, curious, pressed me to tell her all about what was happening between me and "bad girl" Mona Lita, which I did—and Laura acted as if she thought it was amusing. Our relationship remained platonic until a few years later when she phoned me in New York City and said she was nearby visiting her aunt and uncle. She asked me to come over to their apartment. I went there, and on the floor of the rear stairwell outside her aunt and uncle's apartment, saying goodbye, we went beyond platonic.

Skip ahead to 1945. On leave from my job as an organizer with the UE union, I was in Chicago again, this time wearing a second lieutenant's uniform, on my way to the West Coast to ship out to join the 20th Infantry Regiment of the Sixth Division in Korea—leaving behind in Buffalo my wife Rhoda and my three-year old daughter Lorrie. I called the headquarters of the stagehands union, got the phone number of Laura's father and, from him, Laura's phone number. Phoned her to say hello. She wanted to see me right away, would come to meet me, cried bitterly, said she's in a lousy marriage, wants to leave her husband, wants to be with me. Her crying got to me, but I had to tell her that I was married and had a child and it was best for us not to meet, that I'd be leaving in a few hours to take a plane to the West Coast and then on to Korea. She cried, said she still wanted to come and meet me. I felt lousy about it, but I told her it would not be good and I had to go. Said goodbye. And hung up the phone. Since then I've thought of Laura at different times, especially when there was difficulty in my marriage. But we never saw each other or spoke to each other again.—And adding to my feeling of sadness about her, while I can still vaguely remember her face (as it was back then over a half century ago) I still can't recall her real name.

The negative notices that the Chicago critics gave *Sailor Beware* prompted the producers, after a run of a few weeks, to close the show, dropping previous plans to take it to other cities.

Back in "the City" I made the rounds of offices of agents and producers. Because of my red hair, producer George Abbott had me read for a major role in *Brother Rat*, a play requiring a cast of a few young men. I might have looked the part, but at that point I lacked any formal training as an actor, and the small amount of acting I'd done had not yet prepared me for a major role. I remember how nervous I was and how my cheeks flamed hot as I read for the role in the presence of George Abbott. Then actor Garson Kanin read for the part and got it, dyeing his hair red for the role. Kanin went on to become an assistant to Abbott and then a successful playwright and screenwriter.

Kanin subsequently married Ruth Gordon who starred in The Theatre Guild production of John Wexley's play *They Shall Not Die*. That play realistically portrayed what had happened to the Scottsboro Boys, several young black boys who had been framed, falsely found guilty of raping two white girls, and given harsh jail sentences. I played a non-speaking role in that production and I learned a great deal from appearing in it, especially from all the discussion it prompted, not so much about acting, but about discrimination against blacks in the South and also the disputed role of members of the Communist Party in fighting against that discrimination.

While I had flubbed that chance with George Abbott, my red hair still helped me get work in other shows, including the non-speaking role in *They Shall Not Die*. What may have helped me get cast in those productions might have been something more than just the red hair, maybe something added by the different jobs I had had—an indefinable something that working at the Dupont factory and at the Ford hotel and at the A&P and other places somehow subtly reflected itself in my overall appearance and personality. Whatever it was, I found myself getting cast in plays that dealt with working people and/or plays with a radical pro-labor theme and/or plays with a politically leftist point of view. Such plays were not uncommon during that period of the Big Depression in the Thirties.

I believe that acting in those plays contributed greatly to educating me politically, moving my thinking to the left. I drank in the information, new to me, about the "reality underlying our society"—my introduction to the idea of class conflict—that I got from the plays themselves and also from talking with the other actors, some of whom were members of the Communist Party and whom I readily recognized as being much more knowledgeable than I was about the make-up of our society.

There was no question in my mind, probably because of my work history, about whose side I was on. But because I was raised in a family whose income came primarily from our mom-and-pop dry goods store, I thought of myself as lower middle class and—much as my reading of Marxist pamphlets given me by leftist actors made me wish it otherwise—not really working class.

This was especially true of my thinking when I became a member of the left-oriented Theatre of Action. Only years later, long after that group had disintegrated, did I figure out that, despite my family's mom-and-pop dry goods store, I had been the only actor in that theatre company who had worked in a factory, the only actor who personally had a substantial "working class" job history of his own.

With the exception of Perry Bruskin—we're still in close touch with each other—whose father, if I recall correctly, was a union man working in a bakery, most members of the Theatre of Action were university graduates, some from wealthy families, who, generally prompted by reports they had read and heard about the Soviet Union establishing a worker-controlled government following the 1917 Bolshevik revolution, had intellectually arrived at their radical beliefs and their commitment to the working class.

For me, at that point in my life, drinking in this information from my fellow actors *and actresses* who were better educated, better read, more knowledgeable and politically wiser than the ignorant and unsophisticated person I was, helped to dispel a feeling of emptiness and "no point to life" which had intermittently plagued me from the time I was a teenager and, on occasion, had made me think about killing myself. Despite the Big Depression, there was hope. There could be "a point to life." These actors, I believed, I truly believed, were working to make life better for working people, for poor people, for white and black poor people. And this, like a magnet, drew me forcefully to them—to the left.

When I had been hired for the road company of *Sailor Beware* I became a member of Actors Equity Association, the actors' union. Attending the union's meetings, I became aware of a schism between the left and the right, with the old guard part of the right. They dominated the union's executive board and were quick to red-bait any actors who proposed that the union take a stand on issues not narrowly confined to only actors' economic concerns. Supporting Dictator Franco because "he's fighting the communists," the old guard were especially adamant in their opposition to any attempt to put the union on record in support of the loyalists who had been elected in Spain. But even on actors' economic issues the old guard generally supported the viewpoint of the producers rather than the actors.

It was only years later—when I, as an organizer for the UE union, was personally involved in trench warfare between left and right in the labor movement—that I realized that many of the old guard right-wingers in Actors Equity might have been part of a Catholic caucus, like the ACTU (Association of Catholic Trade Unionists) caucus that operated inside our UE local unions in the Fifties and finally, with the help of FBI and other government agencies, succeeded in splitting away a large part of our membership to form a rabidly anti-communist rival.

Our national union convention, supporting Henry Wallace's opposition to a Cold War with the Soviet bloc, had endorsed him, not Harry Truman, for president. This prompted the Truman administration to do its best to destroy our union, enlisting the help of some "labor priests" to pressure AFL and CIO union leaders to launch a continuous series of raids against our UE local unions all across the country.

Years later, in 1976, when the NEA (National Endowment on the Arts) decided to fund a pilot program to involve workers in the arts, Buffalo was one of four cities selected. The announced intention was to involve union members and their families in the arts by getting them to attend professional play productions. I received a phone call from Jack Golodner, head of the national union of professional employees, who had just arrived from Washington and had an appointment to meet with Jim Kane, the president of the Buffalo AFL-CIO Council, to select the person who would be in charge of the new NEA program in the area. Golodner told me he was going to recommend that they support a production of my play *The Dodo Bird*. But he phoned me again several hours later, his voice reflecting dismay as he reported that a Catholic priest—James Healy, the so-called "labor priest" who had openly led a successful campaign to drive me out of my leadership position in the area's labor movement about twenty years earlier—had been brought into the meeting by Kane, and the priest took over, saying the new NEA program was too important to be under the control of anyone but the Catholic Church and he'd appoint the person to be in charge.

To nominally head the new NEA program, Father Healy named Bob Jarnot, an English teacher at South Park High School and, I assume, a devout Catholic. Subsequently I got to know Bob fairly well. He was a good guy, meant well and tried hard. But the program failed to get workers involved because the play productions they were asked to attend at Buffalo's Studio Arena theatre—which then catered to a very elitist audience—did not appeal to working people. There was more excitement for them at the corner gin-mill. Bob, anxious to save the program and his job with it, finally joined me in an unsuccessful effort to get The Studio Arena to do a production of my play *The Dodo Bird*. NEA then cut out funding for the program, which resulted in Bob going back to teach at South Park High School. I credit him for sincerely trying to make the program work.

Father Healy was the chaplain for the St. Joseph Guild, the Buffalo ACTU unit, which he organized early in the Fifties—setting up Catholic caucuses within a wide range of local unions, not only our UE unions—with the publicly stated purpose of driving the communists out of the labor movement. It appeared to me that he was trying to use these ACTU caucuses to try to take over control of the labor unions in the area.

When our union was involved in a strike at the Richardson Boat Company in Tonawanda, the St. Joseph Guild officer whom Healy got named to head the State Mediation Service in the area deliberately helped to prolong the strike—refusing to set up a mediation session—in order to help the employer and the ACTU caucus succeed in getting the striking workers to abandon our union.

At about the same time Father Healy had another of his St. Joseph Guild members, a former business agent for the Machinists Union whom he helped to become a conciliator with the U.S. Conciliation Service—try to extend our strike at the Blaw-Knox plant to the point where our members there would also turn against our union. The government conciliator kept telling me that he had asked the company to meet with us but that they still refused to talk to us. He repeated this even when, with the company manager sitting beside me and listening on a phone extension, I phoned from the company's conference room—immediately after we had already reached agreement settling the strike—and I asked the conciliator if he'd please ask the company again to meet with us. He said he had just spoken to the company manager again and the company still refused to meet with us. I then informed him that we were sitting with the company manager and we had just settled the strike—and I hung up the phone.

Father Healy then got himself appointed by the governor to head up the Mediation Service for all of New York State and he tried to get control of some big downstate unions by using the same tactics his ACTU people had used against our UE local unions. But the leaders of the downstate unions he tried to take over had more political clout than we in UE had and were essentially conservatives who could not be easily labeled Communists. They complained to their representatives in the state legislature, telling them what Healy was doing. The governor withdrew Healy's appointment to head the New York State Mediation Service, a polite way to fire him.

Sometime during this period Father Healy announced he was organizing a tour group to visit Italy. My brother Martin signed on with the group, taking advantage of the cheap fare to visit Italian friends he'd made while he'd headed the Buffalo State College's program in Sienna. Healy knew Martin was my brother and apparently felt the need to explain why he was so openly attacking me and trying to drive me out of the labor movement.

"The majority of the union members your brother Manny represents are Catholic.—This was true of our local unions in the area.—"I'm not opposed to Manny because he's Jewish," he went on. "But he's not Catholic. We should have a Catholic organizer representing our Catholic union members in there."

To avoid unpleasantness during the rest of the trip, my brother told me he chose not to argue.

Chapter 10

I think it was an actor in the rank-and-file group challenging the old guard in Actors Equity who asked me to join the Communist Party.

To be honest about it, I did think at that time that it would be best for my career as an actor—help me get acting jobs with the left-oriented theatre groups—if I said yes when I was asked to join the Party. Later, not too many years later, I like to think that by the time I became a union organizer I had become truly prompted by my concern for other people, with primary concern for working people, for the poor, for needful minorities, etc.—rather than by concern for advancing my own selfish interest.

My red hair, I think, continued to give me an advantage in the Broadway competition for acting jobs, because it was very shortly after the Chicago closing of *Sailor Beware* and my return to New York that I got the non-speaking role in John Wexley's *They Shall Not Die*, the play about the Scottsboro Boys presented by The Theatre Guild. I've mentioned how educational it was for me to be involved in that play, which—one week before my March 1, 1934 twenty-first birthday—opened to mixed reviews.

This was before I became a member of Theatre of Action and I was still essentially untrained as an actor and did not have enough money to pay to attend acting classes. Somehow I learned that Mary Tarcai, who later became a highly respected acting teacher with her own studio classes, was putting together a choral recitation and dance group to give a performance—a fund-raiser for The New Theatre League—at the Civic Repertory Theatre on 14th Street. I believe the idea for establishing the New Theatre League came from the Communist Party, with the intention to encourage formation of worker-oriented theatre companies around the country.

Mary Tarcai accepted me into the group and we performed to benefit The New Theatre League. I remember very well another young actor in the group, also in his early twenties, who went on to become one of the biggest film stars in Hollywood: Charlton Heston.

We performed—with intense choral recitation and modern dance thrusts from the pelvis—a performance piece derived from *Johnny Got His Gun,* the powerful anti-war novel written by Dalton Trumbo. All of us, including Charlton Heston, rhythmically pounded out the words, our fists clenched as we energetically thrust our bodies forward with intense movements stemming from the pelvis: "Johnny got his gun, got his gun, got his gun/ Got it on the run, on the run, on the run/ Johnee-ee-ee!/ Johnee-ee-ee!/ Johnny got his gun, got his gun, got his gun…" It was a strong attack against the use of guns, in which Charlton Heston, now president of the National Rifle Association, ardently joined.—But that was almost 70 years ago, and we all do change over time.

Incidentally, when Charlton Heston a few years back publicly announced his 79th birthday I was then 90, and if Charlton Heston was then 79, he would have been about 10 or 11 years old up on the stage of the Civic Repertory Theatre with the rest of us in our early twenties when—while energetically thrusting his pelvis forward and backward—he belted out, "Johnny got his gun/got his gun/got his gun …" Well, I don't blame a Hollywood actor for shaving a few years off his age.

I had come to New York in 1933 determined to devote my whole life to becoming a star of stage and screen, ready to make whatever personal sacrifice was necessary to achieve that goal. Yet in 1939 I walked away from that, returning to Buffalo to become artistic director of The Buffalo Contemporary Theatre, one of the worker-oriented theatres associated with The New Theatre League.

Examining my life to get at the truth, the deep truth—not the easy surface—as to why I did that, I keep reminding myself that it couldn't be just the candle in the wind. I made choices—difficult choices—conscious and unconscious— resulting in tumultuous changes in the whole direction of my life. What role did money play? What role did sex play?—What role did something other than money and sex play?—I'm still trying to figure it out.

It's easy to see how acting in several productions presented at New York City's Civic Repertory Theatre by the Theatre Union may have contributed to moving me in that direction, where I chose to become artistic director of a worker-oriented theatre. While I did not have specific knowledge about who had gotten together to launch the Theatre Union, I vaguely understood that the intent of the Theatre Union was to educate a trade union audience with plays that dealt in a somewhat progressive/radical way with social problems. As an actor in several of their productions, I did become aware of political tensions up there on top, reflected in disputes about which plays to do and what political/militant actions should be taken by characters in the plays that were produced.

That the plays were intended for labor audiences did strongly interest me, but truthfully when I was cast *in Sailors of Catarro* my main concern had been to get a job as an actor. However, by the time I was cast to perform there in *Bitterstream,* I was beginning to think differently.

If I recall correctly, *Sailors of Catarro* is set in the time of the 1917 Bolshevik revolution and it involves an unsuccessful uprising by some sailors in their navy who objected to the way that the Soviet ruling structure had been established. Again, if I recall correctly, the other play, *Bitterstream,* was a dramatization of Ignazio Silone's novel *Fontamara,* adapted for the stage by Victor Wolfson, brother of actor Martin Wolfson whom I knew well; it was about the unsuccessful revolt of the farmers of Fontamara in Italy.

There was talk among the actors about there being differences within the Theatre Union's governing board concerning these two plays and even more so concerning another play, *Black Pit,* which—again if I recall correctly—was a play dealing with a wildcat strike of coal miners in our own country and was subsequently made into a movie starring Paul Muni.

I was not knowledgeable enough then to be aware of the complicated reasons for the tug-of-war taking place within the theatre's board of directors, which included representatives of the Communist Party and the Socialist Workers Party. After a few years of the Theatre Union's existence this contention, I was told, led to the theatre's demise.

However, even after I became deeply involved in union and politics and was aware of differences "up there" between them, I deliberately ignored—often joked about—admonitions from "up there" in the Communist Party that I should not have anything to do with members of the Socialist Workers Party: "Trotskyites."

In the Buffalo area the so-called "Trotskyites" had splintered into opposing groups. It was possible to work with some of them, lending support to one another in strikes and other matters of that kind. However, even though now I'm again a professional actor and also I'm a playwright with a number of plays produced and, since 1972, I've been a college professor, I'm told that—though I've not been a member of the CP for over half a century—there is a retired union organizer/lawyer, Manny T., who, I've been told, was associated with a small political group in Buffalo that splintered off the Socialist Workers Party, and who still bad-mouths me behind my back, saying about me, "Once a Stalinist always a Stalinist." Maybe that's because I refuse to ape him in demonizing those who might be—or might have been—members of the Communist Party.

Does it bother me that he does this? Yes, it does, though when I'm told about it I laugh and dismiss it as stupid bullshit. I had no connection with Stalin. Didn't defend him or attack him. He was someone "up there and far away" with whom I had no close connection. As an actor and communist in the Thirties, and as a union organizer and Communist in the years immediately after that, I dedicated myself to organizing and improving the lives of the working people with whom I was in direct contact.

Sometime in the mid-Nineties I received a phone call from a friend, LouJean Fleron, who headed Cornell University's Buffalo Labor Studies program, and she told me that two men, who were scheduled to speak at a seminar about the Bell Aircraft strike which had taken place back in the Fifties, said that they would promote a boycott of the seminar by survivors of those striking workers if I—as had been announced—was to be one of the speakers.

"One is supposed to be a good friend of yours," she said. "You'll never guess."

I was not able to guess. She told me he was Manny T. That surprised me because whenever I ran into Manny T. he always flashed a big smile and vigorously shook my hand. LouJean told me the second man was Don Slaiman who had just "retired" from the chairmanship of the national AFL-CIO Civil Rights Committee in Washington. I knew that newly elected AFL-CIO president John Sweeney had cleaned house, getting rid of the Shachtmanite clique whom the two former AFL-CIO presidents, Meany and Kirkland, had used as advisers.

I prepared for the humiliating blow, expecting that LouJean had called to gently take back the invitation for me to speak at the seminar. This especially bothered me since I assumed LouJean, like me, suspected that Manny T. and Don Slaiman were followers of Max Shachtman, formerly the secretary to Leon Trotsky who had broken with Lenin and Stalin, and that they and others, who had been colonized into Buffalo, had supported FBI efforts to undermine our UE union and the Mine and Smelter Union in the Forties and especially in the Fifties during the McCarthy Period—when FBI set up "ultra-revolutionary" political groups to attack the left from "further left."

But I felt better when LouJean Fleron told me that she and UAW Regional Director Tom Fricano—the seminar was sponsored by UAW and Cornell University—had no intention to withdraw the invitation for me to speak. They just wanted me to know what was going on.

A few days later I received a phone call from Frank St. George who had been one of the leaders of the striking workers at the Bell Aircraft plant. What he told me made me feel good. Manny T. and Slaiman had contacted him and several other men who had been involved in the strike, urging that they refuse to participate in the seminar if I was to speak. Frank said he reminded them that I had brought over about a thousand of our UE union members to reinforce their UAW picket lines. He said he told them that if I were not permitted to speak, he and the other surviving workers from that strike would not participate in the seminar.

When I entered the union hall on the night of the seminar, I had to consciously hide my disgust as Manny T. and Don Slaiman rushed over to shake my hand and tell me how glad they were to see me there. I acknowledged their enthusiastic greetings with a fake smile and said nothing. Frank St. George and several of the former strikers had stationed themselves where they could watch the performance of Manny T. and Slaiman. They gathered around me, shaking my hand, and then escorted me into the meeting room. I felt good. Triumphant.

Chapter 11

My political education continued with my non-speaking role in Elmer Rice's play *Judgment Day* presented at the Belasco Theatre in September of 1934. In retrospect, that play is especially important to me because years later when I appeared before HUAC in 1954 and again in 1964 my mind could not help but flash back to compare the witness who named me and others in 1954 and 1964 with the witness in Elmer Rice's play.

In his play Elmer Rice presents his dramatized version of the trial of Communist Party leaders in Hitler's court in Leipzig. They were accused of having burned Germany's parliament building, the Reichstag, in 1933.

In the play the cooperating witness is so drugged that only with great difficulty is he able to stand and speak. He is badgered repeatedly by the prosecuting attorney to get him to mumble that the Communist Party is responsible for burning the Reichstag. Years later, on the internet, a Dutch citizen, a member of some revolutionary group opposed to the Communist Party, is reported to have testified—without being drugged—that he set fire to the Reichstag. And a supposedly reliable source stated that Nazi leader Goering did it.

Anyway, in 1954 and again in 1964 when I was called before the House UnAmerican Activities Committee I had to laugh at myself for having been so naive as to believe that getting a witness to testify the way the witness did in Elmer Rice's play requires that he be drugged. The FBI's cooperative witness who testified against me and other union organizers in HUAC's 1954 and 1964 hearings was definitely not drugged.

In 1954 I was surprised when I saw who was being called to the witness stand to identify me and other UE union organizers as Communists. The cooperative witness was a UE union organizer who had worked with us for years. I always thought Jack was a nice guy, not the most brilliant in his ability to organize and negotiate, but competent enough, and easy going and generally likeable, though always seeming a little too anxious to please and be accepted by the rest of us.

He had been kidding around with us at a meeting of the organizers just a few days before he appeared to take the stand and testify that that very same meeting was a Communist meeting to plan how to control what direction the union would take. He and the committee's lawyer questioning him made it seem like we were plotting to overthrow the United States government—comparable to "setting fire to the congressional Reichstag in Washington."

The National Labor Relations Board had set a date for an election between UE and IUE at the Schenectady GE plants, and the 1954 HUAC hearing had been set to take place just prior to that election. The hearing took place in a courtroom with the apparent intent to make it look like it was a legal trial, which of course it was not. We were allowed to have a lawyer with whom we could have whispered consultations, but the lawyer was not allowed to speak out on our behalf. We could not present witnesses in our defense. We could not question our accusers. The courtroom was filled with officers and members of Local 301 and the purpose of this HUAC hearing was to affect the election about to take place between UE and IUE by creating some kind of hysteria about Communism and the so-called ulterior motives of Communists in the union.

At one point Leo Jandreau was called to the stand. Formerly president of UE Local 301, he was now president of IUE Local 301. He was asked pointblank if he had ever been a member of the Communist Party. Under oath he swore that he had never been a member of the Communist Party. One of the UE union organizers sitting next to me leaned over and whispered into my ear, "They know he's lying. He knows he's lying. From now on he's their boy. They can get him to do anything they want, because anytime they want, they can get him on perjury."

Jack slipped in through a door behind the judge's bench. He did not look out into the courtroom. Head down, he took the stand and swore he'd tell the truth and nothing but the truth. In response to questions from HUAC's lawyer, Jack testified that the Communists met in caucus before union meetings and talked about what policies they would advocate in the meetings. When he was asked to name those who were present at those meetings, he named me along with several others. The congressman chairing the hearing thanked Jack for being a good patriotic American Then Jack was quickly whisked out through the door behind the judge's bench.

Some of the other UE organizers who had worked very closely with Jack and knew him and his wife socially, told me that Jack's wife had been upset about the red-baiting our union was taking and she had pressured Jack until finally he had given in and agreed to cooperate with HUAC. Whatever happened to their life after Jack cooperated with HUAC must have been too difficult for his wife to handle. I was told that shortly after Jack named names the way he did at the HUAC hearing in 1954 his wife killed herself.

While my response to the witnesses in Hitler's court in Elmer Rice's *Judgment Day* back in 1934 had been purely intellectual, an addition to my political education but with no emotional involvement, my response to the witnesses in the HUAC hearing in 1954 was much more complex. My whole life, including my marriage, was endangered. Yet I still felt sorry for Jack. Though I never had the opportunity to speak to him after the hearing, I like to think that he was decent enough not to rationalize that his cooperation with HUAC was a great act of patriotism. And I still wonder if his wife killing herself might have prevented him from thinking that way.

Chapter 12

By accident—*the candle in the wind*—I received what I believe is the best training an actor could possibly get at that time in this country. My appearance with the Theatre Union in *Sailors of Catarro* may have combined with my red hair to bring me to the attention of the Theatre of Action who were looking for an All-American-Boy to play the lead in *The Young Go First*, a play written by George Scudder and Pete Martin, about young men in the Civilian Conservation Corps (CCC).

The Theatre of Action, a collective of young theatre people, had developed from the Workers Laboratory Theatre, which was reputed to have been a Communist theatre troupe. Theatre of Action performed agit-prop (agitational propaganda) sketches at political meetings, in union halls and on street corners. They developed the Living Newspaper technique, dramatizing economic, social and political issues. I believe *The Young Go First* was their first effort to produce a play other than agit-prop.

The CCC was established by President Franklin Delano Roosevelt to provide jobs for unemployed young people. In the play a group of young men, in a CCC camp run by an army colonel, revolt against the camp's living conditions. My thought now is that there really wasn't much to the play. The conditions we revolted against may have been better than the environments we had left behind. But we, the young men in the CCC camp, wanted representation and a grievance procedure to resolve complaints. My character stepped forward, becoming the organizer of the revolt against the iron fist of the colonel.

What was most important for me, far beyond this play, was that the Theatre of Action had been taken under the wing of some of the most talented theatre people in our country, members of the Group Theatre.

The Group Theatre is credited with establishing the Stanislavsky method of acting as the most important tool used by actors in our country. Constantin Stanislavsky, artistic director of the Moscow Art Theatre, studied what good actors did and then wrote several books defining the craft of acting. In the United States this is known as the Stanislavsky Method or just The Method; in Russia it is called The System. Elements of The Method are also often used by playwrights, screen writers and novelists. Scott Fitzgerald revealed his use of The Method in notes that have been included in the preface added to publication of his novel *The Last Tycoon*.

Members of the Group Theatre, including Elia Kazan, Morris Carnovsky, Bobby Lewis, and Harold Clurman gave us, actors with the Theatre of Action, acting lessons. Through my association with these Group Theatre members I was admitted into classes that their actors were taking with Benno Schneider, an acting teacher who later became one of the most highly acclaimed acting coaches employed by Hollywood movie studios.

Further, flowing from my association with the Group Theatre actors, I received a scholarship to study modern dance with noted teacher Ben Zemach, and then studied with Anna Sokolow and Jane Dudley—developing enough skill as a dancer that I was later cast as an actor who performed with modern dance movement under the direction of dancer/choreographer Martha Graham on Broadway in Archibald MacLeish's verse play about the Great Depression: *Panic*.

Group Theatre actor Julie Garfield—he became John Garfield when he went out to Hollywood—helped me get private lessons with his singing teacher. Highly skilled actor/speech teacher Arnold Korff gave me private speech lessons—again on a scholarship—and taught me voice exercises I still do every morning, with a cork clenched between my teeth. Doing that and also still doing warm-up singing exercises every morning—exercises learned when not too many years ago I sang in a production of *Cabaret*—may explain why during telephone conversations I'm occasionally told that my voice doesn't sound like the 95-year old man that I am.

Actor friend Cornel Wilde—an Olympic team fencer and not yet the Hollywood movie star he was to become—gave me private fencing lessons, again without charging me.

It must have been obvious to all my teachers that I couldn't afford to pay for their lessons. And maybe it was that they thought I had possibilities. My red hair may have also helped here. And also maybe some kind of unsophisticated and unpolished patina that I retained from working at the Dupont factory and the A&P and the Ford Hotel prompted this extra kindness from them.

What is very interesting for me—as I think about this now—is that at that point in my life all my energies and hopes were aimed at making it to the top as an actor. *More than anything else in my life I desperately yearned to become a stage and movie star!* Yet about ten years later, when I definitely was given the opportunity to make it up there to the top as an actor—*to become a star!*—I voluntarily chose to walk away from it, choosing to go back to the little recognized, controversial, certainly not glorified, but often reviled job as a rank-and-file union organizer, where I negotiated contracts establishing wages and working conditions, and handled grievances, arbitrations, walkouts, slowdowns and strikes, involved day after day after day with thousands of factory workers in unglamorous heavy industry.

While it's easily evident to me now how much I had changed, I am still trying to dig out the truth of the *why*.

As I recall, conscious political responsibility had nothing to do with it. Conscious loyalty to the working class had nothing to do with it. The Communist Party had nothing to do with it—I did not say one word about the impending choice to anyone connected to the Communist Party. Except for Charlie Cooper—who died only a few hours after I spoke to him in the hospital—I did not talk to anyone connected to the union about it. I did talk to Rhoda about it. Yet it was without any clear understanding as to the *why* that I instinctively chose to reject director/friend Elia Kazan's offer to launch me on a movie career and chose to return to my slogging job in the trenches as a union organizer.

When Kazan directed me in the lead role in *The Young Go First in 1935*, he became my idol, the man I looked up to, the man I wanted to emulate with my life.

In 1954, guided by highly respected editor Angus Cameron—who contacted me after the story a week I was writing for the Buffalo CIO union's newspaper was called to his attention by the UE union's legislative director Russ Nixon—I wrote the first draft of *The UnAmerican*, an autobiographical nonfiction novel about my confrontation with HUAC—where, following the public advice of Albert Einstein, I refused to answer any questions, charging that the enabling resolution establishing the committee was unconstitutional and therefore the committee had no right to exist and question anybody, and I sought to be indicted so the courts would decide whether I go to jail or the committee goes out of existence; the committee said they would ask the House of Representatives to indict me, but possibly fearing that the courts might rule against them, the committee apparently ducked and I was not indicted.

I did something with that first draft of *The UnAmerican*, which I would not have the energy to do today. Since copying machines were not yet available, I—a one-finger typist—typed the script of over 500 pages onto stencils and ran off and assembled 75 copies of the manuscript and distributed them to officers and stewards of the UE local unions I was working with in western New York.

And I mailed a copy of the manuscript to Elia Kazan, expecting praise from him because—though I had not been in touch with him since 1946 when I'd walked away from his kind offer to launch my movie career—I remembered his fierce dedication to the cause of the left and the working class. The script was immediately returned, apparently unread and with no comment. Puzzled, I took advantage of a trip I had to take to New York City—a meeting at our union's national headquarters—and phoned Martin Ritt, a friend from the disbanded Theatre of Action with whom I had written a play, *Behind the Eight Ball*. Marty's wife, Adele Jerome, said she had good news to tell me, invited me to drop by. When I got there she told me Marty had phoned from Hollywood, telling her that he had just signed a contract to direct a film. Since she and Marty had been good friends with Kazan, I told Adele about Kazan returning *The UnAmerican*. I learned from her what I found hard to believe—that Kazan had appeared as a friendly witness before HUAC and named his close friends and fellow actors in the Group Theatre who had been members of the Communist Party, destroying their careers.

Marty identified himself as a humanist. But his career had been hampered because of guilt by association: his friendship with people on the left. The complexity here is that Kazan, who had been accepted as a Hollywood film director because he had cooperated with HUAC, may have used his influence to help partially blacklisted Marty get accepted as a director in Hollywood.

Once I became fully involved as a controversial union leader in Buffalo my rough-and-tumble life separated me completely from the actors I'd worked with in the Theatre of Action. For some reason I'm not sure of myself I made no effort to keep in touch with them, not until I was forced out of the labor movement and blacklisted. At that time, out of a need to counteract the inner turmoil and sense of defeat that poisoned my success with my "day job" as an independent life insurance broker with Canada Life Assurance Company, I turned back to acting and playwriting..

Encouraged when my play *Mark of Success* (later re-named *David and Son*) won the New American Playwrights contest and was produced at Catawba College in Salisbury, North Carolina, I wrote my labor play, *The Dodo Bird*, about a working stiff. Dodo has been automated out of his factory job. With his drinking he has destroyed his family. His internal action or intention in the play is to fight to put his life back together to regain his self-respect. (The underlying secret that drives *The Dodo Bird* is my own fight—after I'd been blacklisted out of my job as a union organizer—to put my life back together to regain my self-respect.)

The Dodo Bird has had more productions in the United States and Canada than all my other plays combined. In 1967, seeking advice about putting on a New York production of the play, I contacted Perry Bruskin, with whom I'd acted when we were part of the long-gone Theatre of Action. It was almost thirty years since I'd last spoken to Perry. I phoned him, said it was Eddie Mann calling, and then explained to cautious Perry that playwright Emanuel Fried— call me Manny—was the old friend he once knew as Edward Mann—call me Eddie. It still took several years after that for him to drop Eddie and call me

Manny. But Perry and his wife Charlotte and I, ever since that initial phone call, have remained in close touch,

I'm not sure why, but I seemed to have developed a strong need to integrate my union life and my theatre life. While fearing a rebuff from the two prominent Hollywood film directors who had been my closest friends back in the Theatre of Action, I took a chance and reached out to contact director Marty Ritt (*Norma Rae, Sounder, The Molly Maguires, The Front*) and—a few years after that—director Nick Ray (*Rebel Without A Cause, Johnny Guitar*).

In 1979 Rhoda and I took a plane flight to Los Angeles after visiting her aunt and cousins in Seattle. Marty's phone umber was unlisted. I phoned and left a message for Marty at the Film Directors Guild. He phoned back and invited Rhoda and me to his home in Malibu. While I had spoken to Adele, Marty's wife, after I'd sent *The UnAmerican* to Kazan, I had not spoken to Marty since I left New York in 1939.

His hand extended, Marty came out of the house to greet me, warmly growling, "How ya doin', kid?" as if that gap in time had never existed. We had a nice visit with him and Adele. He invited us to see a preview screening of *Norma Rae* which he had just completed filming and indicated his awareness of what I was writing by saying that he hoped that *Norma Rae* would open the door for my labor plays to be made into movies.

He said that since *Norma Rae* included labor union material he and the writers had had difficulty getting it financed and they had worked "on spec"—they would get a percentage of the gross.

"If it does very well," Marty joked, "I'll buy Buffalo."—And *Norma Rae* did do very well.

We visited Marty and Adele again in 1981 when my play *Drop Hammer* was produced at Los Angeles Actors Theatre. And shortly before he died of a heart attack in 1990, Marty phoned from Toronto—there to shoot a film starring Jane Fonda—and he invited Rhoda and me to drive up from Buffalo and have dinner with him and Adele, which we did.

The Dodo Bird has been optioned four times by film producers. Though I got the option money and wrote the screenplay, the film producers couldn't raise the money needed to make a movie that digs further than *Norma Rae* into how factory workers, deeply involved in their union, are emotionally torn by layoffs, strikes, and plant closings.

Before I resumed my friendship with Marty Ritt I had read in The New York Times that Nick Ray, having returned to this country from where he'd been living in Europe, was teaching film making at State University of New York at Binghamton. Since I was teaching at Buffalo State College, part of the same state university system, I felt that we had strangely arrived at similar places in our lives. It was a relatively short drive from Buffalo to Binghamton. I phoned Nick and after I cleared up that Eddie Mann was now Manny Fried, we talked like old friends. Nick invited me to come to Binghamton with Rhoda.

I recognized that Nick was a talented film director, as was Marty Ritt. But my meeting with Marty, which took place *after* getting together again with Nick, highlighted how different from each other these men, whom I had not talked to since I worked with them in the Theatre of Action, had become.

My admiration for the contribution to American life by Marty's films, combined with the decent human being that it was obvious he had become—along with the good family life he'd developed with Adele and their adopted daughter—caused me to wonder if I had chosen to follow a path similar to his in regard to stage and film, might I have made a better contribution to American life than I had with the path I'd taken as a union organizer and a not very well recognized writer about union and working class life?

In contrast to my thought that Marty, though heavier, still looked essentially the same as when I'd last seen him, I remembered how I searched Nick's wasted face and decayed skinny frame to find something to recognize from the younger man I had last seen in 1939. While Marty seemed mostly to enjoy talking about his films and his adopted *shiksa* (non-Jewish daughter), Nick had talked mainly about the women he had fucked, including two sisters he lived with in Europe—"the three of us in the same bed." Rhoda thought that with Nick's conversation being so preoccupied with his fucking he had been angling to get into bed with her, with me, or with the two of us. I had dismissed that because wasted Nick didn't look like he was physically capable to fuck anybody.

My insistent questioning finally got Nick off the subject of fucking long enough to explain how he'd ended up teaching film-making in Binghamton down in the southern tier of New York State.

"I was having trouble getting work as a director in Hollywood because of my politics," he began.—Somewhere I'd read that it was not politics, but too much booze that destroyed his film career.—"Then I got an invitation from the French government." His thin lips seemed blood red, in contrast with the white face that was bony and pinched, with sunken cheeks. "The French love me. They invited me to come over there for a retrospective showing of the films I'd directed. And then a department chairperson from the New York State University at Binghamton, who attended the retrospective showing of my films in France, invited me to teach filmmaking at the university.

"So I had my students shoot a film about a famous Hollywood director who couldn't get work because of his politics. Then the French government invites him to attend a retrospective of his films. And a department chairperson from The New York State University at Binghamton, who attended the retrospective showing of his films in France, invites him to teach filmmaking at the university.

So he has his students shoot a film about a famous Hollywood director who couldn't get work because of his politics. Then the French government invites him …"

With my mind's eye I can still see Nick breaking off, chortling, his hollowed face split with a grin, as if by having his students make this film, he had cleverly slipped a subversive blow past the ever-present guard of the wary establishment. Somewhere in our conversation Rhoda had briefly mentioned to Nick that after my clash with HUAC I had been blacklisted. I wondered if that had challenged Nick to try to show us that he was still actively subverting the system.

Shortly after renewing my friendship with Marty in 1979 I read a New York Times obit reporting that Nick had died of cancer. That reminded me how Rhoda and I had nervously laughed along with Nick when, as if he was proud of it, his wasted face spread into a ghoulish grin while he chortled that he was constantly bleeding from his rear.

Chapter 13

It's probably no use to speculate, but I still wonder whether I would have become more like Marty or more like Nick if my appearance in the Theatre of Action's *The Young Go First* when I was only 22 years old had resulted in a Hollywood film career.

"One more leading role and we'll bring you out to Hollywood," Universal Pictures talent scout Charlie Beahan told me after he saw me perform in *The Young Go First*.

And only a few months after *The Young Go First* closed, the chance to get that next leading role came when The Theatre Union announced that their next play in the fall would be Maxim Gorky's play *Mother* and they wanted Edward Mann who had appeared in *The Young Go First* to play the son, the leading male role.

But disheartened and disillusioned, deeply depressed, with no money and no immediate job prospects following the closing of *The Young Go First,* I had already returned to Buffalo, moving back in with my parents and brothers and sisters. I had been so despondent that I'd not told anyone in the Theatre of Action that I was leaving or where I could be reached.

The Theatre Union tried for several months, I was told, to find me. They even looked for Edward Mann in Buffalo. But having returned home, Edward Mann had again become Emanuel Fried.

Since I was depressed and didn't know what to do with my life, my brother Martin, trying to help me, convinced me to resume my college education. I read in the newspaper that Canisius College, a local Jesuit institution, had hired football coach Jimmy Wilson as the first step in an effort to emulate Notre Dame's success in building an outstanding football team as a good source of revenue.

Jimmy Wilson had built a local reputation as a football coach at Lafayette High School and I had played against his team when I attended Hutchinson Central. I contacted him and, based on my having been on the freshman football squad at the University of Iowa, he arranged for a waiver of tuition at Canisius. My brother Marty spoke to a Jesuit professor he knew who arranged for my registration and selection of several courses he thought would interest me. Jimmy Wilson put me in as a quarterback on his "ringer" freshman team. That was when a reporter for the local newspaper, having become aware of my theatre experience, labeled me "the matinee idol quarterback."

This was my second year playing freshman football. There were other players on this freshman team who had already played three or four years with other college or university football teams. I assumed they were being paid some way for their services. We played exhibition games against the freshman football teams of Cornell University and Columbia University and did too well. Although we fielded only a first team and a second team against their five or six teams, we beat them. Unfortunately, our victories over these prestigious outfits attracted the attention of other teams in the minor league that Canisius was a part of. They filed a successful protest about the use of ineligible players and ended the Canisius effort to emulate Notre Dame's financial success with a football team.

I didn't know it then, but Jimmy Wilson was to surface again in my life when I would be involved in an arbitration of some grievances filed by workers in a Jamestown, New York, factory who were represented by our UE union. I was the union rep on the arbitration board. The company had named their rep on the board. The American Arbitration Association sent a list of names from which the union and company board members were to pick the so-called impartial third party. And Jimmy Wilson was the name we selected from that list. The same Jimmy Wilson.

I don't remember the outcome of that arbitration. But I guess I enjoyed our changed situation. A wiry short man, a soft spoken lawyer, unmarried, living alone at the University Club, Jimmy was hesitant, retiring, even apologetic, possibly because I had become the publicly maligned militant and outspoken labor leader representing thousands of blue collar workers in Western New York, no longer the moody young quarterback he had barked at and ordered around when I was on his football team at Canisius.

When I played football for Jimmy Wilson, I was the only Jew attending Canisius College. Back then I believe most of the professors were Jesuit priests. I became a favorite of one who taught a course titled Forty-nine Reasons for the Decline and Fall of the Roman Empire. (The main purpose of the course appeared to be to prove that the Catholic Church was not responsible for the empire's demise.) My professor, a Jesuit priest who always wore his stiff collar and black robe in class, took me aside one day and suggested that I was excellent material to become a priest. He meant it as a compliment. Possibly he had been impressed by some pro-labor comments I made in class, which—though at that point I had

had no contact with the Communist Party since returning to Buffalo—stemmed from what I had learned in New York City as a member of the CP and Theatre of Action.

When I told my Jesuit professor that I was Jewish, he said, "Oh, I didn't know that."

That was it. He never mentioned it again.

Still, considering the public confrontations that I, as a leftist labor leader, had not many years later with the area's so-called "labor priests" Boland and Healy, and considering the public clash that I had around that same time with the priest in charge of adult education at Canisius—he publicly labeled me the most dangerous man in Western New York as he called upon the public to boycott The Park Lane because my wife Rhoda was part owner—it's somewhat amusing that my Jesuit professor believed I had evidenced in class what it would take to become a Catholic priest, possibly a "labor priest."

Somehow—I'm not sure why—while attending classes and playing football at Canisius, I got over my depression and again developed a compulsive need to make it as an actor: *I needed to be somebody, to be recognized!*—I poured out my feelings in an emotional letter to Peggy Craven—stage name adopted by Peggy Hirsdansky, daughter of a Columbia University professor—an actress associated with the Theatre of Action. Touched, she wrote that I should come back to New York and I could stay in the upper East Side apartment where she lived with her husband.

When the football season ended I stopped going to classes at Canisius. Without notifying anyone at the college that I was leaving, I hitchhiked to New York and moved in with Peggy and her husband Bob. But I apparently had attended the school long enough to qualify to receive letters from the college right up until recently, letters addressed to me as a Canisius alumnus asked to make financial contributions to his alma mater.

Chapter 14

Through Peggy Craven I met Dolly (Eleanor Stokes Ridgeway) and for the first time in my life I was deeply in love, so deeply that I turned down a role in the road company of George Kaufman and Moss Hart's *Stage Door* because I believed Dolly needed me to take care of her.

I had never known anyone like Dolly. I don't believe she had ever known anyone like me. It was rich girl meets poor boy. Upper class highly sophisticated young woman who was polished in exclusive private schools meets unsophisticated young actor, with little formal education, who had worked in a factory.

Peggy brought Dolly and me together in her apartment. Dolly was leaving her husband—to whom she had been recently married. He was a young man who belonged to her social group. She did not want to move back into her family's Princeton, New Jersey, home because she did not get along with her stepfather. Dolly said her stepfather was a kept man, supported by her mother who had inherited money.

Dolly's deceased grandfather had been a governor of New Jersey. His wealth had come from ownership of coal mines. His will provided Dolly with a modest but sufficient annual income with provision for a big chunk of money when she got older. When I met Dolly she was in her early twenties, about my age. I thought she was beautiful and vulnerable and highly intelligent and well educated and extremely well read.

With me she deliberately dressed down and wore no make-up. But one time when she was to meet her uncle at the bar in a nice hotel she dressed up and put on make-up, and as I watched her I became aware of a tremendous gap between us. She seemed to shed her relationship with me as she prepared to go off to her world, which did not include me.

She felt it and so did I. (I included that memorable scene—recognition of the reality of our relationship—in one of my unpublished novels: *The Birth and Death of David Lee*.)

We eventually talked seriously about that with a declared effort by both of us to bridge the gap between the different worlds we came from. I don't know which one of us had the harder time with that. Especially since I was Jewish and Dolly said her grandmother—who dominated everything connected with the family—was viciously anti-Semitic. The grandmother controlled the family fortune, and Dolly said that her grandmother hated Jews so much that it would be impossible to ever bring me into her grandmother's home. I think that if Dolly had told me this at the start of our relationship I might not have allowed myself to become so deeply attached to her. But she told me about her grandmother's hatred of Jews only after we were living together in our own apartment—not married—telling everyone that we were married.

We had to find a place to live when Peggy decided to give up the apartment as part of the complicated process of gently breaking the news to Bob that she was leaving him to go off with her new love, actor Norman Lloyd, whom she had met through their association with the Theatre of Action. I was asked to ease the complications involved with that change. Bob asked to have lunch with me and hopefully felt better after spilling his guts about how much he still loved Peggy and he hoped she might get over this thing with Norman Lloyd and come back to him. Peggy and Norman asked me to meet with them and I listened to them tell me how much they loved each other, intended to get married after Peggy got her divorce, and how sorry they felt for nice Bob who, they thought, had a meaningless civilian occupation unrelated to theatre. Peggy said she would help Bob.

The next day Peggy phoned Bob and asked him to meet her in the apartment. I was there. She took Bob by the hand and led him back into the bedroom. When she emerged with him a little while later she kissed him goodbye and sent him on his way. But not before asking him if he felt better now. He mumbled that he did feel better. I guessed that Peggy fucking him had somehow eased the pain.

Peggy and Norman did get married. In my tattered theatre scrapbook I came across a wire they sent me opening night when I played a waiter in *Having Wonderful Time* at the Lyceum Theatre, with Julie Garfield in the leading role. Peggy and Norman wished me a good opening night and thanked me for being their "loving counselor." That was the last communication between us. Norman went on to make it as an actor in Hollywood and then became the assistant to Alfred Hitchcock. Years later when I was in Los Angeles in connection with the production of my play *Drop Hammer*, I thought about getting in touch with Peggy and Norman, but decided not to. I'm not sure why. Maybe because my life had veered so far away from theirs—Norman having become notably successful in Hollywood—I feared that he and Peggy, unlike warmhearted Marty Ritt, would not welcome hearing from me.

The Theatre of Action acquired a brownstone house below 34th Street on the East Side to house the members of the company. I was assigned a room. Dolly accompanied me. She brought her record player and classical records and introduced me to the music of Schubert, Beethoven, Berlioz, Wagner, Debussy, Tchaikovsky and Sibelius. She also introduced me to the novels of Dostoyevsky and Tolstoy; I read *War and Peace, Anna Karenina, The Brothers Karamazov* and *Crime and Punishment*. With her guidance I also read some of Balzac's novels, all the novels of Thomas Hardy, and all the novels by Fitzgerald and Hemingway I could get my hands on.

When Dolly and I were living together I was too much in love with her— or possibly was too deeply impressed, unconsciously, by the slice of society she represented—to recognize how much of the traits of Daisy in Fitzgerald's *The Great Gatsby* (carelessness about the feelings of people not in her class) and Brett in Hemingway's *The Sun Also Rises* (with the same carelessness as Daisy, but also with an ingrained dislike of Jews) were there in Dolly. At one point Dolly made me feel good, telling me that what she loved in me was my Jewish sensitivity, but then she undermined my good feeling by adding that there was something stemming from that Jewish sensitivity—she said she could not define what it was—that, though she tried not to feel that way, she found gratingly offensive.

Loving her—perhaps really dazzled by the patina of wealth and sophisticated social graces embodied in her—it's only now that I can admit to myself that Dolly had anti-Semitism deeply ingrained in her. Recognizing that now, I don't like the behavior of the young man I was. I don't respect him. He was too slow to decide that he must wrench himself away from her.

Our sex life had problems. Dolly had a dropped womb, which made any attempt at intercourse involving penetration painful for her. Speaking French to convey the message delicately, she educated me in other ways to help her achieve climax. But then she went home to her mother's place in Princeton and had an operation to correct the dropped womb. When she returned we had sexual difficulties because of premature ejaculation on my part, which I tried to counteract by recalling that bloodied rat from years earlier, desperately—and ignorantly—trying to bring that into my head to divert my mind away from whatever was causing the premature ejaculation. Dolly at times was not kind about my failure. We had terrible fights and at times I must have sounded distraught and loud enough to be overheard outside our room, prompting the teenaged daughter of our theatre company's cook to confront Dolly with a butcher knife, threatening to kill her for treating me badly. The young girl scared the shit out of Dolly and I had to intervene to persuade my teenaged defender that she must let me act like an adult and handle my own problems.—Dolly did go with me to see a therapist who gave me several books to read. He said they would help me, and they did help to relieve my intense emotional anger at myself, but they did not provide any quick complete turnaround. My agonizing fear of failing to satisfy my sexual partner remained until my difficulty was resolved—my confidence fully restored—with my wife Rhoda.

It was only after Dolly and I had lived together for about three years that I realized that she was acting out the role of glamorous Brett in Hemingway's *The Sun Also Rises*, a book she loved, she seeing me as Robert Cohen, the Jew depicted by Hemingway as an annoying asshole who is continually insulted by Brett while she expects him to continue chasing after her. Of course, Cohen had a background much different from mine. He was rich and he had an Ivy League education. But we were both Jewish, which seemed to be the bottom line that undercut everything else for Brett and Hemingway—and Dolly.

Inevitably the time would come when I would have to decide which fork in the road to choose: the one taken by Robert Cohen who swallowed Brett's insulting putdowns to be near her, or—fuck Hemingway and Brett—make a wrenching break from Dolly and all the rich and sophisticated life she represented.

My experience with Dolly must later have played some role, of which I was not then aware, in the development of my loyalty to the factory workers I represented as a union organizer, giving me the strength to resist tremendous pressure from the FBI and a host of other powerful forces in the community, who tried to compel me by confronting me with all kinds of personal difficulties—or to lure me with bribes of all sorts—to break my tie to the union men and women I worked with.

The Theatre of Action, after the production of *The Young Go First*, seemed to be floundering, not sure what direction to take. There were performances of the company's agit-prop sketches at various union and political meetings and at street demonstrations, none of which involved me. A great deal of time was spent every day taking classes in acting with the Group Theatre guys to hone our acting skills.

Trying to find another play to do, the company commissioned playwright Victor Wolfson—I performed a small role in his adaptation of Dostoyevsky's *Crime and Punishment*—to write a play for us about a strike of meat packing workers in the Midwest. The play he wrote was very important for me. It taught me what NOT to write when I later wrote several plays based upon my own experience with some very tough strikes I led as part of my work as a union organizer. Victor's characters were simplistic stereotypes. The workers had haloes around their heads. The management guys were all bastards. The play consisted of an external clash between these two stereotypes. None of the characters came alive.—Our theatre group did a lot of improvisations for Victor, trying to help him breathe life into the characters but since we, including me at that point, didn't know any better than Victor what it's really like for both workers and management —specific individuals—in a strike situation, we didn't do very well. The play, finally considered beyond repair, was discarded.

By the time I wrote several plays that included a strike I had been involved with many strikes, including some very tough long ones that I had learned to conduct like a military leader. Also, I had learned that the play has to be primarily concerned with how the central character is changed as the result of going through the experience of a strike. The strike should not be the embracing skin or the inner girder, the through line of the play. The main conflict driving the play—its all-embracing skin and its inner girder, its through line—is the action flowing from the conflict inside the head of the complex central character, as he or she deals with his or her personal situation during a strike and is changed in some way by going through that experience. Whether the strike is won or lost is important for a union organizer, but the playwright in concerned with the experience of the central character, while what's happening in the strike— whether it's won or lost—is presented truthfully, as honestly as the playwright can depict it—as it really is—not how he or she might wish it would be.

I got the "Dear John" letter from Dolly—breaking off our relationship—while I was performing up at Green Mansions, a left-oriented "borscht belt" summer retreat in the Catskills north of the City. Green Mansions consisted of a main lodge, a dining hall, cabins, tennis courts, a swimming pool and a rustic theatre. For a number of years the Group Theatre had been hired to provide summer entertainment there. When the Group Theatre became successful enough to no longer need that summer gig, they paved the way for some of us from the disbanded Theatre of Action to perform at Green Mansions. Happy for me, that I had been offered the opportunity to perform at Green Mansions, Dolly had decided that she would visit her mother in Princeton, that she could tolerate her stepfather for the summer weeks that I'd be gone.—I had a good character role in *Night Must Fall*. Marty Ritt, who directed the play, had just complimented me on my growth as an actor—I was feeling great—when the "Dear John" letter arrived from Dolly.

The letter was unexpected. We had had problems, but I thought we had worked through them. I went over in my head what had happened between us, trying to search out what I could or should do. Feeling utterly destroyed, I was desperate. I went to John Latouche for advice. John was part of the Green Mansions song writing team who had been hired to develop mini-musical numbers to entertain the Green Mansions guests. The highly sophisticated lyrics he wrote led me to believe he might be in tune with Dolly's thinking. He and I had become somewhat friendly and I was distraught enough to risk confiding to him about my relationship with Dolly. I let him read her letter, in which she said how much she cared for me and in which, while telling me how hard it was to do it, she said she had to break off our relationship, and then finished it off by thanking me for all I had done for her.

"This is something that comes from being separated," John said. He urged me to leave Green Mansions immediately and go to Princeton to talk to Dolly in person. "When you're there and the two of you talk it through together—it'll be different from her just writing you a letter."

I was not sure I wanted to go into her mother's territory. For several days I walked around, thinking, going off by myself whenever I could get away, walking in the nearby woods, thinking and thinking, reviewing and examining, creating scenes in my head, going over what had already taken place between us and projecting what might take place if without advance notice I suddenly appeared at the front door of her mother's stately home. I went over what had happened with us after the Theatre of Action had to give up the brownstone house: how she went out to Reno and got a divorce there, and then we moved into an apartment in a house on Charles Street in the Village, and I turned down the role of the young Texan in the road company of Kaufman and Hart's *Stage Door* because she was afraid to be left alone, and then after that I had a long run performing in *Having Wonderful Time,* which enabled us to rent a top floor loft on Eighth Street, and she decorated it beautifully, but when the play closed and I was with her in the apartment one night, someone on the main floor pressed the doorbell and I buzzed the person in, and I heard a man shouting Dolly's name as he raced up the stairs and burst into the apartment, and Dolly introduced me to Steve Didier who, I learned later, was a member of the former European nobility who had become one of Marshall Tito's representatives from Yugoslavia to the United States, and he stopped his joyful shouting when he saw me, and he and Dolly lamely explained that they were old friends and that he hadn't seen her for a long while because he'd been out of the country, and he quickly left, and I cowardly did not confront her about this, afraid to lose her to this nicely dressed affable guy who was clearly a more acceptable match for her, while I sensed that during the time I had been gone evenings all week for over a year, performing in *Having Wonderful Time,* an intimate relationship had developed between them.

Reading and re-reading Dolly's letter, I tried to find some encouraging signals that weren't there. I still loved her very much—or, being brutally truthful now, perhaps I loved what she represented to someone like me who then did not think of himself as someone equal to her socially. But I must have had some redeeming characteristics: some sense of pride and some need to respect myself. I decided that I was not going to emulate Robert Cohen who had chased after Brett. I tore up her letter and stayed at Green Mansions and performed there until the summer season ended. Back in the City, I packed her clothes and all her other possessions into cardboard boxes and, without including a written note, mailed them to her mother's home in Princeton—and I moved into a cheap furnished room on West 55th Street, on the north end of the Times Square theatre district.

I heard from Dolly's friend Peggy Craven that Dolly married Steve Didier, and then sometime later divorced him and married someone named Karpa. (I don't think I ever knew Karpa's first name.) Dolly had always told me that she dreaded that she might end up like one of her aunts who had married many times. Not counting as a marriage that Dolly and I had told people that we were married when we were not married, Karpa was Dolly's third marriage. I don't know if there were more after that.

Here's an amusing anecdote. Years later, in the Sixties, I was in Times Square, briefly visiting the City to see some plays after I'd been forced out of the union because of my politics and, while blacklisted, was selling life insurance for the United States Division of Canada Life Assurance Company—their corporate vice president having met with me and then rejected the FBI effort to get the company to fire me. I ran into Sam Garlen, the owner of Green Mansions. I was surprised that he remembered me. I stupidly tried to impress him, telling him how well I was doing selling life insurance. "I'm earning more money than I'd ever earned as an actor or union organizer." I was wearing a conservative business suit, what I usually wore during my life insurance period, and I must have looked prosperous, because Garlen tried to sell me Green Mansions. I dismissed his pitch with a laugh, deliberately being condescending to him as I remembered how years earlier he'd been so patronizing and dismissive toward me and the other actors.

I don't want to leave the impression that Dolly was a bad person. She was politically on the left, was concerned about the poor, the blacks, and workers, and did use her social skills to organize a successful fund raising party for the Daily Worker in our loft apartment. And she did a great deal for me. But the social gap between us was too much at that time for both of us. A major fault of mine was that I, in my head, placed her on a pedestal high above me. I was too impressed by her background, her family's wealth and their place in society. She did try to narrow the gap by dressing me like the young men in her social group. The first time in my life that I wore pajamas was when she bought them for me. She provided the pork pie hat, the tan sport jacket, the gray flannel trousers, and the appropriate shoes that I wore when I was with her. But she also started my lifelong interest in classical music and the world's great literature. We wrote a play together about trying to overcome our class differences. (I still have it. It's not well written. But the idea is there.) We wrote a very long poem about how black slaves were brought here from Africa. (Well meaning, but not good.) Dolly did mean well, but her deeply ingrained contempt for Jews—it seemed to be a class thing, possibly absorbed by osmosis from her grandmother—was clearly evident to me, and no matter how it hurt, and it did hurt, in order to respect myself I could not and would not let myself follow John Latouche's advice to chase after her.

But I was not happy. I realize now, many years later, that in the years that followed the end of my relationship with Dolly I was deeply depressed and that that depression seriously affected the choices I made about what to do with the rest of my life. At the same time, though I was young and had a lot to learn, I was determined then not to let the loss of my relationship with Dolly prevent me from living a useful and satisfying life, not to end up like the young man in one of Fitzgerald's novels—I think it's *The Beautiful and the Damned*—who, jilted by the beautiful upper class young woman with whom he had developed a love relationship, retreats to a small town in the southern tier of New York State, becoming a broken nobody with a dead life. I was not going to let that happen to me.

I did intensify my study of Marxism, attending classes sponsored by the Communist Party. I acted in several sketches that were presented at fund raising events connected with providing support to the Loyalists in Spain who were under attack by the counter-revolutionary armies of Francisco Franco. A leading Party functionary, an older woman to whom I had unburdened the source of my general feeling of sorrow, suggested that I go to Spain to join the Americans in the Abraham Lincoln Brigade. Since Franco had the support of Hitler's air force, the Loyalists were not doing too well. I seriously considered taking the CP functionary's advice. But then those of us in Actors Equity learned that one of our union members—a young actor in his twenties, whose name, I think, was John Lenthier—had gone to France, slipped over the Alpine border into Spain to join the Loyalists, was given a rifle and told to fire a couple of rounds into the woods—his total training for combat—and was immediately sent into battle. Only about a week since leaving the United States, after about two minutes in combat, he was shot and killed. I decided that while I fully respected and was in awe of the bravery of people like John Lenthier and the men in the Abraham Lincoln Brigade, I was not going to let what happened with Dolly lead me that way to commit suicide. That apparently was my rationalization for avoiding admitting to myself that I was afraid of being shot and killed, like young John Lenthier.

Chapter 15

In the few years that I remained in the City after the "Dear John" letter from Dolly, I was unable to develop a successful intimacy with other young women or to take satisfaction in some good developments in my acting career. I made the effort with several young women, all involved in the arts, most of them actresses, all probably as lonely as I was, who responded favorably—several saying yes when I asked them to marry me—and then, still depressed about Dolly, I walked away. I was not nice, and often since then I've wished I could apologize to Ann Lawrence, Helen Golden, Jane Wilson, Peggy Clark, Dottie Green and others whose names I don't remember—all of whom may be dead by now. Years later, trying to get a deeper understanding of my strange conduct, I made the mistake of trying to talk about this with my brother Maury. He didn't want to hear it. He, cut me off, snorting with a nervous laugh, "If any woman is nice to you, you immediately ask her to marry you."

Though my acting career was doing fairly well and I had started to do some directing, I couldn't shake off the dark cloud that constantly engulfed me. Two plays that I appeared in, *Man on the Dock* and *Dance Night*, were trashed by the critics, despite the latter being directed by the Group Theatre's Lee Strasburg. This didn't help to dispel my dark mood. But my role as the punch-drunk fighter in the Brooklyn production of Odets' *Golden Boy* got a good review, and that helped. Also, I had a long run in Kaufman and Hart's *The American Way* at Rockefeller Center. This gave me the chance to meet well-known pianist Oscar Levant who was romancing a young actress in the cast. When I was given permission to use the stage one afternoon to show a small audience of agents and producers a production of *Behind the Eight Ball*, a play Marty Ritt and I had written, Levant told me that Moss Hart would be glad to help me with my playwriting. The play obviously needed that help, but I was still too depressed to ask for it, especially since Moss was rumored to be gay and I didn't feel that I was ready to cope with that. My friends now in Buffalo include gay men and women, most of them in the arts, and I know that it was stupid, really ignorant of me, to be afraid to accept the very kind offer that Levant passed on to me from Moss Hart.

My depression had not been helped by the bad periods between shows. For many weeks I had eaten my evening meals with other unemployed actors in The Actors Fund's "soup kitchen." Those meals were paid for by contributions from working members of Actors Equity. Remembering the help I received back then, I still make my donation to The Actors Fund every year. For a short while I worked with the Federal Theatre, which had been established as part of Franklin D. Roosevelt's New Deal welfare program to provide jobs for unemployed theatre workers. I was given the part of Tranio in a touring production of Shakespeare's *Taming of the Shrew*. We performed mostly for audiences in small towns in Upstate New York. But then we did what became a somewhat strange production of the play in the jail at Ossining. The prisoners quietly whistled and hooted—sort of under their breath—at some gay members of the cast who had decided to wear unusually heavy make-up for that one special performance. But the Federal Theatre job ended for me when Congress terminated the program, charging that it promoted the cause of communism.

I was not earning much money as an actor. Between acting jobs I was often hungry. I searched out cheap hole-in-the-wall eating places where back then you could get a very thick bowl of soup for about a dime. This often was my big meal of the day. Once, after a whole day with no food and no money, I humiliated myself by begging a handout from an older actress I had worked with. Though my mind's eye can still clearly see her face, I unfortunately can't recall her name. Another time, after being told by a man at the Automat's personnel office in Times Square that he had no job openings, but that I could probably get a busboy job and something to eat if I spoke to the manager at their restaurant at 125th Street, I started out—having no money, my face flushed with some sort of fever from lack of food—and walked up Broadway to the 125th Street Automat. Exhausted and fighting back tears, I hoarsely blurted to the manager, "Mister, I'm hungry, can I work here to get something to eat?" The manager was kind. He told me to get a tray and take anything I wanted to eat before I started work clearing the tables. Some weeks later, when I told him I was leaving to appear in another play—I think it was *The American Way*—he generously offered that if I stayed on he would train me to be his assistant. I thanked him, but told him that the only reason I would stay in the City would be if I could succeed as an actor.

I think it was in 1939 that I fell into a situation that might have grounded me firmly on the road to a solid acting career. It was another instance of the candle in the wind changing the direction of my life, as it provided a door through which I was again thrust into contact with what I sensed might be that segment of society that Dolly represented. I read an item in the newspaper—I believe it was the New York Times—announcing that the renowned director and acting teacher Michael Chekhov, having moved his acting workshop from England to New York City because of the dangerous war situation developing in Europe, was holding auditions to fill vacancies in the acting company he was creating. I'm not sure that Beatrice Whitney Straight, a wealthy socially prominent actress, financed the workshop in England, but in our country she had purchased a large estate near the City to house the transported workshop. An announcement in the newspapers invited actors to audition to become members of the company. Requesting an appointment to audition, I assume I cited my acting experience, including the plays I'd appeared in, along with my study with Benno Schneider and The Group Theatre guys, also my work with the Theatre of Action. I remember that I auditioned onstage in a big theatre, with Michael Chekhov and Beatrice Straight seated together far back in the darkness.

I had memorized the defense attorney's summation to the jury in *They Shall Not Die*, the John Wexley play about the trial of the Scottsboro boys, produced by The Theatre Guild. While I had had only a non-speaking role in that production, in performance after performance I had studied how leading actor Claude Rains delivered that dramatic monologue. I didn't know how well my imitation of Claude Rains impressed Michael Chekhov and Beatrice Straight. They conferred briefly, and then Michael Chekhov asked me to repeat the monologue, but this time as if I were a feeble old man addressing the jury. With my body slightly bent and with a bit of a quaver in my voice, I immediately replicated the defense attorney's dramatic appeal to the jury. My performance apparently was good enough to get me accepted into the company and to be provided room and board in the palatial estate, along with a modest weekly stipend. Since I was on the verge of being penniless again, I thought I was very fortunate.

I don't remember how I got to the estate. I might have taken a ride in a bus or someone connected with the company might have taken me there. I remember the wide stretch of green lawn leading up to the magnificent house, because it reminded me of what Thomas Wolfe had written. Was it in *Look Homeward, Angel* or *You Can't Go Home Again*? He described how he felt when he visited a similar palatial estate to which he'd been invited for a weekend.

A young actor about my age, a member of the company, cheerily guided me to my room, and as he rattled away about how glad he was that we would be working together, I rightly or wrongly thought that the way he was dressed identified him as coming from that section of society I associated with Dolly, and his overly friendly manner of speaking reminded me of Dolly's cousin who, the one time we briefly met, kept calling me "a good chap," which had bothered me, though back then I didn't identify why I felt that way. Now I think I might have been feeling that Dolly's cousin was patronizing me, "the rich boy" trying too hard not to be condescending to "the lower class poor boy," with whom his gorgeously beautiful cousin Dolly was having an interesting but certainly temporary affair.

Like Thomas Wolfe—who, without a word to his hosts, walked away from that luxurious home to which he'd been invited for the weekend—I, without a word to Michael Chekhov or Beatrice Straight or anyone else, walked away from that palatial estate and that posh theatre company into which I'd been accepted.

Shortly after that, with the conscious wise or unwise—sensible or nonsensical—decision that "I do not wish to be a court jester to entertain the rich," I responded to a notice of a job opening posted at the office of the New Theatre League and I hitch-hiked back to Buffalo to serve as artistic director for a newly formed workers theatre company, The Buffalo Contemporary Theatre.

Not knowing that thirty years later, in 1969, I would for two weeks temporarily replace actor John Randolph in the Off-Broadway production of my play *The Dodo Bird* while he went out to Hollywood to act in a film, I had made the wrenching decision to permanently give up all my dreams about becoming a star on stage and screen, and I had formally withdrawn from Actors Equity, though thirty years later my temporarily replacing Randolph in the production of my play required me to reinstate my membership.

Back in Buffalo, Edward Mann again became Emanuel Fried, a much changed Emanuel Fried, highly politicized by my experience in the City. I made no effort to contact those who years earlier had been my closest friends. Having learned that they had become used car salesmen, realtors, jewelry store clerks, saloon owners, an optometrist and a podiatrist, I assumed, perhaps wrongly, that they would not share my commitment to organized labor and the working class.

At the same time I made no effort to maintain contact with those I knew from my life in the City—perhaps because it was harder, much harder than I could consciously admit to myself, to part company with the theatre world I had become part of in the City. Though I did not know it then, this was not to be a final and complete break with that world. Many years later—after my years as a union organizer and after I had begun to embody that labor experience in plays that I was writing—I contacted Perry Bruskin in connection with the 1967 Off-Broadway production of *The Dodo Bird*, and then about ten years later contacted Marty Ritt when I was in Los Angeles in connection with the production there of *Drop Hammer,* and then also contacted Nick Ray when I read that he'd been hired to teach film-making at State University of New York at Binghamton—and my friendship with these three, with whom I had been very close when we were part of the Theatre of Action, resumed with an easy familiarity as if we had never been apart all those years. It had been emotionally difficult for me to gear myself up to approach them—fearing a cool rebuff—and I was surprised at the warmth of their responses.

This reminds me of a brief conversation, somewhat relevant, that I had with Julie Garfield one evening before I left the City. We unexpectedly ran into each other in Times Square. Now that he was a movie star, he'd become John Garfield. Since I had acted with him on Broadway in *Having Wonderful Time*, I instinctively called out, "Hi, Julie." He responded, "Hi, Eddie." We stopped and we talked. I got around to asking him how it felt to be a movie star.

"I don't feel any different," he said. "But my old friends treat me different. They're afraid to get in touch with me or to say hello to me."

I knew what he meant, both from how hesitant I felt about talking to him and from how I had shied away from getting in touch with actress Dorothy McGuire once she became a stage and movie star.

Before Dorothy McGuire suddenly achieved her new status as a star, we had taken long walks together, holding hands, exchanging confidences, though I did not tell her about Dolly. I must admit now that I became aware that there was a worm eating at the core of my developing relationship with young Dorothy McGuire—much like the worm that had eaten at the core of my relationship with Dolly. However, there was a slight, but important, difference. Having learned that Dorothy McGuire was somehow related to a wealthy meat-packing family who were publicly known for their financial support of right-wing anti-Semitic organizations, I cowardly avoided repeated opportunities to let her know that she was holding hands with a Jew. Once I left the City, I think that that worm eating at the core of that might-have-been relationship undoubtedly contributed to my reluctance ever to try to get in touch with her.

At this point I must interject that I am not obsessed about being a Jew. I simply am a Jew and am proud of my Jewish heritage. But whether there is a God, or whether someone else is a Jew, or a Christian, or a Muslim, or a Buddhist, or an agnostic or atheist or whatever, I frankly confess is in itself not something I'm deeply concerned about. I try to conduct my life in accordance with the basic Jewish philosophy my parents tried to teach me when I was a child: "Do unto others as you would have others do unto you."

But I'm still trying to grasp a deeper understanding of why I didn't make the effort to keep in touch with some of the other theatre people I'd come know very well, especially Fredric March and Florence Eldredge. The well known acting couple played the leading roles in *The American Way*, and though I was only a minor member of the large cast, they went out of their way to be kind to me, continually inviting me to come into their dressing room, seeming to enjoy talking to me, asking me about my background and my ambitions. Maybe my red hair initially brought me to their attention. Or it might have been the play I wrote with Marty Ritt that was presented on that stage one afternoon. But as we got to know each other Fredric March began to query me about political groups and economic and political situations, often asking my opinion on how he should respond to requests that he got from all kinds of organizations. With the difference in our ages we developed what in some ways approached a surrogate father and son relationship.

105

"Eddie!" he would call out, inviting me into the dressing room, where he would hand me an opened letter. "Who are they and what does it involve?"

But then *The American Way* closed, and Fredric March and Florence Eldredge, leaving for the West Coast, told me to keep in touch with them, to let them know what I was doing. But I did not get in touch with them until—I'm really ashamed about this—not until I desperately needed the help it would provide me to have the internationally famous film star Fredric March write a letter to the Defense Department in Washington, supporting my effort to be reinstated to my job in the mold loft at Curtiss Wright Aircraft—where the Army Air Force colonel assigned to the plant, charging that I was "a subversive," had ordered that I be removed from the airplane factory. Fredric March wrote the letter, and I wrote and thanked him.

Though I thought about Fredric March many times after that, I never again tried to contact him. Why? Lacking in self-esteem? Possibly. Also—thinking about it now—not wanting to be obligated, I hesitate to ask anyone to do me a favor, fearing it might be interpreted as "exploiting the friendship."—I was bothered, felt guilty about having asked Fredric March to write the letter to the Defense Department. This is probably why—when years later I contacted director Marty Ritt—I quickly let him know that I was in Los Angeles in connection with production of my play *Drop Hammer* and was not seeking anything from him, only looking up an old friend. I made the decision to never ask Marty—or any other friend—to consider a play of mine for a film. I would not exploit their friendship. They would have to initiate the suggestion to me.

My experience in the years ahead, especially as a union organizer for a union which was continually under attack by a broad coalition of federal, state, and city officials, other labor union leaders, the right-wing hierarchy of the Catholic Church, the FBI, the press and other parts of the establishment, toughened me up and gave me the backbone—no matter what the cost—to refuse to surrender an inch of respect for myself in order to curry favor and soften the unrelenting personal attacks to which I became subjected.

Part Two

"But not a court jester for the rich!"

Chapter 1

The Buffalo Contemporary Theatre actually had a space of its own, above a sleazy tavern in a rundown three-story building on the corner of Eagle and Ellicott Streets in downtown Buffalo. The second floor performance space, a bare loft, is where I met the woman to whom I was to be married for 48 tumultuous years, until her death separated us.

She did not look like the usual audience member that this primitive workers theatre would attract. When I asked one of the actors—a middle-aged man who was a civil servant of some kind—who the well-dressed sexy young woman was, he contemptuously identified her.

"She's a drunken decadent rich bitch connected with The Park Lane."

This immediately attracted me to her.

Later I learned that Rhoda had been reluctantly persuaded by her politically left-oriented older sister Ruth to attend that Saturday's opening night of our first production. It was a variety show made up of several worker songs and some satirical political sketches that I had written and directed. The actors had asked me to say a few words about my theatrical background and the mission of our theatre before I introduced the production numbers which were listed on mimeographed programs distributed to our audience. There were about twenty people sitting on wood folding chairs in front of the rudimentary platform that the actors had built to serve as the stage.

The first item I introduced was one of the sketches. Lights out. The actors took their places. Lights up. The actors began to speak. Then suddenly silence. Then an actor spoke to fill the silence, hesitantly, unsure about what to say. He gave up and stopped. Embarrassing silence. Another actor spoke, but still did not get the sketch back on track. He stopped. Again silence. Two actors started a conversation, stopped, started, stopped, started and stumbled on, wandering completely off the basic thrust of the sketch.

"OK," I called out, laughing to hide my embarrassment as I stepped out onto the front of the stage to interrupt the obvious misery of the actors. "Opening night and our actors are a little overexcited. So let's calm down and let's start over from the beginning." That's what we did, with the actors settling down, and the performance flowing smoothly ahead.

Something about what I did and the general feeling that that might have conveyed when I stepped in to interrupt the performance must have registered very strongly with Rhoda because sometime later, after we had married, she told me that that was the moment—before we had even spoken to each other—that she had decided that she was going to marry me.

At that point in her life Rhoda was a 21-year old spoiled brat. She reveled in being known as Miss Park Lane, recognition that her family, the Luries, owned Buffalo's leading upscale apartment complex. Its attached restaurant and cocktail lounge, with a wide front porch and impressive columns at its entrance, facing Buffalo's expansive tree-lined Delaware Avenue and the sparkling fountains inside Gates Circle, had been the home of the architect who designed the apartment house. When he died, a long hallway was built to link the home to the main building. The restaurant and cocktail lounge's luxurious interior, including the paneled library with its marbled fireplace and the large fish pool at the end of what had been the living room, was left as it had been when the home was occupied by the architect. The Park Lane was reputed to be the finest place in town to eat and drink—and to dance to the music of a live orchestra on Saturday nights. Other nights a piano player entertained the diners and kept playing for the late night drinkers. For several years Rhoda's father brought in professional singers and musicians to provide late night entertainment for those who came to drink and talk until a few hours past midnight. Liberace, the swishy piano player who became internationally famous for his garish costumes and displays of candelabra, tested his wings here, playing classical music on the piano with a whole orchestra behind him, provided by a back-up recording.

Night after night—after I had finished working all day as a union organizer— Rhoda and I would end up here, drinking, talking, exchanging quips with other guests and the bartenders and waiters and waitresses and the entertainers and the Lurie family's loyal flamboyant hand-kissing maitre d'—Peter Gust Economou.

Until Rhoda's brother barred us from the place—fearing that my involvement in frequent emotionally searing labor-management battles, with negative publicity in newspapers, radio and television, would harm the business—this retreat into the dining room of the restaurant and cocktail lounge almost every night was a soothing escape from the intense crises continually erupting in connection with my work as an organizer representing a very militant union.

But I'm getting way ahead of myself, touching the edge of the development of deeply troubled waters. So I leave this for now, except to cap it by telling a little more about the exchange that took place between me and the man who became my closest friend when I started as the artistic director for the Buffalo Contemporary Theatre. George Poole was an Abraham Lincoln Brigade veteran who had fought against dictator Francisco Franco's forces in Spain. Our views on politics and writing and people—our hopes for a better society—were so much alike that we became as close as brothers, feverishly working together on political, literary and theatrical projects for several years, confidently trusting our fate to each other when government intelligence agents separated us into adjoining rooms at the Curtiss airplane factory and told each of us that the other had confessed that the other was part of a subversive organization. (I told them, "He'd never say that." And George told me that he told them that I would never say that.)

That was our intense brotherly relationship—until we both returned from service in the army in World War II, resuming positions we had come to occupy in the labor movement, and I was surprised to learn that George had become an active opponent,

joining in the fierce effort of some anti-Communist local labor leaders—who were collaborating with FBI—to drive me out of the labor movement. But when we were still close friends, and when Rhoda and I were recently married, and when I was newly hired as an organizer for the UE union, which was charged with being communist-dominated, is when George expressed his deep concern about what he saw as my difficult predicament: that I was in an impossible situation "because the UE and The Park Lane can't sleep together," which I laughed off, telling him, "But we are, we are."

And we were—and it often was exciting—often filled with a quiet joy from intensely stimulating experiences—and yes, also extending over a long a period of years, too often it became absolutely hell—too hard—almost unbearable with tensions developing between me and Rhoda—prompting dark thoughts—fleeting—quickly rejected—thoughts about killing myself.

*****

The community outside, most specifically those on the left who knew about us, were not aware of the dark side in the relationship between the blacklisted lefty and the glamorous lady who, through the death of her father, had inherited her share of ownership of The Park Lane. This was strongly revealed to me not too long ago when my daughter Mindy, having enrolled at Brandeis University to get her doctorate, told me that one of her professors said that he'd been a student at the University of Buffalo and he and his radical friends had thought that Rhoda and I were something like the famous sophisticated dance team of that period, calling us "the Fred Astaire and Ginger Rogers of the Left."

*****

111

The first play produced by the Buffalo Contemporary Theatre, in 1939, was Irwin Shaw's *Bury The Dead*. It was a powerful anti-war play, with soldiers killed in a war refusing to be buried. Playwright Irwin Shaw—after our country got into World War II—refused permission for anyone to produce the play. The Buffalo News drama critic, Ardis Smith, praised our production, and contacted me. We got together and he treated me like someone important. After he'd read a new play I'd written, then titled *Mark of Success*, he asked me to read a play he'd written. I suggested some ideas for rewrite, and he seemed very pleased. He invited me to his home and all the while I was artistic director for the Buffalo Contemporary Theatre he was very supportive of my work. But when, through some unexpected developments—the candle in the wind—I became an organizer for the UE union, he turned against me, literally sneering at me when we crossed paths, quickly averting his eyes, refusing to recognize my presence. In retrospect, I think of him as being similar to Mark Hopkins, my high school physics teacher who got me the job at the Dupont factory on River Road in Tonawanda—a "genteel" not-rich WASP, willingly subordinate to the truly wealthy establishment, smugly certain of the correctness of his views about culture, taking a paternalistic pleasure in helping me, as long as I did not take off in a direction contrary to his beliefs about culture—and politics.

Taking a quick jump ahead to the early 1970s, it was about 15 years after I'd been forced out of the union and I was still blacklisted. It was a few years after I'd had *The Dodo Bird* produced Off-Broadway in New York City with great reviews by the critics. Married to Rhoda for over thirty years, I had become accepted by her family and had changed sufficiently to feel comfortable in The Park Lane milieu. Trying to raise the money needed to produce my play *Rose* Off-Broadway, I invited potential investors to a cocktail party in one of the restaurant's party rooms. Two of the guests, outstanding members of the city's moneyed establishment, Max Clarkson and Calvin Rand, after hearing the reading of the play, went to work on me, pressuring me to abandon writing plays that included anything about labor if I wished to get money to produce my work. I listened quietly while they went on and on, taking turns at haranguing me, until I got fed up with their seeming expectation that I, as a subordinate to them, was expected to change my ideas about what I want to write because they were telling me what I should or should not write. Knowing fully what it meant to my future relationship with them, I made a crucial decision—and I deliberately shocked them into silence by exploding, "You guys are full of shit!"

Calvin and Max were both old money and were sufficiently sophisticated not to react overtly with anger at my outburst. They simply turned around and walked away, and later quietly indicated their displeasure by each putting a measly $100 into the production of *Rose*. And unfortunately I was stupid enough to accept their $100 checks instead of giving the checks back to them with some kind of snide remark like "You need this more than I do."

Calvin Rand had told me how much he appreciated "that the line of communication has been established between us"—I, in his mind, apparently representing the view of labor and the left, and he, in his mind, apparently representing the view of the upper class establishment. But following the incident at that cocktail party, I refused for many years—when our paths crossed—to speak to him or Max. It was not until not long ago when I was acting in *The Streets of Dublin*, produced by The Irish Classical Theatre Company, that their executive board member Calvin Rand—who later became president of their board—went out of his way to approach me and extend his hand and speak pleasantly to me, praising my work in the play, and I responded pleasantly, thanking him. Since then we have frequently spoken to one another in a friendly, but still slightly guarded way—slightly guarded especially on my part.

From where I am now at age 95, looking back past my long years of involvement with labor, past my blacklisted years as a successful businessman selling life insurance, past my years as a playwright with productions of my work Off-Broadway and in other cities across our country and in Canada's Toronto, past the years of my renewed career as an actor, and past over 30 years as a college professor, past my involvement in political skirmishes all along the way, including incessant bumping back and forth between me and the FBI for fifty, sixty, or seventy years—looking back past all that to my experience as artistic director for the Buffalo Contemporary Theatre to evaluate what I did or did not accomplish in that role, I feel sad, having to say that, contrary to what I thought back then, it doesn't seem that I contributed very much with that theatre to improve the lives of working people.

Even before Dec 7, 1941, when Rhoda and I listened to Franklin Delano Roosevelt on the radio, reporting the Japanese attack on Pearl Harbor and our formal entry as a combatant into that war, the Buffalo Contemporary Theatre had disintegrated in anticipation of its actors and technical staff being drafted into the armed services.

Before that happened, if I recall correctly, one of our few major projects had been a full production or a public staged reading of Clifford Odets' *Waiting for Lefty*. When I had been an actor with Theatre of Action, I had acted in a forgettable short play that was the companion piece to the first Group Theatre production of *Waiting for Lefty* at the Civic Repertory Theatre on 14th Street in New York City. The play was hailed then as a strongly pro-labor play because the taxi drivers overcome their fears and vote to stay out on strike, (I concede that that's a simplistic summary of its plot.) The play was then moved to a Broadway theatre where it was strongly supported by the essentially middle class and upper class audiences. Years later, having become a union organizer working with blue collar workers in heavy industry, I recognized that the majority of the taxi drivers presented in the play had formerly been middle class white collar professionals who felt that the conservative establishment had punished them because of their radical ideas, forcing them down from the middle class into the working class, where they hated that they were now "ordinary" members of the labor class, driving taxicabs. This inherent and I'm sure unintended message from the playwright—a demeaning attitude toward those who are "ordinary workers"—may explain, at least in part, why workers in heavy industry unions, especially outside New York City, have not been strongly attracted to the play.

My dear friend Perry Bruskin, with a lifetime of professional theatre experience in New York City undoubtedly will disagree with my view about *Waiting for Lefty*. He and his partner worked very hard trying to develop *Waiting for Lefty* into a musical. I hoped he would get it done on Broadway and it would be a smash hit. With his constant effort to use theatre to promote social justice he would have earned it. But it never happened.

Perry told me that he and his partner hoped to get composer Liz Swados to work with them in development of the *Waiting for Lefty* musical. Redhead Liz and my redhead daughter Mindy were inseparable childhood playmates until—as Liz reported in her autobiographical novel —her father forced her to break that friendship when I refused to act as he demanded. He said he was conveying a threat directly from the FBI—that I must publicly repudiate my left politics and join in the red-baiting attack against my UE union or I'd end up in jail. Liz's mother Sylvia, who had been like a sister with my wife Rhoda for many years, gave Rhoda the ultimatum: divorce me or that's the end of their friendship. A few years later, after our country got through the worst of the McCarthy red scare period, Sylvia tried to re-establish the friendship with Rhoda. Having been put through hell during the McCarthy period, Rhoda bitterly rejected having lunch with Sylvia. Shortly after that Sylvia killed herself.

Now I think that the Buffalo Contemporary Theatre was not much of a workers theatre. With the exception of former sailor and member of the National Maritime Union (NMU) Jack Kramer—he and George Poole were Buffalo's veterans of the Abraham Lincoln Brigade—our actors had no strong ties, no connection to the large body of union workers in the area: the steel workers, autoworkers, machinists, rubber workers, carpenters, painters, bricklayers, clothing makers, etc.

Most of our theatrical productions were the Saturday night collections of worker/folk songs and satirical political sketches, with performances sparsely attended by two or three leftist labor leaders (with generally middle class backgrounds) and a few more middle class progressives (with no hint whatsoever of any connection with labor). We were preaching to the choir, even to only a miniscule sliver of that group in the community.

But because of my membership in the Communist Party I did get to establish personal friendships with some important local labor leaders in the Congress of

Industrial Organization (CIO) unions. Contrary to the generally negative stuff that has been said about such Communists, these men and women, whom I got to know very well, were highly dedicated, highly intelligent, highly idealistic, highly skilled workers, whose primary intent was to improve the lives of the many thousands of skilled and unskilled factory workers in the area. A few of them, including Al Larke, secretary of the Greater Buffalo CIO Labor Council, did quite regularly attend performances of our theatre company. Al Larke—he's long dead now—was an experienced newspaperman, the editor of the Council's weekly newspaper, The Buffalo Union Leader.

When Al asked me to become the newspaper's unpaid film critic, the columns I wrote introduced me to thousands of union families in the area. I did not recognize it at the time, but now I think that writing that column was part of the process by which I started to move over from being primarily a theatre person to becoming a union organizer deeply involved in a very close way with factory workers in heavy industry—and with their families whom I got to know through them.

A quick jump years ahead, temporarily, to the period when CIO President Phil Murray finally gave in to pressure from the right-wing of the Catholic hierarchy and joined in the FBI effort to purge Communists out of all positions of leadership in the labor movement. Al Larke, purged and blacklisted along with many others—including lawyer Dave Pressman, Murray's brainy closest advisor—was quickly hired off the blacklist by the Wall Street Journal to write about labor situations. When I joked about that with Al in a long distance phone conversation, he quipped that wealthy investors"the capitalists"—were willing to tolerate him because "they really have to know the truth about where they're going to put their money." But not very long after he started to work for the Journal, at a relatively young age he died of respiratory complications.

Incidentally, shortly after I was purged and blacklisted—about the same time that Al Larke was booted out of the labor movement—Peter Andrews, old money Buffalonian now living in Washington (more later about our relationship) suggested that I could get a job evaluating labor situations for a consortium of the local banks. "Manny, they want to know what's going on with labor in places where they and their clients may be financially involved."—I thanked Peter, but told him that that was not something I wanted to do.

Married to Rhoda, with her Lurie family owning and managing The Park Lane, I gradually had come to know some of the old money and new money members of the establishment who were tenants in the apartments or, not living there, regularly came into the restaurant and cocktail lounge to eat and drink and dance and enjoy the entertainment.

One of the regular diners I got to know very well was Tommy Ryan. Tommy was a down-to-earth nice guy who was always neatly dressed, including dark suit and a tie. He had been a policeman before he married well, becoming

115

attached to a well-established Buffalo family. He was well taken care of, as he himself let me know when I had lunch with him in The Park Lane dining room. This followed an earlier meeting with him in the office of the Niagara Frontier Transit Authority. Tommy had been appointed the NFTA's chief executive officer (CEO). He had asked me to drop by his NFTA office. We talked generally while I, puzzled, tried to figure out why he'd asked me to drop in. He asked how I was getting along. I said I was doing fairly well. (This was during my years on the blacklist, when I was selling life insurance for the U.S. Division of Canada Life, the company that had refused the FBI effort to get them to fire me.)

Tommy asked about Rhoda and momentarily probed my relationship with her Uncle Louis Lurie. He made some comment about Rhoda's Uncle Louie being a big real estate mogul in San Francisco who's probably listed in Forbes magazine as one of the wealthiest men in the country. He asked if I'd ever met Louie. I said I had, a number of times, had dinner with him and the family every time he came East to visit his brother, my father-in-law. Tommy asked how I got along with Louie. I said we got along all right. I didn't tell him that Louie had offered to set me up in the taxicab business with my own fleet of taxis, an offer that I had laughingly dismissed.

Then Tommy got down to the purpose of our meeting. He said that the FBI had told him that although I was a Communist I was an independent thinker who made up my own mind. I warily listened while he added some compliments about my intelligence, my writing and my integrity. It sounded like he was preparing to offer me a job or to ask me to do something—that he was checking me out to see if I was open to what he was about to propose. But after about a half hour of genial conversation he wound it up by telling me that he admired my courage and my devotion to helping factory workers, and he wished me well. I left, disappointed, thinking that somehow I'd missed finding out the real reason why he had invited me to drop in to see him.

Then Tommy changed jobs, becoming chairman of the Republican Party in Erie County. He phoned me. "Manny, I want you to meet me for lunch at The Park Lane. I've got something I want to talk to you about."

We started with martinis. Then we ate lunch. We were seated in the small room that my father-in-law recently had had added, off to the side of the bar, separated from the main dining room to provide an element of privacy. There were only a few tables in this side room. Tommy waited until the few other diners in there had finished their lunches and left. Then, preparing to get to the point, he repeated what the FBI had supposedly told him about my thinking independently despite my being a Communist, and he again complimented me about my writing ability and my supposed political savvy.

Then he got to his main purpose. "Manny, I'd like you to write the speeches for our Republican Party."

While I assumed he meant speeches for the Erie County Republican Party, it wouldn't have made any difference if he'd been talking about speeches for the National Republican Party. I couldn't help it. I quietly laughed at what to me seemed to be a ridiculous idea.

Where the hell did he get the notion that I would be stupid enough to swallow that kind of bait, to put myself in a position that would isolate me from the thousands of union members in the area who still trusted me and whose support was preventing J. Edgar Hoover's FBI from doing more than they had already done to try to break me.

My laugh did not discourage Tommy. He had so much to offer me that he apparently assumed that for a guy like myself, struggling on the blacklist to support my family, it would be too good an offer for me to refuse.

"Manny"—he leaned forward, smiling in expectation of what he apparently thought would be my overjoyed response—"in return for writing the speeches for us, you will be taken care of financially for the rest of your life!" He repeated the important phrase: "Taken care of financially for the rest of your life!"

He leaned back, with a warm look on his face, seeming to take it for granted that I would respond positively.

"Tommy." I still thought it wise to maintain his friendship. "Tommy, thank you. I appreciate the offer. But to be honest with you, I can't write something like that, something that I don't believe in. But I thank you."

The friendly way I refused his job offer seemed to encourage him, possibly thinking that it was my way of negotiating a better price from him. Taking out his bulging leather wallet, opening it and slipping out a fistful of laminated cards, which he dealt out like playing cards over the white cloth on the dining table, he explained, "We'll take care of you the same way they're taking care of me. I'm a paid officer for all these organizations."

Because I found it surprising, I still clearly remember the name on one of the laminated cards: The Boy Scouts of America. Tommy showed his big teeth, grinning, seeming to think that this would clinch it. "We'll take care of you the same way. For life."

I was quietly amused, but was careful not to show it. In a way, I thought it was insulting that he—and his FBI prompters—thought that I was that naïve that I couldn't see that, even if I was so lacking in dedication to my principled beliefs that I would accept their offer, I would be putting myself in a position where they could dump me any time they wished and I would have no recourse, no backing from anyone—I would be a destroyed miserable unprincipled jerk held in contempt by those on the right as well as those on the left.

I suppressed the luxurious impulse to tell him to tell his FBI friends to go fuck themselves. Instead, in a friendly and very polite way, I thanked him for trying to help me, but very firmly rejected his offer—politely and smiling—rejected it several times as he repeated his sales pitch, pointing to the plastic cards on the white table cloth again and again with what he seemed to think was his special kind of warmly persuasive charm that could not be resisted.

But finally Tommy had to reluctantly give up. He still tried to be upbeat as he told me to think about it. Donning a smiling mask, I told him that unfortunately, being the kind of person I am, there was no chance that I could allow myself to change my mind. Then shifting to an extremely confidential mask, I again earnestly thanked him for trying to help me.

We stood up and shook hands. Out of the corner of my eye, as I walked out of the dining room, I saw Tommy talking earnestly to a neatly dressed man at the bar. Tommy's reporting to the FBI guy, I guessed—and I wondered if the FBI guy, in some sophisticated technological way, had been tuned into my conversation with Tommy. The thought flashed through my head that they really had no respect for my intelligence if they thought that I could be taken in by this kind of stupid shit. Fuck you, I muttered to myself, angrily stalking out of the dining room.

Thinking now about the source of my insistence on resisting the effort to lure me into backing off from my principled beliefs, I believe that that came out of my worry that, being married to Rhoda, I was in danger of becoming a nobody if I gave in to the constant pressure to adjust my values to those of the business and money oriented members of her family.

But perhaps more important than my concern about my relationship with those members of her Lurie family was my concern about my personal relationship with leading members of the establishment in the community, people like Peter Andrews, Calvin Rand and Max Clarkson. As one who wanted to remain firmly rooted to his belief in living a life committed to improving the lives of working people and their families, I was determined to face these establishment guys on a level playing field, not in any way subordinate to them. If I had surrendered in even the slightest degree to adopt their values, accepting their ideas about how I should make my living—or what I, wearing my playwright hat, should write about—I believe that I would have lost my ability to look them squarely in the eye, secure in the feeling that by standing firm in rejecting what they offered, I was their equal, if not better than they were. I was able to walk away from them and their subordinate Tommy Ryan and mutter fuck you or, even better, tell them directly to their faces that they were full of shit—preferably politely, if I could— and still have them desiring "to keep open the line of communication."

Chapter 2

George Poole and I, expecting we would shortly be drafted into the armed services, decided to fill in the time by going to work at the Curtiss-Wright aircraft plant. The Buffalo Contemporary Theatre, its ranks depleted by the draft, had folded. George and I still continued as co-editors of *UPSTATE*, the mimeographed worker-oriented literary magazine we'd founded. But as we became deeply involved in trying to organize Curtiss workers into a decent union to replace the so-called independent union, The Aircraft, we had to suspend publication of *UPSTATE*.

Citing my early machine shop experience (I didn't tell them it was in seventh and eighth grade in grammar school) I was assigned to work as a template maker in the mold loft. The job required that I be able to operate a number of machines, including drill presses, a planer, a lathe and grinders, and use various measuring and marking instruments, to develop the first step in the actual building of the P-40 and C-47 airplanes, transferring the engineers' blue print layouts with precise dimensions onto sheet metal, and going on from there to construct the basic templates and tools that would be used in creating the dies and other tools to make the airplane parts related to the instrument panel. George Poole was also assigned to the mold loft.

Since it was years since I had done any of this kind of skilled machine shop work, I was afraid I would soon be found out and get fired. But the candle in the wind saved me when I was assigned to a crew working under supervision of a young lead-man who looked familiar.

"Chester?"

He grinned as he recognized me. "Manny!"

I used to buy Chester ice cream cones when he was a young kid. He still was a fresh-faced youngster, maybe about twenty years old, who I later learned had been well-trained in a vocational high school.

"Chester, cover me. I haven't handled this stuff, these machines and these tools, since grammar school."

Chester covered me, and I very soon got back what I'd previously learned about handling machines and tools, and quickly developed further from there. When the C-47 aircraft work was started, I was selected to develop the instrument panel. Working within tolerances of three thousandths of an inch, I created the full-scale detailed layout of the panel on a wide metal sheet—to which all the instrument panel's added parts would be fitted—and then I designed and built the tool templates which would be used in making all the added parts that would tie into the instrument panel, deriving all this from the complicated blue print provided by the engineers. I took great pride in the good job I did, and I received a letter of commendation from Air Force headquarters in Washington for suggestions I made to cut the time it took to build the aircraft.

In retrospect, the life I was living then—working at Curtiss at the same time that I was living with Rhoda—was somewhat bizarre, not that I thought of it that way at that time. Rhoda and I had just been married by the leading rabbi in the city in a ceremony performed in the glamorous glass-enclosed porch off The Park Lane's main dining room. This was followed with a very fine reception on the porch, with an orchestra playing and with lots of guests in evening clothes dancing, and lots of food, lots of booze—and everything served by a battery of bustling uniformed waiters and waitresses. I wore a tuxedo borrowed from a friend of my brother Maury.

(A few weeks after I returned the tuxedo, that friend—a lonely unmarried man, unsuccessful in a small retail business venture—hung himself.)

While we were trying to find a place to live that we could afford with what I was being paid at Curtiss, Rhoda and I began life together, rent-free, in a luxurious suite in The Park Lane. Early each morning, carrying my brown bagged lunch, I walked down the heavily carpeted main floor corridor of Buffalo's most exclusive apartment house—home for some of the area's wealthiest families— to go to work to earn my fifty cents an hour in the mold loft at Curtiss. The Park Lane decorator told me that he had designed that main floor corridor "to look and smell like money"—which, at least to me at that time, it definitely did.

Rhoda married me over the objections of her father, Mandel Lurie. He predicted that the marriage would not last six months. Having asked to speak to me in his private office before the wedding date was announced—with a glamorous full-length photo of Rhoda on the Buffalo Evening News society page—Mandel told me that Rhoda and I came from backgrounds that were too different for the marriage to work. I assumed that he was talking primarily about money, my inability to support Rhoda in the style to which she was accustomed. I told him that that was exactly what I had told Rhoda but I had not been able to convince her. He then caught me by surprise, offering me $5000 to disappear. I suppose

I should have felt insulted, but I was really amused that he thought I was the kind of person who could be bought off. So I just shook my head and suggested that he talk to Rhoda and see if he could convince her.

Rhoda had told me how much she enjoyed humiliating all the young men who were attracted to her because they thought of her as Miss Park Lane; she let them think that they were getting somewhere with her, leading them to propose marriage, so that then she could punish them, cut them down, taunt them, make fools of them. She probably did not realize it, but by telling me that she had convinced me that I was never going to ask her to marry me. But then *she* proposed that we get married. Frankly, though I was dazzled by Rhoda being Miss Park Lane and I wanted very much to marry her, I argued that it would be wrong for us to get married, giving essentially the same reasons later cited by her father. Trying to be honest about it now, I admit that I very easily allowed her to overrule my objections.

But there must have been something very complicated at work in my head, something that I am now trying honestly to define. On one of the early days of our marriage, while we were still living in this luxurious suite at The Park Lane— where I, hiding it from Rhoda, was intimidated by the fine furniture and linen— Rhoda came into the apartment with a look on her face that triggered something inside me, that prompted me to grind out from deep in my gut, "It must be nice to come back here and find your toy waiting for you."

The changed look on her face! She was stunned! She protested. But I think what I said had hit home and may have been the beginning of Rhoda doing some serious thinking about our relationship: why she had married me and whether or not it was a marriage she wanted to stay in. I was also seriously questioning it, damning myself for being impressed by The Park Lane, for being corrupted by the upscale life style embodied in Miss Park Lane, by the money—feeling that I was selling out, that I had willingly helped myself to be bought.

That feeling ate at me. It was not much later, when we were having a slight argument, that Rhoda, maybe not too seriously, questioned why I was so concerned about the problems of workers and unions, and she said something to the effect that now that I'm married I should be less political and think more about our problems. We had a quick exchange of words, with Rhoda flippantly pressing me and with me getting more and more defensive and frustrated by my not being articulate enough to adequately defend myself, until again from deep in my gut, unplanned, the words ground hotly out of my mouth. "Listen! You bought the body! Not the mind!" (I should have said, "*I sold* the body not the mind.")

But inexplicably—I'm still not sure why—our sex life at that time was good. Despite all kind of tensions and emotional arguments about my being away too many evenings in connection with my political and labor activity, our sex life was good—and Rhoda, late at night, languidly relaxing with her after-orgasm drink and cigarette, seeming to be smugly happy that she did not have the problem of some of her married lady friends, would let me in on the secrets of those who had told her that they never had had an orgasm. With Rhoda's help, perhaps unwitting help, for which I was very grateful, I had overcome the sexual problems that had led me to picture in my head the terrified rat that I had seen in my early youth and with whose bloodied anguish I had identified whenever I had had difficulty trying to sexually satisfy some woman I cared for.

Moving from our temporary home at The Park Lane, we rented a one-room apartment that I could afford with what I was earning with a lot of overtime pay at Curtiss. Our new apartment actually had a tiny bathroom off a corner of the somewhat larger one-room in which there was rudimentary kitchen equipment along one wall and a Murphy bed folding up into the side of another wall. But Rhoda's father sent over The Park Lane decorator and he dressed up the place with white wall-to-wall thick carpeting on the floor, luscious curtains and drapes on the windows, fine linen including a pink satin coverlet on the bed, and good furniture, along with a full set of dishes, pots and pans, and silverware—all supplied, without charge, from the plentitude of these things at The Park Lane. The silverware was stamped with The Park Lane insignia. The decorator had chosen a quietly sexy color of paint for the walls, and the painters from The Park Lane maintenance crew had painted the whole apartment. It was a fairy wonderland into which I entered each day, empty metal lunch bucket in hand, when I returned from my work in the mold loft—and from my union organizing activity—at Curtiss. It took years for my head to change to where I no longer was intimidated by living in that kind of atmosphere, which well-meaning Rhoda considered to be "living like a poor person," a challenge that she sought and felt prideful that she could handle without serious complaint.

We were married only three months when Rhoda became pregnant. Though urged to do so by her mother and father, she refused to have an abortion. But she did keep jumping off the loading dock to the cement pavement below in the rear of The Park Lane, landing hard on her heels, with the idea that this might jar loose that creature growing inside her. But fortunately it didn't. I yearned for a redheaded daughter, and luckily we got one.

(Actually we got two of what I wanted, because our next child, born eight years later, was also a redheaded girl.)

Both Rhoda and I loved this happy gamin-faced baby that had refused to be aborted by her jarring jumps from the loading dock. Rhoda asked that we name her Lorrie, derived from Rhoda's maiden name of Lurie. And Lorrie not only changed our lives, but also changed the life of Mandel, Rhoda's father. He adored Lorrie. He came over almost every morning to take her along to breakfast with him in The Park Lane dining room, setting her in a high chair beside him. As soon as she was old enough to start walking, he would come over and, holding her hand, take her for a walk. When Lorrie years later was asked what she remembered about her grandfather who had died while she was still a young child, she said, "He loved me."

Rhoda and I—and her father and mother—agreed that we needed a larger apartment to have a room ready for the baby. Mandel arranged a good rent deal for us to be able to move into roomier quarters in The Gates Circle Apartments right next door to The Park Lane. Rhoda—with the help of The Park Lane decorator and painters, and with new beds, linen, drapes and more furniture, all provided by largess of The Park Lane—again created what at that time was for me a kind of fairy tale atmosphere in the apartment, with which I still felt strange and from which, while we lived there, I always felt somewhat alienated.

Maybe somewhere deep down inside me, living in this apartment so fancily furnished by The Park Lane was just too far and just too quick a jump from how I had lived as a child, my parents and all nine of us children taking turns for our weekly baths in the small copper tub set down in the middle of the floor of the kitchen behind the dingy dry goods store on Genesee Street. I don't know why, but remembering those weekly baths we took in the copper tub in that roughly furnished kitchen, I have to fight to hold back tears blurring my eyesight.

I believe I was unconsciously afraid that by letting myself be drawn into fully accepting and enjoying what then was to me a fairy tale environment, I might be undermining my deep-seated determination to remain true to my commitment to improve the lives of working people, including the thousands of men and women working at Curtiss. And *that* helped to reinforce my stiff resistance to several highly lucrative offers to buy me off and also helped to reinforce my ability to stand firm, not giving an inch, when I was confronted with life-threatening and family-destroying attempts to make me back off from that commitment. My concern that I might have let my body be bought, though that might have been a somewhat crude and perhaps inaccurate attempt at encapsulating how I thought about it, intensified my resolve not to relinquish my mind.

But looking back at it now, it appears that my life back then—divided as it was between my world at Curtiss and my fairy tale world which included frequent, almost nightly, trips to The Park Lane next door where, without charge since Rhoda signed the checks, we'd dine, drink and dance until well past midnight—was somewhat schizophrenic. And it was inevitable that the time would come when it would no longer be possible to continue living simultaneously in both those worlds. It was inevitable that the time would come when Rhoda and I would have to re-assess our marriage and make our choices.

At Curtiss, George and I joined The Aircraft independent union. But we quickly heard from other workers in the mold loft that The Aircraft had been set up with the connivance of the company to keep out the CIO or AFL, and if anyone challenged the do-nothing policies of the leaders of The Aircraft, the company would find an excuse to fire him.

I learned that The Aircraft was affiliated with the Federated Industrial Union (FIU), an umbrella organization set up by local lawyer Edward Hamilton, into which he had gathered several local unions, similar to The Aircraft, that had also been set up with company connivance at other factories in the area. I assumed that Mr. Hamilton was drawing a very good income from the dues collected by all these FIU local unions.

Through my union activity at Curtiss and later through my work as a union organizer, I got to know a lot more about the FIU, including what I finally learned from Edward Hamilton himself when, trying to get rid of me as an opponent, he took me into his confidence and offered me the lucrative opportunity to work with him to build the FIU into a national organization. He summed up his offer in a letter he wrote to me, which he concluded with something like this: "I would like you to be my friend, but if you choose to be my enemy, I am.../ Sincerely yours/ (signed) Edward Hamilton"

To begin with, the strategy that George and I developed at Curtiss was to form a caucus of workers in our mold loft department to push for resolutions to be adopted by The Aircraft membership, instructing the present leaders of the organization to demand that the company provide an across-the-board wage increase and other benefits for all Curtiss employees. If The Aircraft leaders blocked that, we would then propose that the caucus organize a campaign to elect new leaders. It was a strategy that George and I—both still members of the Communist Party at that time—formulated without direction from or consultation with any CP officials, just by talking about it ourselves when we stopped off after work for a beer at a nearby bar.

We did believe that Curtiss workers would have greater negotiating strength in a union that is affiliated with the CIO and that if our caucus could successfully lead the way to make The Aircraft into a truly democratic union, we would be in a position to urge the caucus to propose that The Aircraft members vote to affiliate their organization with the aircraft division of the UAW union, a unit of the CIO. If the effort to make The Aircraft into a truly democratic union was blocked by top officers of The Aircraft, we believed that a majority of Curtiss workers might then be persuaded to quit The Aircraft and sign cards to join the UAW.

It was a tactic that later, when I was a UE union organizer, was used successfully in organizing campaigns at other factories, including the Pratt & Letchworth foundry and machine shop in Buffalo, where the workers established a UE local union to replace one of Edward Hamilton's FIU outfits.

My union experience led me to assume, rightly or wrongly, that most companies formally or informally develop their own underground—shall we say "spy"—network to counteract, soften or undermine whatever their employees may be planning in the way of asking for a wage increase or doing anything else that might affect production or profit. I also assumed, based on that experience, that it is wise to take it for granted that within minutes after a union or caucus meeting is adjourned, the company personnel responsible to use that information has received a full report, usually phoned in, telling them exactly what took place there, including names of potential trouble makers.

At Curtiss someone in the mold loft caucus, probably one of our "best friends" in the department, most likely had been brought into the company's network to be an informant—less kindly labor men and women might call him a stoolpigeon—resulting in George and me being quickly singled out for special treatment.

Looking back now, I laugh at one especially ludicrous action performed by our department foreman to rein me in. I think that the foreman was a decent well-meaning man who, to keep his job, thought he had to do what he was told to do. One morning he came down to my area in the department and, avoiding my inquiring look, he used a piece of white chalk to draw a large circle around the bench where I worked. Still finding it hard to look directly into my eyes, he told me that if I thought I had a legitimate reason to step out of the circle I must raise my hand to get his attention and, after I tell him where I want to go and why, he would decide whether to give me permission. The other side of the coin was his order that no other employee in the department was to cross the chalk line to go into that circle to talk to me without first getting his approval. Workers from other departments who came in and crossed into the circle to ask my help to solve problems they might be having with tools and/or parts developed from my layouts were immediately challenged. The foreman charged down from his raised platform to confront them and, monitoring our conversations, he would stay there until they left.

The ever-present grapevine—my experience has led me to believe it's there in every factory—must have spread the word about the chalk circle throughout the whole plant, because for a few days following the chalk circle's creation a larger than usual stream of workers came into the mold loft department to ask me questions about tools and parts and blueprints, seeing with their own eyes the chalk circle drawn to wall them off from contact with the redhead. The company's underground network must have reported that the chalk circle was having exactly the opposite of the intended effect. The chalk circle lasted less than a week. When I came to work one morning it had been mopped away.

Most of the time the work itself at Curtiss—like the work back at Dupont—was, at least for me, not a very interesting pastime; for me, being stuck in the factory was too often like being stuck in a prison, the repetitive nature of much of the work boring me to the point of flipping me out of my mind. Fortunately, at Curtiss, the intense challenge connected with trying to overcome the company's resistance to our effort to develop decent union representation made my life there—and I believe the lives of others in the mold loft, including George of course—not only tolerable, but even compellingly interesting. That may explain why George and I were able, with relative ease, to develop an active caucus of mold loft department workers who two or three times a week willingly rushed from work to the nearby bar for 15-minute meetings where the caucus decided what to do next.

George and I expected that the company was receiving reports about what was happening in our caucus meetings. So I was not too surprised when two well-dressed men came into the department one morning and spoke to the foreman before walking down to my bench. One of them spoke quietly to me.

"Hello, Manny."

"Hi."

"Manny, have you ever been in California?"

"No, sir."

It was true that I had never been in California. Years later I learned that there was an Emanuel Fried who did live in California. But I wasn't that Emanuel Fried. However, being questioned, even this briefly, by these two men intimidated me, truthfully frightened me. I assumed that they were FBI agents. And this was the first time in my life that I was aware of the FBI paying attention to me. I had no idea then that this was the beginning of an off-and-on bumpy relationship with FBI, which would continue right up to the present. Fortunately, the early frequency of my brushes with FBI quickly toughened me, hardened my resolve and strengthened my willingness and ability to confront them publicly head-on every time they tried to curb what I write, what I think and what I say, especially since I believe that it is/was they, not I, who are/were doing what is not right.

My answer—that I had never been in California—seemed to satisfy the two visitors. They turned and left the department. But a week or two later they returned and came directly to my bench.

"Manny, how'd you like to have your own radio program?"

I knew why they were making the offer. We had expanded our mold loft caucus to include workers from other departments, backing a man named Leo Kriegbaum to run for president of The Aircraft. George and I had met with Leo and he had agreed to run on a progressive program that we worked out with him. We had written and distributed leaflets publicizing his program and his candidacy. It looked like Leo might defeat FIU head Edward Hamilton's candidate and get elected president of The Aircraft union. So I assumed that I was being offered the radio program to get me out of the plant as a step toward breaking up our caucus and undermining the support we had generated for Leo.

Needless to say, I refused their offer. Leo Kriegbaum was elected president of The Aircraft. George and I were designated by Leo to put out a weekly newsletter for The Aircraft, which we did—until Leo turned against us.

Chapter 3

It's hard for me to believe—it seems so strange as I think about it now—that I did not tell Rhoda one word about what George and I were doing in relation to the union at Curtiss. Rhoda never asked me and I never volunteered the information. My life with Rhoda and my life at Curtiss were two separate streams. Neither Rhoda nor I had any idea that sometime in the years ahead those two streams—with help from the FBI who thought it would bring me to heel and end my involvement with labor—would inevitably be made to collide with tumultuous and agonizing force by FBI agents deliberately and maliciously acting to destroy Rhoda's proud sense of herself as Miss Park Lane.

From the time she was a child Rhoda had wanted to become an artist, a painter. She got her mother to enroll her in Saturday morning painting classes at the Albright Art Gallery. When Rhoda graduated from high school she studied painting for a year at the Art Institute in Philadelphia. When she returned to Buffalo she became—as she herself described it—"a Sunday painter." But when she married me she seemed to become possessed with a desire to prove to me that I was not the only one who worked at a job. She arranged with her father to use a small room on the first floor in the rear of The Park Lane as her studio, going there every day to paint. She generated commissions to paint portraits, at that time using only water colors. A few years later she drove back and forth to Toronto every week to study oil painting with one of Canada's leading portrait painters until she became proficient using oils—and from then on called herself "a people painter" and tried to embody the sum of her model's whole life in the face and body she painted.

Rhoda's mother, Rae, felt that her husband did not fully appreciate her capability because she did not "work." When he died before she had fully developed distribution of the hand cream she had created in a chemistry class at the University of Buffalo, she cried out to Rhoda, "I didn't get a chance to show him." Anxious to support Rhoda's intense effort to become a good professional artist, Rae paid for a maid and a cook, young African-American women, to relieve Rhoda of housekeeping and cooking chores and give her more time and energy for her painting. Rhoda had grown up in a household with a full-time maid and cook; but our having an African-American maid and cook—the maid serving our evening meal prepared by the cook—contributed further at that time to my uncomfortable sense of living a lifestyle completely alien to me, a feeling exacerbated by the contrast each day between what I came home to and the mold loft work and union involvement I had just left at Curtiss. Rhoda readily agreed when I told her I'd feel more comfortable if she would tell the maid and cook to go home early each day to allow us to serve ourselves the already prepared meal.

Rhoda's sister Annette told me that I was good for Rhoda and that she herself would have become active with labor if she had married me. She and Bunny lived in a large apartment in The Park Lane. Their beautiful African-American maid proudly dressed herself like the stereotypical movie French maid. Moments after Rhoda and I ever entered Annette and Bunny's apartment, which we did almost every day, the maid quietly served us what she knew was our usual drinks, martinis, from the ornate bar that filled a whole corner of the richly decorated living room. (With my friends at Curtiss my usual drink was beer on draught.) Annette enjoyed pampering Rhoda, bought her clothes, advised her concerning makeup and hair style, protected and counseled her. Annette apologized to me that she herself was apolitical. But she liked to joke in an accepting way about the different radical experience I brought into the Lurie family.

Rhoda was the youngest of the five children. Annette was the oldest. She had worked for a short while as a reporter for the Buffalo Evening News, a job that Bunny, her wealthy husband, had persuaded her to quit when they married. Surprisingly, Bunny and I got along very well. He had contempt for the establishment and enjoyed talking on a fairly intimate level with working people. Years later when he and Annette moved to Florida he enjoyed telling me how he had become very friendly with the garbage pickup man and how he was advising him regarding investments in the stock market.

*****

Bunny had grown up working for his father in wholesale distribution of foods. For many years, using his phone at home, he bought and sold humongous quantities of foods on the commodities market, especially perishables, where the risk was great and the profit or loss equally great. I listened to him making phone calls, checking out weather and potential markets in city after city while, as a train moved eastward from California, he bought and sold the whole load of strawberries packed into that train's long string of freight cars.

Sometime later when I was in charge of a tough strike already lasting almost a year at an electrical equipment manufacturing company whose owner belonged to the same upscale club as Bunny, I was told by Bunny that the word at the club was that the company's president had already lost a million dollars because of the strike. "Hold out another year," advised Bunny, "and you've got him licked, he'll cave in." I ruefully laughed, telling Bunny that our people were in desperate straits and might not be able to hold out even another month. Bunny said he was sorry to hear that. Shortly after that the company made an under the table deal with another union and wiped out our strike and our local union there.

*****

Ruth was the middle daughter, a severe manic-depressive. Today that would be termed bi-polar. Politically, Ruth was intellectually way to the left, but she did not belong to any political organization. She welcomed me into the family and confided how she had tried, but failed, to persuade the elevator operators, cleaning women and switchboard operators in the apartment house side of The Park Lane to form a union to deal with her father.

Rhoda had two brothers, Howard and the younger George. In the early years of my marriage I had little to do with Howard. He lived in Rochester where, funded by rich Uncle Louie, he operated an outdoor drive-in movie theatre. It didn't take me long to learn that by reading what was printed on the editorial page of the Wall Street Journal I could tell what Howard's view would be on the important political, economic or social issue of the day. When my father-in-law died, Rhoda resented that she was not even asked if she had an interest in taking over management of The Park Lane. Uncle Louie owned 60% of the business; Rhoda and her mother and brothers and sisters owned 40%. Howard was told by Uncle Louie to sell his Rochester drive-in movie business and to move back to Buffalo to take over operation of The Park Lane.

"I want to stop paying off this business agent from the waiters and waitresses and bartenders union," Howard said to me. *"I'm sick of him coming in and telling me I forgot his birthday. How do I stop it?"*

"Don't pay him off," I said.

"Then he'll ask me for a raise for his people."

"You really don't want to get rid of him," I said.

Like Ruth, George was also a manic-depressive, bi-polar. Before he ended up spending months at a time in mental institutions, his frustrated father, usually a very kindly man., not knowing how to handle his son's widely swinging moods, including being depressed sometimes to the point of being almost catatonic, would urgently exhort him, "C'mon, son! Pull yourself up by your bootstraps!"

George was a lawyer. After passing the bar exam he had worked for about a year with one of Buffalo's most prestigious law firms, quitting because it would take too long working there to achieve the one-of-the-richest-men-in-the-

United-States status of his Uncle Louie. When he was emotionally sailing high, way up there out of control, he thought he was running the world. Years later, when the Off-Broadway production of my play *The Dodo Bird* got a great review in The New York Times, it for some reason sent George sky-high and he walked into the New York Hilton Hotel, asked to speak to the manager, told him he was considering buying the hotel—George did give the appearance of being old money rich—and the manager politely gave him a tour of the kitchen facilities that George said would reveal the general condition of the whole property, after which George told the manager that this convinced him to buy the hotel and he gave the manager four one hundred dollar bills as a down payment. That fiasco finally ended with two policemen, responding to a phone call from Rhoda, subduing a vigorously resisting George to cart him over to Bellevue Hospital.

But back in Buffalo, before he started soaring that sky-high and sinking that way low, George and I got along very well. Night after night—while I was still working at Curtiss—Rhoda and I would meet George and his current date back at The Park Lane for a nightcap that extended past midnight, leaving me sleep deprived the next day at work. Rhoda fondly called her favorite brother "Gentleman George." He was always precisely dressed in a well-fitted suit, with a nice tie and a handkerchief, folded with its corners showing, stuck in the pocket on the upper left side of his suit jacket. Though he was slightly built, George was handsome and well tanned, usually spending a lot of time playing tennis at the club, where young women of his social group—who generally did not work at any job—were attracted to him, the Park Lane connection probably adding a special sheen to his image.

George was also a proud member of the Buffalo Junior Chamber of Commerce. While we were having a drink at The Park Lane bar he mentioned that he had been introduced to my brother Maury at a Jaycees meeting, referring to my brother in such a patronizing way—putting him in a class beneath him—that I instinctively resented it, though I let it pass. But I felt guilty, that I was betraying my brother, when I went on to tell George that Maury—active in a Jaycee membership drive—had asked me to do him a favor by signing up to become a Jaycee member, promising me that I wouldn't have to do anything that would publicly connect me with the Jaycees, dismissing as irrelevant my labor and my leftist activity and connections.

When Howard took over management of The Park Lane property, George who was listed as an officer of the family's closed corporation insisted on also playing a management role. Howard designated George to be his assistant, managing the restaurant and cocktail lounge. Subsequently George told me that when the business agent of the union of waiters, waitresses and bartenders came into his office and routinely asked for the usual birthday present, "I kicked the son-of-a-bitch out of my office."

However, the business agent then went to Howard and collected the birthday present from him. Rhoda was involved in the resulting bitter clash between George and Howard, with George accusing Howard of cowardice. Howard said he was doing what's best for the business and that Uncle Louie had approved what he had done. George said that since he himself did not wish to be associated with that immoral way of doing business he would move to New York City. Rhoda insisted that George still be paid his regular salary. Howard agreed.

To give George a sendoff when the time came for him to leave, I joined him and Rhoda at the bar in The Park Lane dining room where we had a few drinks.

Since marrying into the Lurie family my drinking habits had changed. When I had been living at home with my parents and brothers and sisters, my alcoholic drinks were usually restricted to wedding receptions, bar mitzvah celebrations, and Passover meals. Married to Rhoda, with The Park Lane bar in the family, we drank the hard stuff every day. No special occasion was required. When I drank with my Park Lane family evenings after coming home from work at Curtiss, I usually had a martini and maybe one or two scotch-on-the-rocks, with on rare occasions a Bloody-Mary inserted before or in between. I never thought of any of us as alcoholics, but years later when I learned that our younger daughter, Mindy, was going to Alateen, a group meeting for teenagers affected by alcoholic family members, I recognized that Rhoda and Howard and Ruth were definitely alcoholics, and George was borderline. I don't believe I myself ever approached becoming an alcoholic.

My drinking regimen with my Park Lane family contrasted with the single beer or the single whiskey-shot-with-beer-chaser that I drank "to be one of the guys" with George Poole and other members of our caucus at Curtiss, and that for the same reason, later when I became a UE organizer, I drank with our union members and their families.

Looking back, thinking about it now, those contrasting drinking patterns revealed the somewhat schizophrenic nature of my life, which became emotionally more difficult for me—and yes, also for Rhoda—to handle as I moved from my job at Curtiss into my years as a UE union organizer, where I drew increased attention from FBI and other opponents who employed the red-baiting weapon associated with McCarthyism. To respect myself, no matter what the cost, I would not let myself give up my labor and leftist activity and permit my life to become completely assimilated into the world of my Park Lane family where with only that as my life I feared that I would be a nobody, of no importance. But I also liked the life that I had with my Park Lane family. To feel fulfilled and secure, I was cocky enough to believe that I could keep both worlds fairly balanced in my life.

133

Chapter 4

Within a few weeks after our mold loft department caucus led the way to get Leo Kriegbaum elected president of The Aircraft union, Leo made a deal with the old guard we'd helped him defeat.

George and I were each notified by registered mail to appear before a special meeting of The Aircraft called to vote on a motion to expel us from the organization for being in violation of the clause in The Aircraft constitution barring from membership in the organization those Curtiss workers who are guilty of "Communist association."

We knew that the constitution also barred "Communists" from membership in the organization. Since the FBI certainly knew that George and I were members of the Communist Party, we found it strange and somewhat amusing that we were accused only of *associating with Communists* but not actually being Communist Party members. We speculated that the reason for that might be that the FBI—we assumed it was the FBI who prompted Leo's action against us— did not want to reveal their "plant" within the local branch of the Communist Party whose testimony might be required to prove membership. Since we thought that restriction also would affect proving "Communist association," we wondered what Leo—even with information secretly supplied by the FBI— might use to back up the charge.

We believed that a majority of the thousands of workers employed by Curtiss at that time liked the effort of our caucus to make The Aircraft into a real union and, given a fair chance to avoid being red-baited themselves, would vote to keep us in the organization.

The meeting hall was jammed with an unusually large turnout of Curtiss workers. We expected that Leo and the old guard, possibly with the help of the company's undercover network, had brought out those Aircraft members who were most likely to back their effort to expel us. We had worked hard to get a good turnout of those we believed would support us.

Leo slapped the gavel down on the podium and called the meeting to order. He announced that there was only one order of business that could be brought up at this special meeting. He then read the motion presented by the executive board to expel George Poole from the organization "because he is in violation of the constitution barring from membership those guilty of Communist association." To prove that George was guilty of Communist association, Leo called on the former president of The Aircraft to read aloud a newspaper article that identified George as a veteran of the Abraham Lincoln Brigade that had fought in the Spanish civil war on the side of the Communists against the anti-Communist troops of General Francisco Franco.

"We are a democratic organization," announced Leo. "The membership will act in a democratic way to decide this." Then without opening the floor for discussion of the motion to expel George, he continued. "We'll now vote on the motion to expel George Poole from membership in The Aircraft because of his admitted Communist association. All in favor say Aye." There were some Ayes in response to that. Leo rushed on. "Those opposed?" The Nays far outnumbered the Ayes. Leo slapped his gavel down on the podium. "The Ayes have it. George Poole is expelled."

Leo ignored the grumbling protests from the audience. A loud gruff voice, badly imitating the blasting horn of a railroad locomotive, yelled, "Choo-choo! Choo-choo! Rail-road! Rail-road!"

I was sitting with George Poole, both of us surrounded by a good turnout of members of our mold loft department caucus. My mind racing, I tried to think of some way to derail this freight train, Leo running roughshod over any attempt to have an honest vote count. I sensed that we had the majority on our side if we could very quickly—no time to discuss—no time to exchange ideas—very quickly, instantaneously, create a roadblock to derail the rushing freight train.

Leo hurried on, trying to get the whole thing done before we had time to re-group. He presented the second motion: "Emanuel Fried is hereby expelled from membership in The Aircraft because his association with George Poole is clear proof of his guilt of Communist association." With a sharp slap of his gavel he concluded, "All in favor say Aye!"

I leaped to my feet, waving my arms, yelling to short circuit the railroading tactic that Leo confidently thought he could repeat. "All in favor of keeping me in the union," I shouted, "come over to this side of the hall!"

There was a loud clattering of shoved and collapsing folding chairs as an unquestionable majority of those in the hall delightedly grabbed this opportunity to stop Leo's railroad train, ignoring his gavel's loud hammering as they jostled one another, while yelling out loud, gathering around us on our side of the large room.

"That's your vote, Mr. Chairman!" I yelled to Leo who was momentarily stunned into silence. "Motion to adjourn!" I yelled. "All in favor!" The shouts of Ayes drowned out the feeble attempt of Leo to regain control, and the crowd noisily churned toward the exits. The meeting was over.

Celebrating this partial victory, some of us from the mold loft department stopped off at a nearby tavern for a quick beer. From there I went to join Rhoda in the Park Lane dining room. We had a few drinks. Nothing was said about what had happened in the union hall.

Chapter 5

I have a need to digress. Last night my dear friend, actress Rosalind Cramer whom I admire and respect, pressed me to answer why I had so stubbornly stuck to my beliefs about labor even though it had been so difficult. I answered, and she questioned my answer. I answered again, and she again questioned my answer, and this went on and on and on, until I finally angrily blurted out that it was only by defying those on the other side of the fence that I had been able to compel them to respect me.

Having started, I could not stop. From deep within, it poured out of me. "As their dangerous opponent who refused to retreat and did whatever was necessary to maintain my ability to threaten their domination of our society, I was their equal. If I had folded because of the anguished difficulties they imposed, not only upon me but also on Rhoda and our two children, when they tried to break me, or if I had allowed myself to be bought over to their side, whether by money or blandishments of various kinds, I feared, unconsciously, instinctively, that I would become a nobody, no longer the threat that, despite social and financial differences, compelled them to accept me as someone equal in my strength to their strength—my defiant and stubborn refusal to abandon my dedication to advancing the cause of labor placing me on a level playing field with them— they could not ignore me."

Roz was kind. She quietly asked, "And where did that come from?"

Upset, I slammed the door shut. "You can read my memoir when I'm done with it. See what I find out there."

But that did not quiet my unrest. I went to bed but could not fall asleep. I did not like myself. I thought that the reason I had given for stubbornly sticking with labor meant that I was a selfish person concerned more with my own ego then with the rightness of the cause of labor, the needs and rights of working people. My thinking kept me awake for hours until I thought through to an idea that helped me think better of myself. Admittedly, since I had not grown up in an environment where—like some who had followed in their family's footsteps to go to Harvard, Yale or its equivalent and from childhood were ingrained with the belief that they were superior and above others and entitled to rule—I had a constant need to lift my ego to where I was on an even keel, eye to eye, with those who had been raised to believe that they were superior to me in knowledge and intelligence and rightly ruled me along with others like me. Angrily thinking about it, I dug out the thought that to build my ego I could have made choices other than lining up with the ranks of labor. Knowing that well established movie actors can look ruling class sons and daughters squarely in the eye and tell them to go fuck themselves, I chose to turn down Kazan's offer to build my career as an actor in the movies. Also, when I began to get recognition as a playwright I stubbornly resisted pressure from the FBI and from others I knew in the theatre and movie business to abandon writing plays that enhanced respect for working people, for labor people. They held out offers for higher praise for my play productions and greater recognition as a playwright if I would write material that did not go against the grain, material that did not contribute to challenging those who were ignoring and exploiting working people and the poor. If I had made the choice to write the kind of stuff which is acceptable to those who behind the scenes are exercising great control over the arts and our society, my ego might that way have gained the prestige to act with equal strength to deal with that inner circle of our privileged class. I readily confess that the choice I did make was made in great part to build my ego, but I like to think that stubbornly living out that choice despite the cost to my family and me, choosing to stand shoulder to shoulder with the rank-and-file of labor, may ameliorate the selfishness that my choice carried with it.

However, I myself am not fully at peace with that rationalization. It was Socrates, I've been informed, who first stated that the life unexamined is the life not lived. I have the need to examine my life deeper—and then deeper beneath that—to find out what I was *really* doing with my life—and *why*.

Chapter 6

Back to 1941 and Curtiss.

Following that meeting where George Poole was expelled from The Aircraft and I was not expelled, the tempo of events shot up into high gear. I was transferred from the plant on Kenmore Road to the plant in Cheektowaga. Both George and I were dropped as editors of The Aircraft newsletter. The FBI interrogated us separately, telling each of us that the other had identified the one being interrogated as a member of the Communist Party. When I was summoned out into the assembly area to check an airplane part that wasn't fitting properly, a foreman yelled to several men who were hauling an assembled P-40 fuselage down the aisle toward me, "Roll over that Commie sonofabitch! Kill him!"

The organizers for the United Auto Workers convinced us that our best protection against getting fired was to come out openly as volunteer organizers for the UAW, so that if the company fired us it would be clear that it was because of our activity on behalf of the UAW and then a good case could be made for the Labor Board to order the company to rescind the discharges and reinstate us to our jobs with reimbursement of pay we would have lost. When they named George and me co-chairmen of the UAW Volunteer Organizing Committee, I resigned from The Aircraft and pinned a row of large UAW buttons across the front of my shirt.

Advised by the UAW organizers that during our lunch periods we had the right of free speech, I gave impromptu talks during lunch breaks, describing gains that would flow from joining the UAW, to workers gathered in the plant yard while they were eating. For several successive days no one tried to stop me from doing that. Then, on a day when I had just started to give my usual talk about the UAW to a gathering of workers in the yard, a uniformed company guard, who I assumed was acting on instructions from his superior, came to me and interrupted to tell me that it was against company rules to conduct a union meeting on plant property. I told him that I was not conducting a union meeting, but that I was just speaking to some men—who had the right to listen or not listen—in accordance with my constitutional right of free speech. Without saying a word, the guard walked away.

For a few more days I continued to make these impromptu speeches on behalf of the UAW to workers in the plant yard. Then the company acted. The head of plant security and two other men, all in plain clothes, came into the mold loft department and briefly stopped to speak to the foreman. Then, with everyone in the department watching them, they came to me at my workbench. The head of plant security quietly told me to get my tools and other personal property. With the head of plant security leading me and the two other men flanking me, they silently marched me out of the plant and out to the front plant gate.

All along the way I thought I was maintaining a surface calm as I tried to accept what was happening with an air of dignity. But my heart was pounding so strongly that I worried that my escorts could hear it.

The head of security handed me a letter signed by Colonel Simonin, Army Air Force liaison officer overseeing work done at Curtiss, informing me that my removal from the plant was ordered on the grounds that my conduct was subversive. Carrying my metal toolbox, I walked away, trying not to let my escorts become aware of my panicky feelings.

Needless to say, my discharge caused problems at home. I was not sure what to do immediately to replace the missing paychecks. Fortunately Rhoda agreed that I had been discharged because of my union activity, not for doing anything to interfere with production. My father-in-law, though he did not agree with my union activity, was a realist and readily took it for granted that that was why I had been discharged. His attitude contributed to my decision to launch a fight to be reinstated to my job.

The UAW organizers I'd been working with told me that they were urging their national officers to make a fight for my reinstatement. They said they were arguing that failing to do that would hurt the Curtiss organizing drive. Their problem was that their immediate boss, the UAW regional director, had been elected on a program of opposing the Communists in the union, and he was not anxious to push for my reinstatement to my job in Curtiss. Faced with that reality, I launched my own campaign, using every important contact I could develop, including people I got to know through Rhoda and her Lurie family at The Park Lane, to produce a stream of letters to the Defense Department in Washington, testifying to my character and my active support of the war effort. Even my father-in-law, though he told me that he disagreed with my union beliefs, wrote a letter of support, asking as a matter of justice that my discharge be rescinded. I made getting these letters of support my full-time job, and as the letters accumulated it became easier and easier to get more letters. By the time

142

I secured letters of support from the mayor and other elected public officials, I had enough letters to almost guarantee a positive response from anyone else I asked to write a letter on my behalf.

On Sunday, December 7, 1941, Rhoda and I sat in our living room and listened to Franklin D. Roosevelt's radio talk to the nation, his famous speech categorizing the Japanese attack on Pearl Harbor as "a day of infamy." We were at war, joining the allied forces of Great Britain, France, and the Soviet Union. Especially important was the development of cooperation between our country and the Soviet Union. In that changed situation it became temporarily *un*fashionable in our country to viciously attack members of the Communist Party. While the anti-Communist thrust of our country's corporate-dominated establishment was never really eliminated, only temporarily masked from open antagonism, a great show was made of public cooperation between capitalist and Communist leaders on a local, state and federal level "to win the war." The atmosphere flowing from this cooperation made it even easier to get the letters from elected government officials and prominent members of the community, asking the Defense Department in Washington to reinstate me to my job at Curtiss.

This international alliance to win the war also contributed to open, but somewhat uneasy, cooperation between some leaders of the Congress of Industrial Organizations (the CIO union) and Communist Party leaders to organize the unorganized production workers in factories all across the country. It was normal for some Buffalo CIO union leaders to regularly cross the street from their offices in the Root Building to discuss tactics and get assistance in difficult organizing and strike situations from CP leaders in the Party's office. In a strange way this was reflected in a conversation I had with CIO Regional Director Hugh Thompson, during which he told me that any union leader who is not called a Communist is not doing a good job for his members. But many CIO leaders who asked for this help from Communists were hypocritical and when it served their purpose were prone to openly—or secretly—attack those same Communists whose help they had secured. Generally those of us Communists involved in these situations were fully aware of this potential duplicity but—counting on the defense we hoped to get from the rank-and-file workers in the union—we did our best in those difficult organizing and strike situations to help those same CIO guys that we expected would later try to knife us in the back. It took brassy United Mine Workers Union leader John L. Lewis to openly state what many CIO leaders were not honest enough to reveal—that he used the Communists to organize the workers into his union because their dedication made them the best organizers, but once the Communists got the workers organized into his union he kicked the Communists out.

The UAW organizers at Curtiss were well aware that George Poole and I were members of the Communist Party. When I was walked out of the plant they told our supporters at Curtiss that the UAW would provide me with financial help to support my family. This support was exceedingly meager, consisting of a token few dollars slipped to me now and then. With the men I had worked with at Curtiss knowing that I was blacklisted and unable to get a job elsewhere, I was an embarrassment to the UAW organizers and an obstacle to their attempt to get Curtiss workers to join their union. I sensed that they wished that I would just disappear. But the letters of support I had accumulated made it difficult for them. Finally even the UAW regional director set aside his anti-Communist bias and enlisted the help of the top UAW national officers to exert their influence in Washington to try to secure my reinstatement to my job at Curtiss.

Meanwhile, the head of the Western New York branch of the Communist Party told me that the United Electrical, Radio and Machine Workers, the national union known as the UE, was looking for an organizer to add to their local staff. The UE office was in the same Root Building where the CIO regional office was located, across the street from Communist Party headquarters. I met with Al Clough, who was heading the UE campaign to organize workers at the Buffalo Bolt factory in North Tonawanda. Contrary to the ugly stereotype some people may believe about union organizers, Al Clough was actually the most gentle and soft-spoken man I've ever met in my whole life. He was a big man who listened intently and seemed to completely absorb whatever was said to him. Workers trusted him. He was a Communist and I believe also a Quaker.

There are several interesting odds and ends worth tying up here before I try to fully capture what it was—deep beneath the increasing tension created by the sharpening clash between my union organizer world and my Park lane world— that kept driving me. Also I need to try to identify as best I can *why* and *how* that impending clash and the climactic clash itself changed me.

My testimony before the National Labor Relations Board, which included my report about the foreman exhorting the workers hauling the assembled fuselage to run me over and kill me, contributed to the Board's decision to rule that The Aircraft was an illegal organization formed and operated with assistance and control by the company's management and that the company could no longer recognize The Aircraft as the union representing its employees.

Leo Kriegbaum, who had turned against George Poole and me after we had helped him get elected to head The Aircraft, had the chutzpah several years later—when he had weaseled his way into temporarily becoming an organizer for the Service Employees Union—to ask me to talk to my father-in-law about making the cleaning women, maids, elevator operators, switchboard operators, handymen and other custodial employees at The Park Lane join his union. Leo confidentially advised me to tell my father-in-law that he promised not to ask for a wage increase or any other financial benefits for the employees, that he only wanted their dues money to finance organizing employees of other apartment buildings. Not wanting to reinforce my father-in-law's negative feelings about "union bosses," I did not pass on Leo's message, which I knew

144

would have drawn a grunt of contemptuous disgust. Fortunately, not long after that the Service Employees Union dumped Leo.

It took several years but finally the Defense Department acted in response to the unrelenting stream of letters and phone calls challenging Air Force Colonel Simonin's rationale for removing me from the job at Curtiss. An investigator from the Defense Department—civilian clothed Mr. Knox—set up a meeting with me. He seemed to be a decent guy and we got along well. With a secretary recording our conversation, he asked questions about my background and why I was so interested in the union. In response to his question—"Why don't you just take care of your own potatoes?"—I told him I felt a responsibility to be concerned about people who are less well off.

As if to catch me off guard, "Manny," he shot at me, "where do you get the money to eat and drink at The Park Lane?"

So that was it. Colonel Simonin had drawn the conclusion that I was living a lifestyle beyond what I could afford on my Curtiss wages, and therefore I must be getting paid to agitate and disrupt production by opposing The Aircraft and urging Curtiss workers to join the UAW union.

"My wife's family owns the place," I said quietly, unable to repress a sardonic grin. "It's the cheapest place for me and my wife to eat. We don't pay anything. My wife just signs the bill."

In our more relaxed ensuing conversation I told Knox that Park Lane tenant Frank Carr, a powerful Democratic Party leader—asked by my father-in-law to check into why I had suddenly been upgraded by my draft board for immediate induction into the armed forces—reported that he'd been told it was to get me away from my union activity at Curtiss. Knox said he'd look into it. Carr told me Knox checked with him. A week or so later I was informed that my draft status had been put back to what it had been, not immediately subject to be called into the armed forces. (Not long after that, in part to prove I was not ducking my duty, I volunteered and served in the infantry for two and a half years.) I don't know exactly what Knox reported back to his superiors in Washington, but I was subsequently informed that Curtiss had been ordered to reinstate me to my job with pay for the money I had lost because of being removed from the plant. Colonel Simonin was transferred from his fine post overseeing production at Curtiss to a post where he was placed in charge of a warehouse.

By the time this happened, I was already a UE organizer, deeply involved in union organizing drives at Buffalo Bolt and several other factories in Tonawanda and North Tonawanda. To establish a date for calculation of pay owed me, I arranged to come back to work in the mold loft at Curtiss, where I notified the foreman that at the end of the shift on that one day I would be quitting, formally ending my employment with the company. The foreman, apparently following instructions from the front office, made no effort to make me do any work and did not interfere with the steady stream of workers who quietly and quickly came to my bench in the department to shake my hand and just as quietly and quickly left.

To add to the developing complications in my life stemming from my work as a UE organizer, Rhoda gave birth to the redheaded baby girl I had wished for and immediately adored. Anxious to keep the Lurie name alive, Rhoda came up with Lorrie, making the baby's full name become Lorrie Elizabeth Mary Fried, the Elizabeth and Mary inserted to carry on names of deceased members of our families. Not realizing how hard it was going to be, I swore to myself that I would protect my child from any hurt caused by the controversy connected with my work as a UE organizer.

At that point I was not aware that the trains on the two parallel tracks of my life, stretching through my controversial world connected with the UE union and through my glamorous world connected with The Park Lane, were racing with ever increasing emotional tension toward inevitable collision. Somewhat arrogantly, I thought that, though it might be difficult, my stubborn effort to be honest with myself and with Rhoda would create for us a socially acceptable merger of the two parallel tracks into one unusually complicated but wonderfully integrated life track.

Part Three

"Heading for the train wreck!"

Chapter 1

Though several years earlier my father-in-law had died unexpectedly of a heart attack—a ruptured main artery—I could still imagine how Mandel Lurie, sitting behind his desk in his office in The Park Lane, a cigar stub clenched between his teeth and lips, would have held the morning newspaper up in front of his face as he usually did each morning, and would have made a point of looking back and forth from the banner headline to me...and back and forth...and back and forth—shaking his head, not openly approving or disapproving, but definitely bewildered, not understanding what justification there possibly could be for the brazen action that he correctly would have assumed was something that I had organized.

That morning the banner headline—big black letters across the top of the newspaper's front page—blared out that UE union members had stopped work at 13 factories in the area. The article below reluctantly, I thought, conceded that it was not a strike. Thousands of UE members had walked off their jobs in the afternoon of the previous day, August 9, 1953, to go to a mass meeting in the park. The news story made the point that "UE organizer Manny Fried introduced the featured speaker, James Matles, national director of organization for the allegedly Communist-dominated United Electrical, Radio and Machine Workers."

The general tone of the news story seemed to imply that what we had done was a violation of some law, which it was not. I imagined that the newspaper editor—whose treatment of me for several years indicated that he agreed with the FBI's assessment that I was a dangerous man who must be driven out of the labor movement—apparently thought that he had me out on a limb for having organized this kind of interruption of production. Perhaps I was paranoid, but I thought that the editor had had his reporter deliberately try to whip up sentiment in the community against our union, and by prominently mentioning my role as the local union representative, specifically against me.

Editors for both the morning and evening newspapers had been targeting me for years. The Buffalo Evening News reporter Fred Turner, their hatchet man, seemed to take malicious pleasure in shooting at me with frequent "guilt-by-association-with-Marx-Lenin-Stalin" articles. From the personal information he seemed to know about me I believed that he was working with the FBI, trying to demonize me, publicly doing for them what it was illegal for them to do.

I am aware now of how much at that point I had changed from the time when I started to work as a UE union organizer. At first those news stories attacking me upset me terribly, especially when they caused problems for me with Rhoda. But by the time this bold headline would be read by Rhoda, I had learned that while some sections of the community, probably including many people in The Park Lane world, might be bothered by the action we had taken, working families—the great majority in our community—might consciously and/or unconsciously feel a sense of pride that thousands of ordinary working men and women like themselves had the guts and the know-how to boldly challenge the establishment this way. That made it easier for me to hold my ground until the effect of the news story on Rhoda would wear off.

Our union, refusing to join in the purging of the left from the ranks of organized labor, had split from the CIO in 1950. This ushered in the period when labor reporters for the Buffalo Evening News and the Buffalo Courier Express tainted every mention of our organization with the phrase "the allegedly Communist-dominated UE union." While these reporters claimed to be objective, we in UE believed that they were taking sides against us. Frequently when we were in a fight with an employer or with a rival union that was raiding us or with a government agency that was trying to help the rival union or a recalcitrant employer undermine our organization, a reporter would phone and ask me to give a statement. Then the reporter would reduce my statement to a short paragraph or two and use that to provide the platform for a very long statement by one of our opponents, ripping our union's position apart.

Looking back, I can see that by the time we stopped work for that special meeting on August 9th in 1953 I was no longer the novice frightened by the "importance" of those who were attacking our union. I had apparently decided that the best defense was to attack. I had learned by trial and error that when I had the courage to step out in front and lead, taking the blasts that I drew from our opponents and then, not retreating or apologizing, attacked again even more strongly, our union's rank-and-file members backed me up. They seemed to take some sort of pride in the way I openly stood up to the so-called untouchables in the establishment, publicly striking back at the powerful national and international corporate employers and yes, the powerful national leaders of the unions raiding us, and the FBI, the Catholic "labor priests" and the priest in charge of the Canisius adult education program who were assisting our opponents, some federal and state labor-management conciliators and some political office holders, all the way up to some in the president's administration in Washington, who, we believed, were unfairly trying to destroy us because we had opposed the Cold War and had supported Henry Wallace rather than Harry Truman. At times I felt like we were standing up against almost the whole world, while at the same time I was deeply convinced that what we were doing was right and was good for our country.

I always admired the way union leader John L. Lewis told the governor of Michigan that if he, the governor, sent in National Guard troops to break the auto workers sit-down strike, that he, John L., would stand, breast bared, in front of the strikers and challenge the soldiers to shoot him first. And I admired even more the UAW union organizer I knew in Buffalo who told me—even if it might not have been true—that when he had been one of the rank-and-file leaders in that sit-down strike inside the auto plant in Flint, Michigan, and the governor phoned into the plant and imperiously ordered him, the lowly peon, to lead those "lawbreaking sit-down strikers" out of the plant, he responded, "Fuck you, governor," and hung up.

So it was not a big jump for me to follow in their footsteps. Disgusted with the way the newspaper reporters were using statements they sought from me to help our opponents rip us apart, I refused to respond with any more statements, instead coldly responding, "No comment." The Buffalo Evening News labor reporter Ed Kelly, in particular, seemed to enjoy himself by following up to taunt me with one provocative question after another, deliberately forcing me to repeat with a flat cold voice, "No comment...no comment...no comment," over and over. Then in his news story Kelly reported the statements and questions with which he had taunted me, saying I had refused to respond to them, making it look like I didn't have anything adequate to say.

"Fuck you and fuck your newspaper and please quote me accurately!"

Reeking with anger and cold contempt, the words were spat between clenched teeth, a fierce response bursting from me, as unexpected for me as it apparently was for Ed Kelly. It stopped him cold. Rendered him speechless. He did not recover enough to speak before I slammed the phone down.

Our UE strategy committee, composed of presidents and chief stewards from our local unions representing thousands of factory workers in Western New York, who had been quietly listening to hear what I'd say to Ed Kelly in response to questions he might have about what was to happen on August 9th, were taken by surprise and momentarily silenced by what they heard, but as I turned to them—concerned about their reaction—they recovered and, nervously laughing, called out their approval.

For the rest of my years as a union organizer, my response to newspaper reporters remained: "Fuck you and fuck your newspaper and please quote me accurately."

Of course, the newspapers never printed it. I didn't think they would. But they no longer could say that I refused to comment. (I used that response years later in a similar situation that I created in *Drop Hammer*, my play that one Los Angeles drama critic was kind enough to call "a work of genius.")

The positive result we intended to create was to make the newspapers become identified in the community as the biased advocate for our opponents. By not giving the reporters public statements to provide the basis for lengthy diatribes against us, we made the newspapers curb the amount of space they gave to those who were attacking us. Our response to their attacks was given "in house" to our union members. I had learned from my mistakes that if we convinced our union members in very difficult situations to stand firm and not cave in to the opposition, the majority of the community would, possibly after some initial hesitation, swing over to support us, despite what they read in the newspapers.

It was not until long after I had been forced out of the labor movement, and already had productions of several plays drawn from my union life and Park Lane life, that a compassionate woman reporter to whom I did not want to say, "Fuck you..."—since I knew from the articles she'd written that she was a decent person—convinced me from then on to abandon that slam-the-door-shut response.

If my father-in-law had been living I know he would not have said a word while he glanced back and forth from me to that banner headline announcing that our union members had shut down those 13 factories to go to a special meeting in the park. Our relationship had been such that he never said anything to me about what I did as a union organizer. He didn't have to say anything. I could guess what he thought. But I respected him, in part because Rhoda told me that he had refused to be the "token Jew" when he was invited to join the highly restricted Buffalo Club.

(Only recently have a number of Jews been permitted to become members of the Buffalo Club and have women been permitted to enter the Buffalo Club through the front entrance rather than having to come in through the back door and pass through the kitchen.)

I always assumed that Mandel meant well, that he wanted to be fair, but that he had difficulty understanding me or what or why we in the union were doing whatever we were doing. So he and I always tended to be carefully friendly with one another. Without ever verbalizing it, we ostensibly agreed to never talk about my work as a union organizer, probably because neither of us wanted to create a rift between us that would interfere with the unusually close and loving relationship that he had developed with his granddaughter, a relationship that I thought he may have sensed, and perhaps envied or resented, might—as long as *his* daughter Rhoda was not willing to break her marriage to me—be subordinate to my position as Lorrie's father.

I confess—take full responsibility for it—that I came up with the idea that culminated in that August 9th demonstration in 1953. I had wracked my brain for days to come up with some dramatic action to take in response to the warning sounded by our director of organization Jim Matles. He'd summoned the entire organizing staff from all across the country to an emergency meeting at the UE national headquarters in New York City. I was deeply touched by his message that the survival of our union depended on each organizer finding a dramatic way to get the union members in his or her area into motion to protect the gains we had won, that this was the only way we could stop the growing movement on the part of employers with whom we had contracts to refuse to continue recognition of our union.

At our national convention the delegates from our local unions all across the country had voted to follow the lead of Mine Workers Union leader John L. Lewis, not to sign the non-Communist affidavits that the federal government, with the Taft-Hartley Law, had made a requirement for being eligible to utilize the services of the National Labor Relations Board. In Western New York, my area of responsibility, managements at three factories— Wurlitzer, Remington Rand, and Richardson Boat—were already using this vote taken by the convention to try to avoid continued recognition of our union's right to represent their employees in grievance proceedings and wage and contract negotiations.

*****

It was the time of the toad, the beginning of the worst of the McCarthy Period, the early 1950s and—thinking about it now—I realize that this was when I was finally becoming confident enough to develop my own personal evaluation about the political situation. Now I think that I can define my view even more clearly. The labor unions had come out of World War II ready to ask for delivery of the promises made by the corporate establishment to get sacrifices from workers represented by organized labor during the war. The big corporations, with reactionary elements in the National Association of Manufacturers and the Chamber of Commerce leading the way, reneged on their promises and used their financial clout to buy the support of a key chunk of the federal government to whip up the Communist issue, splitting the labor movement, engendering a civil war between unions that resulted in the destruction of the unity and militancy of organized labor all across the country—doing damage that has still not yet been fully repaired.

*****

I don't mind admitting that I was scared, not immediately sure what I should do to follow up on that emergency meeting of the organizing staff with Matles. But I had learned to turn to the membership of our union and to present the difficult problems to them and to go on from there.

153

Knowing what we were already experiencing with managements at Wurlitzer, Remington Rand, and Richardson Boat, and that rival unions were already being prodded and assisted by FBI and other government agencies to connive with these and other companies to launch raids to take away our bargaining rights, I thought that we quickly had to do something dramatic. I called a meeting of members of the executive boards of all our UE local unions in Western New York to decide what action we could take to convince companies that we had the clout to punish them severely—financially, where it really counted—if they tried to deny us the bargaining rights they'd agreed to in contracts with us.

It was my responsibility, I believed, to come up with some specific action to be taken. I first floated the idea of a one day simultaneous stoppage of work by our members in all the factories in the Buffalo-Tonawanda area where our union held the bargaining rights. A narrow majority of the assembled rank-and-file leaders of our union voted that down. They convincingly argued that the companies might sue us for heavy financial damages because a one day work stoppage could be labeled a strike in violation of the clauses that prohibited our union members from striking during the life of our contracts with them. As a compromise between those favoring a one day stoppage of work and those who opposed it, I proposed the special meeting during working hours, letting the managements know—but not until the day of the walkout—that regularly scheduled work would resume immediately after the meeting. After much serious debate that course of action was adopted.

While our contracts also prohibited managements from locking out our union members, I received reports a few days before August 9th that several companies were threatening that if their employees left work to go to the special meeting they would retaliate by permanently locking them out, not permitting them to return to work. A hastily called meeting of our rank-and-file strategy committee unanimously approved my proposal to counter that. *(The best defense is to attack.)* We quickly informed all managements that any company that retaliated with a lockout, with possible intent to break our union or to demand concessions before allowing their employees to return to work, would have that lockout changed into a strike, with our members—their employees—refusing to return to work until that company agreed to a substantial wage increase.

At that time Rhoda had, upon her father's death, already become part owner of The Park Lane Apartments and its prestigious restaurant and cocktail lounge, the prime gathering place for the area's movers and shakers. She shared ownership with her mother, her two brothers, her two sisters, and majority stockholder Uncle Louie. San Francisco real estate mogul Louie Lurie, during his frequent visits to The Park Lane, enjoyed telling the family, including in-laws like me, juicy items about his close personal friendships with important national figures, including J. Edgar Hoover—how the head of the FBI pleaded with him to be included in Louie's big financial deals. I didn't think it wise to mention to Louie that I'd been told that J. Edgar considered me to be the symbol of the left in western New York and that he had ordered his agents to get evidence to indict me under the Smith Act. This piece of legislation, later declared unconstitutional, made membership in any organization designated as subversive by the U.S. Attorney General a crime.

After my father-in-law died, Rhoda, Lorrie and I had moved in with my mother-in-law in her large apartment in The Park Lane. Company executives living in The Park Lane knew who I was. I knew who they were. We were cautiously polite as we frequently passed one another in the long sedately decorated lobby. I thought the situation strange, actually ludicrous, especially on some freezing early mornings when, all bundled up in work clothes, I walked through the richly decorated lobby to join some of our striking union members parading back and forth in front of factory gates. There, I often carried picket signs criticizing something done or not done by company executives who were at the same level in upper management as those living in The Park Lane.

I think my theatre background may have contributed to my ability to involve our union members in creating the drama and excitement that would keep their interest on a high level during the run-up to the outdoor August 9th meeting. Local union officers and stewards handed out printed stickers with that date and nothing else printed on them. Those stickers were plastered all over the place inside and outside factory buildings. Workers with their challenged imagination and ingenuity running wild, sought out unusual places on ceilings and walls and machines and cranes inside the factories to use chalk to scribble "August 9th" in big letters. Over the usual ear-shattering noise inside some of the factories, workers screamed "August 9th!" back and forth to one another.

Adding drama and mystery to the operation, our local union officers agreed to refuse to answer managements' questions about what was to happen on August 9th. Managements played the game, making believe that they didn't know what was going to happen until they were formally given the information on the morning of August 9th. But all of us knew that the companies had sufficient ears placed inside our union for them to know exactly what was planned for that afternoon. And we assumed that company managements had consulted with one another to determine what joint and/or individual actions they would take if and when their employees left work to go to the outdoor meeting in the park.

Managements of three companies—Durez, Blaw Knox and Markel Electric— notified our local union leaders at their plants that if their employees walked off the job to attend the meeting that August 9th afternoon they would not be permitted to return to work. Their employees ignored that threat and left their jobs to attend the meeting. The three companies locked their gates and would not let their employees return to work. In response, we held separate meetings of the workers from each of the three plants. We presented our recommendation. There was little discussion. A vote was taken at each of the three meetings. The union members at all three meetings voted to formally notify the three companies that their illegal action, refusing to let their employees resume work after the meeting, had negated the no-lockout/no-strike clauses in their contracts with the union, and that employees at each of the three companies would not return to work until the company agreed to grant a substantial wage increase.

It was the beginning of a bitter conflict that, in the worst of the three situations, dragged on for many months. All along the way I was fearful of the outcome.

As the lockout/strike dragged on, Matles almost every other day impatiently phoned me from his office in New York City.

"Manny"—like a broken record, his rasping voice insultingly challenged— "what the hell are you doing up there now?"

Angry, feeling that he was unfairly attacking me, my increasingly defensive response was to growl back a string of obscenities, concluding with something like: "Shit, I'm doing exactly what the hell you told us to do!"

I knew that Matles—aping what many factory foremen do regarding workers that they supervise—noted the dates and exactly what I said—entering in his little black book every negative point he could tally about each organizer, no matter how insignificant by itself that point might be, preparing to use the resulting "significant" accumulation to knock down the hapless organizer if and when at some future time it might serve his purpose to do so.

I had an especially stressful problem because Markel Electric, the company giving us the greatest difficulty, was owned and personally managed by close friends of Rhoda's Lurie family. Rhoda said she'd never forgive me if I caused company president Joe Markel to have a heart attack. Joe's son and company vice president, David Markel, had been the closest friend of Rhoda's brother George since the two were young children. And one of my eleven-year old daughter Lorrie's closest friends in her class at public school #64 was Joe Markel's granddaughter.

It was not unusual for Rhoda and me to be having dinner or a drink in The Park Lane restaurant at the same time as Joe Markel and/or Dave Markel sat with their family at a nearby table—we and they making believe that we did not see each other.

156

Chapter 2

"I want you to answer this question! Are you a Communist?"

It was shortly after I had returned from serving as a lieutenant in the infantry in World War II. I was standing in the front of the union hall in North Tonawanda , speaking to a meeting of hundreds of day shift Buffalo Bolt Company workers when our UE Local Union 319 president Gordis Knapp, abruptly rising from where he had been seated with other officers of the local union at a table beside me, shouted that fiercely at me.

"Are you a Communist" And he followed that up, demanding, "Yes or no! Yes or no!"

Although I knew from Knapp's past actions that he was strongly opposed to me and that he wanted the local union to break away from what he called "this Communist union," I was not prepared for his screaming challenge. Thinking about it later, I assumed that since his brother was on the local police force, Knapp might have been prompted to publicly challenge me this way in front of the local union's membership either by his brother or perhaps directly by FBI agents who at that time were visiting our local union officers in their homes, telling them that I'm a Communist and urging them, as patriotic Americans, to pull their local organizations out of "that Commie union."

"Are you a Communist?" Knapp screamed over and over. "Answer the question! Yes or no!"

The meeting exploded. Shouts from the men and women in the hall drowned out Knapp. The loudest shouts I heard from all sides surprised me. "No, don't answer! No, don't answer!"

Thinking about it later, I wondered if they hadn't wanted me to answer the question because they feared that I'd answer with what was generally suspected. In the current political atmosphere at that time—while perhaps wanting to support me because of what I'd done in contract negotiations and in handling their grievances on the job—they might not have wanted to be put in a position of being pressed to publicly support their union representative who admitted that he's a Communist.

But I could not refuse to answer. That would give Knapp and his supporters the ammunition they wanted.

"I'll answer your question!" I shouted above the noise in the hall. "I'll answer, I'll answer it!"

That prompted a swelling chorus: "No! Don't! Don't answer! No! Don't answer! No! No!"

"I'll answer your question!" I yelled again as loud as I could, loud enough to crush the noise in the hall into a momentary breath of silence. Following up quickly to fire an instinctive response—I don't know where the hell it came from—I hoarsely slammed my answer directly into Knapp's reddening face. "It's none of your goddamn business what my politics is!"

The hall erupted with applause and cheers. It was an answer that the majority welcomed, giving them the response that they could more easily defend.

Our UE Local 319 represented almost a thousand workers at the Buffalo Bolt Corporation's old factory in North Tonawanda. Whole families—husbands and wives and their grown children—worked there. The majority lived in Tonawanda and North Tonawanda, where the first generation arriving from Poland and Eastern European countries had settled. Most had never worked anywhere else during their entire lives, a situation that a few years later contributed to great personal tragedies.

This was a plant where the bolts and nuts and related products were made by machines designed and built by the workers in this factory. The machines were old, and operators needed great skill to keep them producing accurate products.

"But when I get up in the morning and I don't go to my machine the whole day is not right. I'm like a tub in the middle of the ocean without a rudder. I'm the only man in the whole plant who knows that machine," cries out Dodo, in my play *The Dodo Bird*, grabbing onto his skill with that machine at the Bolt Works to hang onto as he fights not to be destroyed by his personal tragedy. *"I can cut within three thousandths of an inch. The foreman says he don't know how I do it.— Without my machine I am nobody. So I go to the tavern.— One is two, two is three, three is four, four is drunk."*

Local 319 chief steward Archie Clifford was the most outspoken among those supporting me at Buffalo Bolt. He was trusted by the men and women in the plant because of the way he fought to protect them. Politically he was not pro-left or pro-right. Nor was he anti-left or anti-right. He was just strongly pro-union because of what the union was doing, and he said he liked what I was doing for the men and women working in the shop.

Both Archie Clifford and Gordis Knapp were fully aware of my leftist politics. Archie said my political beliefs were my business and he was happy as long as I continued to confine my involvement with Local 319 to the advice and support I gave in handling their grievances and in negotiating their contracts. But Gordis, at union meetings and in the shop, waxed rabid, blood red in the face, about the need for Local 319 "to pull out of this Communist union." Archie always countered this by pointing out that I did not interfere in the members' control of their local and that with my assistance they had, without a strike, won good contracts year after year.

Shortly before the August 9th rally, hysteria about communists—ratcheted up nationally by Senator Joseph McCarthy—and specifically directed against me in the Buffalo and Tonawandas newspapers, hit a wild peak, enabling Local 319 president Gordis Knapp to get workers at a monthly membership meeting to narrowly approve his motion to bar me from sitting in with their bargaining committee during contract negotiations with the company. But everyone expected that chief steward Archie Clifford would constantly be in touch with me, to let me know what was going on, to get my input.

Shortly after the 1950 birth of our second red-haired daughter, Mindy, our family had moved out of my mother-in-law's apartment in The Park Lane into a house on Chatham Avenue in North Buffalo. Chatham Avenue is a nice street, one-block long, divided in two by a narrow island planted with small bushes and flowers. As the red-baiting attacks against me were being whipped up in the newspapers, FBI agents went up and down the block, visiting our neighbors, seeking their support to put the pressure on me by keeping their children from playing with Lorrie, then age 11, and Mindy, then age 3.

How do I know this? Our immediate neighbors, with children grown and living elsewhere, told us that they argued with the FBI agents, defending us.

Lorrie was dropped out of her Sunday school and dance class car pools. Parents refused to let her sit with their children in the ice cream parlor after dance class. Lorrie sat there at a separate table with Rhoda or with me, whichever one of us had driven her to dance class.

The Meilman family held a block party at their home on Chatham Avenue. We were invited to the party by Sam, who regularly commuted to his small furniture factory in Jamestown. When his wife Eleanor opened the door to admit us, the shocked look on her face told us something was wrong. Later Eleanor revealed to Rhoda that there had been a dispute between Sam and Eleanor about inviting us. One of the women at the party told me that Rhoda, crying, had locked herself in the bathroom. I persuaded Rhoda to come out, and we went home. I learned that Eleanor had told Rhoda that she was going to get all the mothers on the

159

block to keep their children from playing "with your lovely adorable little Mindy until her father gives up his Communism."—For weeks our house was a morgue, Rhoda and I not talking to each other, sleeping in the same bed in order not to disturb the children, but lying there like two frozen sticks, on opposite edges of the queen size bed.

Many years later, when I had had plays produced Off-Broadway in New York and other cities across our country, resulting in my being hired to teach Creative Writing at Buffalo State College, I mentioned the incident with the Meilmans in a review of a film about a blacklisted movie director, starring Robert DeNiro, that I wrote for the Buffalo News. The day after the review appeared in the newspaper, Eleanor Meilman phoned me. Sobbing, she asked me to forgive her for the pain she had caused our family. Since Rhoda had already died and my two daughters were doing very well, Eleanor's belated apology meant little to me. But I forced a friendly laugh and said, "It's okay, Eleanor. It's okay."

But it was back when Eleanor was still contributing her share to turn our home—temporarily at that time—into a painfully quiet morgue, that I had to deal with further difficulty created by Gordis Knapp. Emboldened by his success in getting the membership at the union meeting to bar me from sitting in with the committee during negotiating sessions with the company, Knapp launched a campaign to get support for a motion he announced that he intended to present at the next union meeting, a motion for Local 319 to pull out of our UE union.

"I'm going to call on our union members to show their patriotic support for their country" he told workers in the shop, "by voting to disaffiliate our Local 319 from this communist UE union."

With some other companies already trying to use the red issue to avoid living up to their contract obligations with our local unions, I worried about how much support Knapp was developing for his motion, especially when I heard that the company was permitting him to wander throughout the factory, openly talking to workers on the job, asking their support for his motion that he told them he was going to introduce at the next union meeting.

Archie Clifford telling me not to worry did not stop me from worrying. I could not help quietly wondering if Archie might have decided it was expedient and necessary for him not to oppose Knapp's motion. In that McCarthy Period, with the all too prevalent fear that many of our local union officers had of being attacked as being unpatriotic and/or associated with Communism if they stood up for our UE union, I already had had several surprises of this kind.

At Wurlitzer's North Tonawanda plant the surprises were quite complicated. Since we had had very good relations with the management people on a very personal basis, I was blindsided when their lawyer, with whom we had always gotten along very well, informed me in the presence of our grievance committee, that he wanted me to leave the plant because our committee, headed by chief steward Walter Kwiecen, had informed him that they planned to switch their affiliation from our UE union to the rival IUE union.

I learned later from Sam Brown, the local union president at Wurlitzer, that FBI agents had visited him and other top officers of the local union in their homes, scaring them out of resisting the disaffiliation move. Sam said that according to information leaked from the front office and spread through the grapevine in the plant, the reason why the Wurlitzer management team, which had had such good relations with us, had been won over to turn against us was that they had been offered a business deal too hard to refuse. The Catholic Church leaders who until then had not permitted electrical organs in their churches—Wurlitzer manufactured electrical organs—agreed to permit their use in return for Wurlitzer management's assistance to replace our UE union with the newly formed IUE union, initially dominated, nationally and locally, by the Association of Catholic Trade Unionists (ACTU) caucus.

The IUE petitioned the National Labor Relations Board to hold an election and, over my objection that such elections were never permitted to take place on Good Friday, the Board set that date for Wurlitzer workers to choose between UE and IUE. The overwhelming majority of Wurlitzer workers were members of the Catholic Church. At a very special early morning church service for Wurlitzer workers on Good Friday, the priest told the workers it was their duty as Catholics to throw out "the anti-Christ Communist UE." When workers left the church and drove to work, IUE organizers handed them leaflets with a cartoon showing a figure, labeled UE, crucifying Christ.

Yet just prior to the Labor Board election two strange things had happened.

At a plant gate meeting where I was speaking to a fairly large gathering of Wurlitzer workers, defending the UE, several men standing in front of the crowd, only a yard or two away from me, threw tomatoes at me. I thought that they had been too close to miss me. But no tomato came anywhere near me.

Also, at a meeting of the Wurlitzer local union, my old friend George Poole appeared, invited by chief steward Walter Kwiecen. Walter and I had worked together amicably for several years. Now he refused to talk to me. A burly man, rough looking, he was heading the move to switch the local union from UE to IUE. When George Poole had come back from service in the army in Europe during World War II he had told me that he was disgusted with the brutal way some Soviet soldiers—to him they represented what kind of people Soviet communists were—had conducted themselves toward civilians. At the meeting he and I—who had been like brothers—avoided eye contact and did not speak to one another. Kwiecen gave George the floor to address the meeting. Never referring to me, George attacked the national leadership of our union, accusing them of following the Communist line: that, after Hitler's army attacked the

Soviet Union, the UE national officers prevented our union members from taking militant action to oppose instances of major exploitation by their employers.

When I rose and started to respond to what George had said, a large group of workers in the hall—obviously as planned in advance—stood up and shouted derisively to drown me out. Led by Kwiecen, a bunch of them rushed forward and grabbed me and, while still shouting about getting rid of the Commies, lifted me high above their heads and hustled me out of the hall to the sidewalk outside.

Then something happened that confused me. I still speculate, but am not sure, about what it signified. The men who had roughly grabbed me and held me high above their heads, screaming about getting rid of the commies while they hustled me out to the sidewalk in front of the hall, abruptly—as if a signal had been given—stopped shouting and carefully set me down. Walter Kwiecen held my arms to steady me and softly whispered into my ear, "Are you alright, Manny?"

The IUE won the election by a narrow margin and took over the UE contract with Wurlitzer. Although the union shop clause in the contract required that all Wurlitzer workers, as a condition of employment, must become members of the union, ten of the former UE executive board members and stewards—who proudly labeled themselves "the dirty ten"—were not permitted to become members of IUE. Wurlitzer management and IUE did not contest continued employment of "the dirty ten." Apparently Wurlitzer and IUE feared that if the dirty ten, men and women highly respected by all Wurlitzer workers for their unselfish idealism, were permitted to become members of IUE, they might be elected to replace present IUE office holders and lead the local union back into UE.—This hypocrisy continually produced a lot of dark jokes out in the shop.

The most respected man in the whole shop—respected by both management and workers for his intelligence and quiet dignity as well as his skill as both a tool and die maker and a self taught portrait artist—was Frank Mayer, a man in his sixties, who when he was younger had been a "boomer," the word used to describe idealistic workers who went from one job to another to help establish a union in each workplace and then moved on to do it again in another workplace. Frank made no attempt to conceal that he was a Communist. The acknowledged leader of the dirty ten, he was treated with great affection by all workers in the shop.

Early one morning several years after IUE replaced our UE local union at Wurlitzer I received a phone call. The caller identified himself. It was Walter Kwiecen. We had not spoken to each other since that time when he had whispered into my ear, "Are you alright, Manny?" The fight between UE and IUE was now being bitterly fought at many other plants. Wary, I wondered what the hell Kwiecen wanted from me. Was he going to be stupid enough to offer me some lousy incentive to switch to IUE?

"Manny, I thought you'd like to know," he said softly, almost like it was a secret that he should not be saying to me. "I thought you'd like to know that the old man had a heart attack and died." We both knew that he was talking about Frank Mayer. "I thought you'd like to know," he repeated.

I said, "Yes. Thanks."

"I thought you'd like to know," he said again.

"Thanks ... thanks," I said, awkwardly ending our conversation.

It had been a moment somewhat like what I heard had taken place during World War I when on Christmas Day soldiers from the opposing armies for one day stopped shooting at each other and emerged from their trenches to exchange holiday greetings—and then the next day resumed trying to kill each other.

I did not speak to Kwiecen again until about twenty years later when—after I had been hired to teach Creative Writing at Buffalo State College, getting me off the blacklist—I was a delegate from the college's faculty union attending a meeting of the Buffalo AFL-CIO Council.

*****

A few years after the local National Labor Relations Board director had—over my objections—set the election at Wurlitzer for Good Friday, I asked the same Labor Board director to set Good Friday for an election involving workers choosing a union at the Merwin Wave Clip plant.

"Manny," the director firmly lectured me, "you know we never hold elections on Good Friday."

"You did at Wurlitzer!" I snapped at him, having deliberately set the trap that he'd stepped into. "You did at Wurlitzer!"

His face reddening and tightening, the skinny director leaped to his feet while curtly raising his voice. "We're not going to talk about that." And he left the room.

Realizing that he might have set the Wurlitzer election for Good Friday at that time in response to the pressure of having to avoid being accused of being soft on Communism, I felt sorry for the guy and let the matter drop.

*****

Back then there were a lot of taverns—workers simply called them "bars"—in Tonawanda and North Tonawanda. They were the social clubs for the thousands of factory workers and their families who lived and worked in those twin industrial towns a few miles north of the city of Buffalo. Most workers had a favorite bar where they hung out and I got to know the bars where I could reach our key union people, dropping in to see them there or phoning and leaving messages for them.

My favorite hangout—other than my frequenting The Park Lane restaurant and cocktail lounge with Rhoda—was Andy's Bar across the street from the Columbus McKinnon plant in Tonawanda. Andy Smilinich was a pro-union foreman at the National Roofing plant, which was opposite the other side of the Columbus McKinnon plant. Andy's wife Polly worked behind the bar. Outwardly tough as nails, Polly inwardly was a sensitive highly reflective woman. For some reason that I can't quickly define, Polly and I hit it off well as good friends who could confide our personal problems to each other. There was no hint of anything sexual. We were just good buddies. She knew about my connection to The Park Lane and she often kidded me as she set a boilermaker down on the bar in front of me, a shot of whiskey and a beer chaser ordered for me by one of our union members. She'd whisper, "Not the fancy stuff you'll be drinking later." It was true that later that same day I might be drinking a martini at The Park Lane. Rhoda—ordering her martini ("very little vermouth, please")—didn't like to drink alone, and I readily accommodated her.

*****

I'm developing a play for myself to perform: *Boilermakers and Martinis with Manny*. I performed a half hour version at a poetry reading in the back room of a local book store. Other writers on the program read their poetry. With as yet no script, I told about forty people in the audience how I arrogantly thought I could safely live those two tracks, the union life and The Park Lane life, keeping them apart while being true to those I lived and worked with in both those worlds.

*****

At that time I could talk to Polly at Andy's Bar, but not to Rhoda, about things like my situation at Buffalo Bolt. And Polly would talk to me about things like the affection she received from her grown retarded son when she went to see him in the institution and how she always cried when she had to leave him. Back at The Park Lane, Rhoda and I, drinking our martinis—before my life in my union world forced the collision with her life in her Park Lane world— might be talking about some social things that she had arranged for both of us to do with her friends in her Park Lane world. Or we would be sitting there in The Park Lane, drinking, and—avoiding union and politics—make small talk with those friends of hers, while I brightly concealed an ever-present feeling of an uneasy distance from them, as if we originally came from different planets.

It's become clear to me that in the world connected to Andy's Bar, I often felt pangs of guilt about my life in the Park Lane world, while in the Park Lane world I often felt pangs of guilt, being a hypocrite living a false life. And it may have been these feelings of guilt in both these worlds that combined to help me, no matter what the cost, to become hard and adamant about not surrendering my political and union involvement. At the same time, possibly because my childhood had centered on our family's mom-and-pop dry goods store, I truly felt like an outsider, a lonely outsider, in both those worlds.

At Buffalo Bolt, following up on his campaign in the shop to mobilize sentiment against our union, Gordis Knapp at the next Local 319 meeting handed the president's gavel to Archie Clifford, putting Archie in charge so he himself could speak from the floor. He raised his hand and was recognized by Archie. He introduced his motion for "Local 319 to disaffiliate from this Communist UE union." He then stiffly asked Archie for permission to speak on the motion and I wondered what was going on in Archie's head as he pleasantly told Knapp to go right ahead—"Brother, you got the floor."

Knapp made an impassioned attack about the UE being a Communist union and he wrapped himself in the flag and called on the hundreds of Buffalo Bolt workers who filled the union hall, an equal number of men and women, most of them middle-aged, to support their country and to vote as patriotic Americans for his motion to disaffiliate from this Communist union. He finished his ringing harangue with an ultimatum.

"Either you people vote to pass this motion to disaffiliate from this Communist union or I will offer my resignation as president of Local 319 and from being a member of this Communist union!"

There was an immediate response. As I watched and listened, I realized that Archie had done a lot of quiet organizing inside the plant, preparing for Knapp's motion.

"I move to accept his resignation," one voice yelled

"Second the motion," another voice yelled.

"All in favor of accepting Brother Knapp's resignation please signify by saying Aye," Archie quietly but firmly declared after a sharp tap of his gavel.

There was a roar of Ayes.

Archie firmly tapped his gavel once more. "The resignation of the president is accepted."

There was absolute silence in the hall as all eyes focused on Knapp.

Even though he could have protested that the action taken was in violation of Robert's Rules of Order, Knapp apparently was too stunned by the speed with which this unexpected response had happened to say anything. With his head lowered to hide his tears, he slowly walked out of the hall.

*****

I am more aware of the sadness of that moment now than I was then. Belatedly, I feel sorry for Gordis Knapp who by now is probably long dead. I'm sure he meant well. I believe he was misled by all the demonizing stuff that was being thrown at our union back then. Our union was truly democratic, run by its members, and we had negotiated contracts providing our members with the best wages and working conditions compared with wages and working conditions at similar factories in the area.

*****

Local 319 members voted NOT to stop work to attend the August 9th outdoor meeting in the park, while at the same time voting to give full moral support to the meeting's objective: to let companies know that UE local unions in the area were ready, if necessary, to slug it out to preserve their UE contract protections. Archie told me it was a compromise he had worked out with a section of the Local 319 membership who had been affected by Gordis Knapp's charge that the national officers of UE were all Communists—which, by the way, was not true.

This effort to distance themselves from the national leaders of our UE union—and from me—did not help the union members a few years later when the Ohio-based Eclipse Corporation bought the North Tonawanda bolt factory and—reportedly, as part of some tax-saving scheme—permanently closed the plant. There was no advance warning. The shock to the hundreds of Buffalo Bolt workers, many middle-aged, who had never worked for anyone else—and to the entire community—is hard to adequately describe.

Some guys never did get a job after the Bolt Works, says Dodo in my play *The Dodo Bird*—defending himself to Bull Blatter who has been telling him what a piece of drunken shit he's become. *The president of the union hanged himself in his cellar. My steward stuck a gas pipe in his mouth. And one guy took a dive in the river and went over the falls. Right after Christmas too. They locked the doors and threw the key in the river. But I didn't take no rope or no gas. I got a job.* Bull sneers back at Dodo: *Labor grade fourteen. Bottom grade. They'll never let you run a machine again, you bastard. You're through. You and that lousy multiple threader. You are useless.*

I took that from real life. When right after Christmas the corporation closed the North Tonawanda factory, Arnold Smoyer, the local union president who had replaced Gordis Knapp, hung himself in his basement. A union steward committed suicide with gas. And another worker jumped to his death in the rapids of Niagara Falls.

The closing of the Bolt Works threw fear into the hearts of all workers in the twin cities of Tonawanda and North Tonawanda. If Buffalo Bolt workers could be thrown out of work after the security of working all their lives at that one factory, the thousands of workers employed at Spaulding Fibre, Columbus McKinnon, Remington Rand, Durez, AutoWheel Coaster, National Roofing, and yes, Wurlitzer, feared that this might happen to them. Their fears were well-grounded. In the immediate years that followed, all these companies

166

permanently shut down their factories, moving the jobs of their Tonawandas employees to low wage areas, some elsewhere in the United States, some to Europe, but most to countries in Central and South America, and Asia and Africa.

Rhoda every so often would pull the rug out from under me, dismissing my effort to identify myself with the factory workers I represented. "You like to think you're working class, but the life you're living, you're not working class."—I had no answer. I felt guilty as hell. With that Park Lane world being part of my life, I knew that much as I tried to identify with and feel the feelings that literally hundreds, really thousands, of workers and their families, whom I had come to know very well, were feeling when their wage earners were losing their jobs through plant closings, I never would have to face the situations that they faced, many of them forced to go on welfare.

When I was blacklisted, with the FBI making sure that I could not keep a job with any U.S. employer, The Park Lane loaned me $100 a week until I finally got work as an independent contractor selling life insurance for the United States division of a Canadian company. I was constantly aware of this difference in my situation. But I lacked the courage—though I thought about it—to refuse the loan from The Park Lane.

Rhoda's brother George put it simply, but very well, as he himself struggled unsuccessfully to break away from that world: "The Park Lane life is very seductive."

Chapter 3

During 1941 and 1942, early years of our married life, Rhoda's father tried to convince her that I must be cheating on her all those nights that I claimed to be out doing union business. Rhoda, I believe, accepted that I was going to union meetings and making house calls to get workers to join our union as part of our organizing campaigns at a number of factories, including Columbus McKinnon, Spaulding Fibre, Buffalo Bolt, Wurlitzer, Otis Elevator, and Pratt and Letchworth—companies where thousands of their workers did choose our union to represent them.

My well-meaning father-in-law enlisted the help of city detectives—who, along with uniformed police, regularly ate free meals in the kitchen of The Park Lane restaurant—to check me out. I think he might have been disappointed when they confirmed that on those nights when I was not home I was actually doing union business.

Not yet ready to give up on his effort to get Rhoda to end what he thought was a marriage destined to fail, her father hammered away at Rhoda, arguing that if I really cared for her, I would get out of all that disturbing union and political activity which was making me the target of an unrelenting stream of red-baiting attacks in the newspapers, that if I truly loved her I would be willing to make life more pleasant for her by switching to something non-controversial, something in the business world, like starting the company with a string of taxicabs that Uncle Louie offered to finance.

Rhoda was caught between this pressure from her father and my firm refusal to give up my work as a union organizer, work that I believed was tremendously worthwhile, highly honorable and personally extremely satisfying.

"Rhoda, I'm helping thousands of families have better lives. If I were to agree to walk away from these same people who've joined our union despite all the red-baiting they see thrown at me, it would be the worst kind of selfish cowardice on my part. I wouldn't respect myself and I think that you might lose your respect for me."

Rhoda accepted that.

But my father-in-law did not give up. He sincerely believed that our marriage inevitably was doomed to become very painful, not only for his daughter Rhoda but also for his granddaughter Lorrie whom he adored. In retrospect, I must concede that his assessment of our future was more realistic than mine.

Rhoda reported—as if she were a disinterested party—that her father had asked her if I would agree to go with her to talk to Rabbi Fink. I was aware that Mr. Lurie—I never addressed him any other way—knew that I respected Dr. Fink, chief rabbi of the elitist Temple Beth Zion, because of his constant struggle, often publicly, with his generally conservative congregation. And I assumed that Mr. Lurie had already sounded out Dr. Fink, persuading him that he should advise me for the sake of my family to give up my work as a union organizer. If I were now to refuse to meet with Dr. Fink, it would appear that I did not believe that I could adequately counter the strength of the arguments coming from this friendly progressive community leader.

A meeting of Rhoda and me with Dr. Fink, I realized, would be similar to what happens when I, along with a local union's bargaining committee, meet with an employer's legal and personnel team in a negotiating session. The company representatives and I seem to be trying to convince one another of the rectitude of our positions. But we are really fighting to win the minds of the members of the local union's bargaining committee.

And I knew that Dr. Fink and I would be politely and carefully jockeying to win the mind of Rhoda.

We met with Dr. Fink in his study where he warmly greeted us and seated us in richly leathered chairs across from where he sat behind his polished desk. He asked Rhoda about her family and then about her work as a painter—a sort of cozy kind of conversation to establish a warm and friendly atmosphere. While on the surface I smiled and laughed, internally I was tensely waiting for the attack, worried about my ability to repel his coming effort to capture Rhoda's mind.

He eased into it, asking about our daughters Lorrie and Mindy, and then spoke about how important my family must be for me. Then he praised me for the fine work I was doing for the workers in our union, helping them and their families live better lives. He congratulated me for my courage, standing up to the constant battering I was getting in the newspapers, labeled subversive and an agent of the anti-Christ in a constant drumbeat aimed at turning our union members against me. He said that I could take pride in my ability to stand up in the face of all that, and also take pride in the fact that in the face of all that my union members trusted me and supported me.

"But you must think of your wife and children. They are not as strong as you. They need your protection. You have made a fine contribution. You can be proud of what you've done. But now that you've established these strong organizations to help these workers, it's time to think of your own family and the difficulty that your activity is causing them." He continued, on and on, about my accomplishments, my personal sacrifices, Rhoda's sacrifices, my responsibility to my family, again and again praising me for what I had done, but concluding over and over that I now owed it to my family "to step down off the firing line."

Watching Rhoda's face and trying to read her body language, I thought that Dr. Fink was winning her mind. My insides were seething. I wondered how I could respond effectively as he again strongly stated, "You owe it to your family, to Rhoda, to step down off the firing line." He kept coming back to that phrase, and each time I thought that it was deeply resonating with Rhoda. It was difficult for me—about half the age of this highly respected man who spoke with the quiet authority of someone whose advice was usually given great weight in our community—to challenge him, but I had to stop his flow of words or I would be lost. I feared that the situation was reaching the point where I would have no chance to keep Rhoda from turning against me.

"Dr. Fink!" I harshly interrupted. That stopped his flow of words. But then, unsure what to say, I hesitated. He started to speak. I again interrupted him. "Dr. Fink! You don't know this family!"—I don't know where that came from. Spontaneously I had ripped it out from somewhere deep within my subconscious, astonishing myself.—Rushing on, feeling my face heating up, I tried to keep my voice down as I forced myself to hold in the bubbling explosion inside me, "Dr. Fink, you don't know Rhoda's family!" I spoke quietly, intensely, shooting the words directly into his stiffening face. "You think you know them but you don't really know her Lurie family! You don't know the emotional problems that plague this family! A star-crossed family! Rhoda's brother George! A lovely guy, in and out of institutions all his life. Manic-depressive. Alternating between periods when he's in a frozen catatonic state and periods when he's a financial genius pulling off multi-million dollar real estate deals. Rhoda's sister Ruth! Also a very lovely person when she's not being un-lovely. In and out of institutions. Manic-depressive. A raging destructive drunk when she's high and imagines she's one of the greatest writers in the world. And when she's down, repeatedly attempting to kill herself, cutting her wrists, turning on the gas, swallowing pills. Her brother Howard! His wife says he's not there, he's empty, no heart, no feeling, never really there. Rhoda's sister Annette! Afraid to ever leave the house. Rhoda's mother! Never taught Rhoda to brush her teeth or wash her hands when she went to the toilet. Never taught her how to cook. Rhoda and Annette still laugh and ask each other where Mother was when they were growing up, her body there, but Mother never really there—!" I broke off, and saw that my outburst had affected Dr. Fink. I went on, more quietly.

171

"Rhoda!" I said—asking Dr. Fink to look at her. "Do you know what Rhoda said about me? She said I pulled her out of the fog.—You want to know what she thinks about what I'm doing for the working people I represent?—She zigs and she zags! Depending on what's in the newspapers about me that day and how much pressure she's getting from other people because of me. She zigs between being happy with what I'm doing and what our life is. And when the newspapers and other people make her unhappy with what I'm doing she zags the other way.—The worst thing I could do for her—and for my family—is to zig and zag with her every time she zigs and zags! I'm providing stability here! Stability! For Rhoda! And for our daughters—Lorrie and Mindy!"

I stopped and waited.

Dr. Fink looked to Rhoda for a response. Rhoda sat there, seeming relaxed, perfectly still, with a faint touch of a smile on her face that said only that she was listening.

I looked to Dr. Fink. He stood up and nodded. "Forgive me for interfering. You know what you're doing. Good luck to both of you. I wish you well."

He shook hands with both of us.

As we silently walked back to the parking lot, I was yearning to know what Rhoda was thinking. But it wasn't until our car neared The Park Lane that Rhoda finally spoke.

"That was interesting," she said, very quietly.

"Yes," I said, also very quietly, not wanting to roil the momentarily smooth waters.

Rhoda suggested stopping for a drink in The Park Lane cocktail lounge. We sat at the bar and toasted one another, clicking our glasses of martinis carefully so as not to spill any of the precious liquid. Then I had to leave to attend a meeting of our UE Strategy Committee—the presidents and chief stewards of all our unions in the area—in the labor hall in North Tonawanda, where we made plans to mobilize support for Markel Electric, Blaw Knox and Durez workers who had been locked out by their employers.

The understanding attitude displayed by Dr. Fink led me to turn to him for help several months later when the extended lockout and strike at Markel Electric developed into an agonizing source of disquiet for Rhoda, and therefore also for me.

Joe Markel, I eventually came to believe, had welcomed the opportunity presented by our union members leaving his plant to attend the August 9, 1953 outdoor meeting in North Tonawanda. It gave him the excuse he was seeking to get rid of our union, not because of the public reason he gave—to get rid of the Communist union—but because, with AFL and CIO at that time still intensely rival organizations, the AFL construction trade workers were refusing to install electrical equipment made by Markel Electric workers who were not members of an AFL union. Joe Markel wanted an AFL union to replace our UE union, which then was still affiliated with the CIO.

We felt compelled to respond to his refusal to let workers return to their jobs the morning after they had attended the outdoor rally. Our union members, at an emergency meeting that same morning-after, voted that they were now on strike and would not return to work without a substantial wage increase. We had no idea that this was the beginning of a bitter strike that would last many months, dividing the entire Western New York community. Rhoda's Park Lane world and the overwhelming majority of the Jewish community actively lined up against me, charging me with full responsibility for the lockout and the strike. It was not just coincidental that Joe Markel was then publicly honored—with photos and articles in the newspapers—as a leading financial contributor to local Jewish community organizations.

*****

Prominent Jewish community leaders seemed to ignore that what I, also Jewish, was doing with the union was helping to counteract anti-Semitism among working people in the area. Anti-Semitic remarks about Joe Markel were never again repeated after I reminded our union members that I, their representative, am also Jewish. But it was not until almost fifty years later that a young woman, the new publisher of The Jewish Review, commissioned an article for that local weekly newspaper to let its readers know that it was not Manny Fried who separated himself from the Jewish community, but that some Jewish community leaders had publicly shoved him outside the fold because they disagreed with his politics and his union activity. Actually a few Jewish leaders in the community, including Dr. Fink, had expressed support for what Manny Fried was doing back then, but so quietly and carefully as not to be noticed.

*****

Rhoda was torn between concern for the Markels, long-time friends of her Lurie family, and concern for her husband—and yes, she was also concerned for the striking Markel Electric workers. She thought that Joe Markel was wrong to refuse to meet with the union's committee to talk about the dispute. When I told her the low hourly wage that Markel was paying his workers, she conceded that the demand for a wage increase might be justified, especially when the large financial contributions to community organizations, for which Joe Markel was being so publicly honored, were at least in part made possible by the low wages he was paying his employees. "The Markel Electric workers should be given some public recognition for Joe Markel's philanthropy," I told her.

While adamantly refusing to meet with our union committee to discuss our dispute, Joe Markel sent letters to the striking workers in their homes—but not to those who were members of the strike committee—asking them to repudiate "the Communist pickets" marching back and forth in front of the plant entrance and to return to work. A few workers did cross the picket line, but not enough to create even a slight trickle of production.

This apparently prompted Joe Markel to place a large ad—not mentioning the strike—in The Challenger, the local weekly newspaper for African-Americans, offering "good jobs at good pay." High unemployment in the black ghetto created a steady stream of men and women approaching the plant the next morning. They were met a block away from the main factory building by union teams, men and women, including black workers, who explained why they were on strike. (One of our union organizers, Danny Fitzgerald, a "sad sack" infantry veteran who had plodded his way alongside army tanks into Germany with General Patton, had suggested sending these teams of "scouts out" to meet potential scabs before they got to where club-wielding police on foot and on horseback were waiting in front of the factory to escort scabs through our picket lines.) Not willing to scab on the striking workers, all the blacks turned and walked away.

Markel next secured the assistance of James Healy, self-designated local labor priest, to get the Catholic Charities organization to send "D.P.'s" (displaced persons from Europe after end of World War II) to cross the picket line. They too, more because of confusion than sympathy, when confronted by frightening teams of strikers a block away from the factory, turned and walked away. Since the great majority of our striking workers were Catholics, our chief steward easily gathered a large contingent to accompany him to the headquarters of the diocese. Speaking for the group, he politely told the bishop that, though they were reluctant to do it, they were ready to make it publicly known to all workers, especially Catholics, in western New York that the Catholic Charities organization is sending scabs to cross a picket line composed mainly of rank-and-file Catholic workers. Catholic Charities immediately stopped sending "D.P.'s" to scab.

Thinking that Joe Markel might find it hard to refuse a request from Dr. Fink to have the disputing parties meet with him in his study at Temple Beth Zion, I repeatedly tried to reach the highly respected rabbi by phone, leaving word with his secretary. Wondering if—knowing about our dispute with Markel—he was avoiding my call, I sent him a telegram. It was not until weeks later that I received a reply from him, a telegram informing me that he had been out of town and was not familiar enough with the situation to be helpful. I thought he may have taken that long to reply because in the intervening time he might have been feeling out Joe Markel about meeting with us, and had finally given up on that.

As the strike dragged on, stretching from weeks into months, "labor priest" Healy started sending letters to homes of the striking workers—their addresses probably provided by the company—comparing the strikers' hardships with the economically secure life of their "Communist union leader ... the barefoot boy from The Park Lane." Some strikers kidded me about that "barefoot boy from The Park Lane" but Healy's reference to my connection to The Park Lane strangely seemed to help rather than hurt my standing with them.

I called our chief steward's attention to references in Healy's letters to things that had been said in our strike committee's private strategy meetings, and our chief steward whispered to me that our meeting room must be bugged. But I thought it more likely that Healy had recruited a spy in our strike committee, and I even wondered if he could be our chief steward.

Let me insert here—looking back from where I am now at age 95— that I realize now how being involved that way with complex and powerful surface and secret cross currents connected with a very difficult strike, compelling me to make extremely difficult decisions affecting the lives of many families of workers who were trusting me to provide a solid path through a swirling maelstrom of overwhelming economic and political challenges, and having to quickly devise strong responses to a seemingly insurmountable gathering of attacks from opposing forces, while at the same time contending with difficulties the strike was creating between me and Rhoda in her Park Lane world, was often— strangely, surprisingly—highly exhilarating. But having to deal with all that intrigue and those blazing fires, my mind was too deeply concentrated on concocting counter-offensive tactics to recognize and appreciate the flashes of positive exhilaration I was actually feeling at that time. This may sound strange now. It was strange then.

I should have known that children hear and feel what's going on in the home. My daughter Lorrie was 11 years old, and Joe Markel's granddaughter was one of her closest friends. I was surprised—actually pleased—that one evening while we (myself, Rhoda, Lorrie and 3-year old Mindy) were having dinner in The Park Lane dining room, Lorrie unexpectedly volunteered that she and Joe Markel's granddaughter had talked about the strike. I could see that she—and Rhoda—were looking for my reaction as she went on to tell me that they had agreed that they were not going to let the fight between her father and her school friend's grandfather affect their friendship.

"Good," I said, as much to Rhoda as to Lorrie, and then talked about something else, trying to let them know that, though it might be unusual, it was alright with me for the two girls, the daughter of the strike leader and the granddaughter of the factory owner, to ignore what was happening—that their lives could go on without being affected in any way by the strike.

I can laugh now at my stupidity, not anticipating even the possibility of the anguished nightmare to come, even though I was having a terrifying dream that recurred over and over during that time and in the immediate months and years that followed… that it is night and I am standing alone in darkness on the second floor in a rickety ramshackle house that is trembling, swaying back and forth, threatening to collapse with each tiny move I make, my entire body tensed with fear as I carefully slide one foot at a time across the rough boards on the bare wooden floor, terrified as each slight movement causes the entire house to increase its trembling and to sway and sway and sway—I freeze, paralyzed by fear that one more step will crash the splintering boards of the entire floor and the surrounding rickety house out from under and down on top of me. I ruefully laugh now at how stupid I was *not* to understand the warnings embodied in those paralyzing dreams.

*****

Warnings! My mind's eye unexpectedly sees three witches cackling their warnings over a murky fire in Shakespeare's Scottish play, a scene in the Theatre of Youth's production in the abandoned bomb shelter beneath Buffalo's main library where years later, after I had been maneuvered out of my organizer job and blacklisted, I performed the role of the doctor in Lady Macbeth's sleep walking scene—and met one of the witches, Roz Cramer, who, after Rhoda died, became my closest friend and confidante.

Chapter 4

The Markel strike was only one of a number of fires we had to contend with, each contributing to the unbroken stream of attacks upon our union, primarily targeting me. During the first half of the 1950s our government leaders in Washington kept up a steady flow of inflammatory rhetoric about Communists in the labor movement, strongly affecting our situation. At that time—with our union representing 30,000 workers in over a dozen factories in the area—the Buffalo Evening News labor reporter Ed Kelly told me that the FBI had labeled me the symbol of the left in Western New York who must be broken. This was part of an unrelenting effort from outside our union to use "the Communist threat" to create dissension within our ranks, coordinating this with raids against our local unions launched by other unions, their leaders spurred by FBI agents to prove they were anti-Communists and by some rabidly anti-Communist Catholic priests who formed Unionists United Against Communism, setting up a devout Catholic, the president of the local Bricklayers Union, as their front man to issue their press releases attacking me and our union. Other unions who raided us were motivated solely by greed, trumpeting about getting rid of "the Communist threat" as their excuse to try to snatch into their grubby fingers the additional dues they would get.

Buffalo Evening News hatchet reporter Fred Turner, who I think was acting as the public voice for the FBI, wrote a series of columns attacking me, seeming to assume that by breaking the loyalty of our union members to their union representative he would break their loyalty to their union. With few exceptions, our local union leaders did not appear to be deeply affected by Turner's columns in which he kept trying to link me "by association" to Stalin and Marx and Lenin. Our local union officers had become used to attempts to tar me with that brush. But Turner's columns did cause severe problems for me at home. On those days when he wrote especially tough columns attacking me, by the time I came home Rhoda had insulated herself within the protective cocoon she created with vodka martinis. She would not speak to me and for a few days after Turner's tough newspaper columns appeared, our home was like a morgue, heavy with the silence between us.

All these forces opposing our union seemed to think that our August 9th rally presented them with their great opportunity to destroy our organization. It seemed as if a signal was given to attack our union on a wide front. CIO unions—our union having parted with the CIO in 1950—readily joined with AFL unions to cooperate with employers to try to undermine the loyalty of our union members. In several instances the highly unique tactics they used seemed to smell of the kind devised by some very savvy intelligence agents. This was confirmed by reports I received from local union officers who told me that they had been visited by FBI agents who used anti-Communist appeals to patriotism, threats to deport family members who had not yet fully attained U.S. citizenship, and/or promises of financial benefits to get them to cooperate to pull out of our union.

*****

Johnny Cirrito was the president of our Columbus McKinnon local union. Working together, we handled grievances and negotiated contracts. We became good personal friends. On numerous occasions Johnny vigorously defended me and our union against red-baiting attacks.

One night, while we were drinking a few beers in Andy's tavern across the street from the plant, Johnny confided that he always had wanted to get out of the factory and open a tavern of his own, but because he had a criminal record, a car theft conviction when he was a much younger man, he had been turned down when he tried to get a liquor license. I remembered this some months later when Johnny unexpectedly red-baited me at a meeting of the local union and tried to persuade the union members to pull the local out of our organization. He failed at that, and the union members voted him out of office. Johnny quit the factory and opened his saloon. I speculated that he had made a deal and secured his liquor license.

Bill Bentz, the son of a Pennsylvania coal miner, replaced Johnny Cirrito as president of the Columbus McKinnon local union. Bill, like many workers from Pennsylvania coal mining families who came to the Tonawandas to work in defense plants during World War II, was a dedicated unionist—"a labor man." Bill told me that he had started to work in the coal mine but his father had told him to get the hell out of there and get an above ground job in a factory.

In his late thirties, well built, a nice looking guy, Bill thought of himself as a ladies man. Married with children, he seemed to enjoy telling me about his fights with his wife over his escapades. His self-esteem seemed to require him to be always on the alert to be sexually aggressive, at least outwardly, with women inside and outside the plant. He lived in Tonawanda a few blocks away from the Columbus McKinnon plant.

One evening he did something that shook my trust in him. I had thought of him as a close friend, that we had developed a good personal relationship. But that evening, knowing that I was in Tonawanda at another local union's meeting, Bill came to Buffalo to the apartment that Rhoda and I had moved into in the Gates Circle Apartments, next door to The Park Lane. Rhoda told me how surprised she was when she answered the door buzzer and there was Bill. He asked if I was home. Rhoda had met Bill with me before, but he had to remind her who he was. Rhoda told me that when she caught on to his real intention for being there, she wondered if he was the kind of predator who would get physically violent with her. She admitted being frightened but was proud at how easily she had coolly dismissed his clumsy—overly charming—attempt to engage her in sexual banter, what she thought was apparently his prelude to attempting to get to something more serious.

When this happened we were still in that '50s McCarthy period when presidents of some of our local unions were telling me that FBI agents had come to their homes to get them to work towards pulling their locals out of our UE organization. Bill Bentz never told me that he had received a visit from the FBI. But I learned from other local union officers who were visited by FBI agents that one of the tactics that the agents had in mind was similar to the tactic that the Richardson Boat Company had used to push their workers out of our union. I'm not sure that FBI agents were involved with what Richardson did—though they might have been.

That tactic can be summed up very simply. Create a strike and prolong it until the resolve of the striking workers is weakened and they are so desperate to return to work that they abandon the strike and return to work with no union or with a less militant union. In actuality there were several ways that that kind of strike was created. The Richardson Boat Company made proposals that were impossible for the union to accept. However, at another plant where our union also was the bargaining agent for the workers, the Durez Plastics Company in North Tonawanda, a man who said he was a former coal miner from Pennsylvania, but who—in retrospect—I think might have been a paid undercover provocateur planted inside the workers' ranks, blew up another worker's complaint—(a foreman demoted, taking his job, bumping him to a less desirable job though with no cut in pay)—to a pitch where, with no grievance being filed, he used that other worker's problem to lead a walkout of the entire shift, creating a wildcat strike involving workers from all three shifts, and he then agitated to prevent acceptance of any proposed settlement, while blaming the striking local union's officers for the failure to settle the strike.

In other instances FBI agents added another twist to this. Without informing and seeking cooperation of the company, they visited some of our local union leaders in their homes and appear to have intimidated and/or bribed them to initiate and prolong a strike, rejecting as inadequate any settlement proposed by the company and also any settlement proposed by me, the organizer assigned to work with that local union. In those instances the FBI, in their effort to destroy our allegedly Communist-dominated union, seemed willing to victimize the company as well as those workers who were being kept out on strike.

And so one day Bill Bentz, in the middle of the Columbus McKinnon day shift, came running up the stairs to my office in the labor hall in North Tonawanda. I wondered at how agitated he was as he breathlessly told me that the day shift workers had walked off the job and were on their way over from the plant to hold a meeting downstairs in the hall. And then he vomited.

I don't remember what the grievance was that resulted in the workers leaving their jobs. I do remember that Bill, conducting the meeting in the crowded labor hall, made an impassioned speech about not returning to work until there was a satisfactory settlement. Bill had a record of being a good fighter for the people in the shop. His executive board and the bargaining committee and the hundreds of workers, who filled the hall and overflowed out onto the sidewalks in front of the place, trusted his leadership—as I also still did—because as head of the local union he had done a good job. There was a unanimous shouted vote to back up their president and not return to work until the president and the bargaining committee worked out a satisfactory settlement with the Columbus McKinnon company.

After the meeting I phoned the company's personnel man. He proposed an immediate meeting at the plant to talk about the problem. But Bill said that he had to get a strike committee together to set up picket lines at the plant gates to stop second and third shift workers from going in—to let them know that the day shift people, who far outnumbered workers on the two other shifts, had voted to strike the plant. We arranged a meeting with the company for the very next day. The personnel man proposed that we meet in the front office at the plant. But Bill said that he and the bargaining committee would not cross the picket line. We agreed to meet company representatives at the Lafayette Hotel in Buffalo. The way this situation was developing surprised me because I had expected that Bill and his committee would be anxious to set up a meeting with the company that very same day to settle the problem quickly and get the people back to work.

And I didn't understand Bill, his excessive agitation, his vomiting. Something strange was going on. Normally a loud extrovert—before this he'd confidently handled many difficult problems in the shop—Bill appeared to be deeply torn, much too deeply torn, brooding about something bigger than the grievance cited as his reason for leading the day shift workers out on a wildcat strike.

Maybe I am now reading this assessment into it, since I now know the strange way that Bill conducted himself during the strike, seeming to deliberately stretch it out week after week after week—and especially the strange thing that he finally did that seemed deliberately designed to permit the strike to be settled in a such way that he could not be blamed for permitting it to be settled.

The strike, begun in the fall, dragged on into the winter. Bill torpedoed every effort we made to settle the issue, though I still can't remember what that issue was. I argued with Bill. His burly chief steward, a machinist who still worked his farm, argued and swore at Bill. It was evident that Bill was sweating but he resisted every proposal to settle the strike. His committee argued with Bill during breaks in the negotiations but would not disagree with him in front of the company's battery of lawyers and personnel people.

Bill was tense, jumpy, easily flaring up, and I thought that someone might have an iron grip on him, squeezing his balls, forcing him to prolong the strike in hopes of breaking our union.

Then one weekend, with snow falling, Bill—after agreeing to another meeting with company negotiators to take place at the hotel in Buffalo the following Monday—drove deep into the hills of Pennsylvania to visit his father and mother. Early on Monday morning the chief steward got a phone call from Bill in which he said that the snow had blocked the Pennsylvania roads and while he would try to get back to Buffalo in time for the meeting, "you guys go ahead with the meeting with the company—don't wait for me."

On that Monday morning—without Bill—we met with the company's negotiating team and readily settled the strike. Bill returned late the following day, after a special early morning meeting of union members had unanimously ratified the strike settlement. Bill didn't seem to be bothered by that. On the contrary, he seemed relieved, actually laughed. "I guess you guys did better without me."—I had the idea that he was quietly proud that he had found a way out of the trap into which he had been cornered.

Frankly, it was my guess that FBI agents had been putting the heat on Bill. I was more certain of this some time later when two union officers, each representing workers in different factories in Tonawanda, separately told me that FBI agents had been to see them in their homes and—using the same old charge that our union was communist-dominated—had pressured them to work to get rid of our union. And then, not long after that, each of these two men acted in very strange ways, Lou Vucinich creating a novel scenario to escape from the FBI pressure, Sheridan Creekmore creating a novel scenario to produce a strike which he tried to prolong by knocking down every proposal made to settle it.

*****

I'm deliberately, temporarily, breaking off to jump many years ahead—I think it'll be interesting to know now what happened years later to Lou Vucinich and Sheridan Creekmore. When, in 1972, I became a professor in the English Department at Buffalo State College I ran into Lou in the hall of the building where I taught. He must have been in his late fifties by then and he told me he had registered to take some English courses. Some months after that, abandoning the woman he had been living with for many years, Anna, a co-worker at the National Roofing factory, he married one of my colleagues, his English professor, a lovely woman. It was her first marriage. She retired, and they moved to Cleveland. I guessed that she'd be supporting him. And I chuckled as I thought about what a clever unprincipled conniver Lou was—after all, in addition to abandoning Anna in Tonawanda, he had confided to me that he had left his wife and children back in Yugoslavia. As for Sheridan Creekmore, years later he was elected mayor of Tonawanda —that was after he had phoned me, no longer a union organizer, telling me to keep my nose out of the situation when some old friends working at the Durez factory sought my advice about a problem they were having with the company.

*****

But let's go back now to what happened earlier, in the Fifties—with Sheridan Creekmore and Lou Vucinich—starting with wily, slippery Lou Vucinich..

"Man-nee! Man-nee! In Europe, yes! But not here, not here, I didn't think here in America!" Lou, agitated, speaking with his thick accent, pulled out his wallet and quickly snapped it open, showing it to me, then snapped it shut—as if he was some undercover cop identifying his authority.

I guessed what might have happened. Lou might have had a visit from some FBI agents, and an agent might have pulled out his wallet and flashed a badge or I.D. of some kind, scaring the shit out of Lou who was not yet a U.S. citizen.

A giant of a man towering over my head, Lou was a displaced person—"a D.P."—from his home country, Yugoslavia. Polly and Andy Smilinich had warned me not to trust Lou. They said he had been one of the right-wing special guards in Yugoslavia who collaborated with the Nazis during World War II, and that this formal charge had been made against Lou and he had been voted out of the Tonawandas Yugoslav Club. Andy Smilinich was Lou's boss at the roofing company factory—and his wife, Polly, had told me that Lou knew better than to come into their bar across from the factory because he knew she would not serve him.

Lou was a strange mixture. Elected chief steward by his fellow workers at the National Roofing Company, he did a good job on their behalf, aggressively discussing their grievances with superintendent Andy Smilinich. Because of what I had been told by Polly and Andy, I was careful not to trust Lou completely. He talked to me often, going out of his way to be very friendly, thanking me again and again for advice I gave him about some grievance he was handling.

"Thank you, thank you, thank you, Man-nee, thank you!" said always in a way that had me believing he sincerely meant it.

182

Lou nervously pocketed his wallet. He seemed to take it for granted that I read what his pantomime with the wallet meant. I thought it might mean that FBI agents had visited him and asked him to work with them to get rid of what they considered to be a Communist-dominated union.

"Draw up a letter for me that I resign from the chief steward job. I'll sign it."

Realizing that this might be Lou's way to get out from under pressure he might be getting from some FBI agents, I made no effort to dissuade him. But I told him I would not write the resigning letter for him. He would have to write his own letter, his own handwriting, stating simply that he resigns as chief steward. Lou immediately did this, handing me his signed resignation.

But the next day, even more agitated than the day before, Lou confronted me in my office in the labor hall and told me to tear up his resignation letter. He had changed his mind.—"Tear it up—I'm not resigning."—I guessed that FBI agents had told him to get the hell back in there as chief steward and reminded him that he could be deported back to Yugoslavia where the leftist rulers would take care of him.

I felt sorry for Lou and worried about the pressure he must be feeling. In the weeks that followed Lou changed. He who had been a fighter on grievances brought to him by workers in the shop now blatantly refused to recognize the legitimacy of complaints that workers brought to his attention.

A petition was circulated in the shop and several local union officers filed a charge to remove Lou from the office of chief steward. The charge was presented at a special meeting where I was asked to preside and make sure the procedure was handled correctly with testimony and witnesses. Lou had the right to respond. But he made no effort to defend himself. The vote of the members to remove Lou from the office of chief steward was unanimous, not one dissenting vote.

After the verdict Lou firmly gripped my hand and whispered into my ear, "Thank you, Mann-ee! Thank you! Thank you!" I was impressed by the ingenuity with which Lou had slipped out from under the control of those who were pressing him to be their stoolpigeon —*they* use the euphemism: "informant." In that time—during the McCarthy period—FBI agents made little effort to conceal the fact that they were visiting some of our key people, trying to get them to turn against their "Commie union." So I took it for granted that FBI agents were behind what I, now somewhat amusedly, recall what I term "the Creekmore caper."

Sheridan Creekmore came up through the ranks in our local union at Spaulding Fibre. As the result of his militant leadership in several successful strikes, Spaulding workers elected him president of our local union there. ("Creek" had a habit that made me cringe—again and again, on some controversial issue, he would tell his union membership that if they didn't approve what he advocated he would resign.)

When I was promoted to International Representative for our union in Western New York I hired Creekmore to be a fulltime paid organizer on our staff and assigned him to take charge of negotiations for a renewal of contract at Columbus McKinnon. Negotiations stalled on the issue of the seniority clause drawn up by Creekmore. He recommended a strike on the issue, and the workers walked off the job and set up picket lines.

The strike dragged on for weeks, until my boss in the union, Mike Jiminez, and I confronted Creekmore in a private session in my office in the labor hall in Tonawanda. We questioned him about the proposal on seniority he had put together. It was about a page and a half of fine print that was so complicated and ambiguous it was impossible to tell what he was proposing. We asked him if he was proposing departmental seniority or plant-wide seniority or some combination of the two? Creekmore insisted the clause "speaks for itself and it's up to the company to make an acceptable counterproposal." He conceded that the company had made a number of counterproposals but that none of them had been a satisfactory response to his proposal. He didn't deem them worth bringing back for consideration by the striking workers.

Over Creekmore's vigorous objections, we removed him from the contract negotiations. I joined our rank-and-file negotiating committee and we quickly settled the strike with agreement on a combination of departmental and plant-wide seniority, which was overwhelmingly approved by the striking Columbus McKinnon workers.

One of the reasons I had recommended bringing Creekmore onto our organizing staff was that I respected his courage and resistance to FBI agents who, he voluntarily told me, had come to his home and asked him to work with them "against this commie UE union"—and he said he told them he would not work with them to undermine our organization. But now I wondered if he had been truthful with me. Was he working with FBI agents—deliberately prolonging an unnecessary strike at Columbus McKinnon, a provocateur ploy used successfully, though only temporarily, at Remington Rand—but unsuccessfully at Blaw Knox's Buffalo Foundry and Machine—to get the striking workers to turn against our UE union.

What happened to Creekmore?—Again let's briefly jump ahead a few years to when IAM (International Association of Machinists Union) leaders offered to bring our local unions into their organization to help us, they said, to get out from under all the red-baiting. Their representative personally assured me and the other UE District Three organizers, including Creekmore, that they knew about our radical political affiliations but that was in the past and the Machinists Union—with specific approval by the president of the national AFL-CIO—

wanted our "energy and experience"—our "know-how." With a guarantee from IAM that we would be kept on their organizing staff, we recommended that our local unions vote to affiliate with the IAM. And then IAM fired all of us who had been UE organizers—except for one man—Sheridan Creekmore.

*****

Let's get back to the three companies—Durez Plastics, Buffalo Foundry and Machine, and Markel Electric—whose managements had locked out their workers, members of our UE union, to which we retaliated by our people voting to change the lockouts into strikes for a wage increase.

At Durez Plastics the company, seeing that the striking workers were solidly supporting our UE union there, quickly agreed to a wage increase, settling that strike.

At Blaw Knox's Buffalo Foundry and Machine plant there was disagreement—we learned through the grapevine—within the management team on how to deal with our strike there, paralyzing that situation. I phoned the U.S. Conciliator Service and asked them to contact the company to set up a meeting. The Conciliator they assigned was Clarence LaMotte, formerly a business agent for the Machinists Union and a close associate of "labor priest" Healy—the same "labor priest" who was sending letters to Markel Electric strikers, asking them to repudiate the strike they'd voted for and to return to work, rejecting their "Commie union leader Manny Fried."

Week after week U.S. Conciliator Clarence LaMotte—in response to my pressing him to set up a meeting with the company at Buffalo Foundry and Machine—said he had called the company and they refused to meet with us until the striking workers returned to their jobs. So I took great pleasure in phoning him from the company's conference room after—without his help—we met with company representatives and settled the strike with a substantial wage increase.

"Clarence, it's Manny Fried—I wish you'd call again to set up a meeting with Buffalo Foundry and Machine—" He cut me off. "Manny, I just finished calling them again—and they still say they won't meet with you guys until you call off the strike and get the people back—" I cut him off. "Clarence, I'm sitting here right now with the company and we just settled this whole thing with a wage increase."—I thought of saying, "So thank you, you lying hypocrite!"—Instead I just quietly said, "So thanks, Clarence—goodbye." And I slammed down the phone.

Chapter 5

The Markel Electric strike was different Because of the close relationship between the Markel family and Rhoda's Lurie family, the strike dragging on for months kept increasing the pressure on Rhoda to break up our marriage. Rhoda wanted the strike to be settled. She agreed that the workers were underpaid and deserved a wage increase. But the beating I was taking in the newspapers placed her in a bad position with her older brother Howard who was managing the family's Park Lane business since the death of their father.

Rhoda, trying to help find a way out of the impasse at Markel Electric, suggested that we ask her brother-in-law Bunny, married to her sister Annette, what thoughts he had about the situation. Not expecting anything to come of that, but also not wanting to refuse Rhoda's offer of help, I agreed to meet Bunny. Now Bunny was a very successful trader in the agricultural commodities market—a multimillionaire—a nice guy in his forties—who, I expected, had absolutely no use for unions. The maid admitted us into their luxurious apartment in The Park Lane. Bunny and Rhoda's sister Annette greeted us warmly and we all sat on stools at their private bar and we had a few drinks— and finally talked about the situation at Markel Electric. I learned that Bunny did not like what Joe Markel was doing, thought that—with the strike already lasting more than six months—Joe was not doing the right thing by refusing to meet and talk to his workers' union committee. Bunny seemed truly concerned about how the striking workers and their families were surviving.

"You've got Joe Markel licked," he said. "Word at the club is that he's already lost at least half a million dollars. Keep it up another six months he'll crack."

I laughed, a rueful laugh. "Another six months? I don't know if our people can last a few more weeks."

The Buffalo police assigned to monitor our picket lines at Markel Electric were split in their attitude toward the strike. One friendly cop told me to watch out for another cop assigned there who had accepted an electric heater from the company. And one night I received a phone call from a man who said he was a police lieutenant who regularly played bridge with my younger brother Gerry. He warned me that the company had arranged for mounted police to break up our picket lines in the morning so easy access could be provided for scabs to get into the plant.

I got to the plant very early next morning with a hand held motion picture camera and from the moment the mounted police arrived I kept the camera1 lens focused on them. Several times they tried to ride at me with their horses. But a cordon of strikers surrounding me prevented them from getting through to me—and the threat of being photographed apparently prevented them from blatantly busting up our picket lines. Fortunately, I was the only one there who knew that I had not had time to get any film to load into the camera.

Thinking back, it may be possible that many people might find it hard to believe that the way the Markel Electric strike ended really could have happened the way it did. But it did happen that way it did!

There were a few Markel Electric workers regularly crossing through the picket lines every day, ignoring being called scabs by the picketing strikers—not enough of them to produce anything substantial. A middle-aged woman we'll call Doreen—who defiantly crossed the picket lines every morning—lived in a farming suburb outside the city. One morning one of the picketing strikers told me she had heard that Stanley—our chief steward for the amalgamated union which included Markel Electric and Buffalo Foundry and Machine—had boasted that he was going out to Doreen's home that night and use a screw driver to punch holes in the tires of her car.

I confronted Stanley, a burly loud mouth whom I did not trust. Several years earlier at Buffalo Foundry and Machine he had headed the company union which our UE union ousted in an election conducted by the National Labor Relations Board. Stanley's brother was on the Buffalo police force, and the way Stanley talked—echoing the newspaper propaganda about our national union being communist-dominated—I suspected that, through his policeman brother, Stanley might have been contacted by the FBI guys who had been trying to destroy our UE union ever since our union's national convention endorsed Henry Wallace, who opposed the Cold War, to run against Harry Truman, the Democratic presidential candidate who, in order to avoid being labeled "soft on Communism," red-baited worse than the Republicans.

Stanley admitted he intended to go out to Doreen's place and puncture the tires on her car.

I was as stern as I could possibly be. "Stan, don't you dare go out there and monkey with Doreen's car. All we need to get this entire community to turn against us is for you to get caught doing that kind of stupid shit."

On my insistence Stan promised me over and over that he would not go out to Doreen's home that night as he had planned. It might have been Stan's intent to live up to that promise. But as happened with Lou Vucinich who, after he resigned as chief steward at the Roofing factory, apparently was told to withdraw his resignation as chief steward and continue to undermine our union from within—someone, maybe Stanley's policeman brother or FBI agents themselves, must have ordered Stanley to go through with what seems to have been a well planned charade.

Doreen and sheriff's deputies were waiting for Stanley. A deputy sheriff reported to the newspapers that Doreen caught Stanley in the act of puncturing the tires of her car, and that Stanley was apprehended by the sheriff's deputies—caught in the act of attacking Doreen with a screw driver.

Judge Fisher sent us a message. Call off the strike or he'll give Stanley the maximum sentence of many years in jail. The strikers, taking pity on Stanley, voted to call off the strike. Judge Fisher fined Stanley $3000, which I reluctantly persuaded our national office to pay. And a short time later Judge Fisher was named to serve on the state supreme court.

The strikers went back to work—and Joe Markel signed a sweetheart contract with an AFL union, which was what he wanted from the very start.

Chapter 6

"This is the hand that shook the hand of the most dangerous man in Western New York—Manny Fried!"

That was Father Clancy, the Catholic priest heading the adult education program at Buffalo's Jesuit Canisius College—where I had played quarterback on the freshman football team back in the Thirties during a slack time in my New York City theatrical career.

Clancy, his hand dramatically raised, addressed a crowded St. Joseph's breakfast of post office employees. He called for a boycott of The Park Lane "because Manny Fried is married to one of the owners there"—that was my wife Rhoda—"and every dollar you spend at The Park Lane goes to help the Communists."

Whoever was mapping the tactics to drive Manny out of the labor movement—most probably FBI—must have decided the time was ripe for the big push to get rid of Manny. In addition to a flood of red-baiting articles attacking the UE and me, written by reporter Fred Turner in the Buffalo Evening News, a number of "friendly" approaches were made to Rhoda's older brother Howard, warning him that I, because of my bad publicity, was harming the family's business.

As part of this—apparently since *they* had not succeeded in their objective by directly attacking me—*they* went after my wife Rhoda and my two young daughters Lorrie and Mindy, to create pressure to force me to repudiate my union and my politics.

Father Clancy's harangue at the St. Joseph's breakfast was the follow-up to a series of carefully executed maneuvers. FBI agents visited our neighbors up and down the block on Chatham Avenue where we lived and got one neighbor, Eleanor Meilman, to lead a successful campaign to get parents on the block to stop their children from playing with Mindy, age 3, and Lorrie, age 11. Mindy was still too young for Sunday school and dance classes, but neighborhood drivers dropped Lorrie out of car pools for both those classes. The parents, once good friends, were too embarrassed to speak to Rhoda. They gave their hurtful messages directly to Lorrie.—Years later, after Rhoda had died and Lorrie and Mindy had become accomplished adults, Eleanor Meilman phoned me. Sobbing, she asked me to forgive her for what she had done. Momentarily touched by her crying, I said, "It's okay, Eleanor, it's okay."—But it was—and is—not okay.

Our closest friends at the time, Sylvia and Bob Swados, without telling us in advance that they had a message from the FBI to deliver to us, invited us to their home, served us drinks and briefly engaged us in some polite conversation—and then Bob got serious.

"Manny, I have a message to give you—from the FBI. They said to tell you that you must publicly condemn your union and your politics or you will end up in jail." That threat did not surprise me since I had already read in my FBI dossier I'd secured through the Freedom of Information Act that I was listed for "custodial detention." Bob went on to inform me that unless I did what the FBI wanted me to do I also would not get approval from the bank on my application for a veteran's preferred mortgage to buy our home on Chatham Avenue.

When I told Bob that *they* and the bank could not get away with refusing the mortgage to a World War II veteran, he agreed. He also agreed that the situation in our country was not yet such that it would permit *them* to pick me up for "custodial detention."—"Custodial detention" is what was done to Japanese-Americans during World War II.

But Bob went on to say that I owed it to my wife and children to do what the FBI said I must do. I told him, perhaps a little too sharply, not to tell me what I owed to my wife and my children. "That's between them and me. You stay the hell out of that!"

Following up on that confrontation, Bob and Sylvia invited a long list of our mutual friends—predominantly those in Rhoda's Park Lane world—to a grand party in the Hotel Statler ballroom where Bob and Sylvia passed the word along to their invited guests that they should break off all association with Rhoda to get her to bring pressure to bear on Manny "to make him come to his senses and repudiate his radical union and his radical politics."

Then Sylvia asked Rhoda to meet her for lunch at The Park Lane, where—Rhoda told me—Sylvia presented her with the choice: "Divorce Manny or I will never again meet with you or speak to you."

*****

A few years later, after I'd been forced out of the labor movement and I began to write, trying to dig out what might have been behind my desperate effort to hang on to both my union life and my Park Lane life, Rhoda told me that while she was picking up Mindy after grammar school, she by chance ran into Sylva who was picking up her daughter Liz. (Mindy and Liz, two red-haired beginners as guitar players, had been inseparable until Bob and Sylvia broke up their childhood friendship.) Rhoda told me how she had said to Mindy, "Let's go for lunch." And then Sylvia, mistakenly thinking the invite was addressed to her, enthusiastically responded, "Yes, I'd love to do that!" Rhoda told me how she then coldly told Sylvia, "I was not talking to you!"—I don't know to what extent, if any, that encounter had something to with what happened very shortly after that—Sylvia killed herself. It was many years later that Liz Swados wrote her musical play *Runaways*, which got great reviews from the New York critics. I haven't seen *Runaways* performed but I've been told that in it Liz refers to her mother as a runaway, that Sylvia killing herself was "running away."

*****

When Catholic priest Clancy—at the St. Joseph's breakfast attended by post office employees—painted me "the most dangerous man in Western New York" and called for a boycott of The Park Lane because I was married to one of the owners, I wonder if he had already been made aware of the difficult situation in our marriage because of the Markel Electric strike—and was his call for a boycott part of a deliberate effort to force the issue there?

Rhoda was a very decent highly principled person. She adored Lorrie and Mindy. Though she had directly threatened to divorce me because she could no longer take the negative pressure she was getting from her Park Lane family and friends, she was very careful to keep this away from Lorrie and Mindy—they were completely unaware of the threat of divorce—until one day it was unintentionally revealed to Lorrie.

I was sitting in the living room of our home on Chatham Avenue when the front door swung open and eleven year old Lorrie, crying, dashed in and threw herself into my arms. Rhoda, also crying, but not as wildly as Lorrie, came rushing in immediately behind her.

Rhoda breathlessly explained. "She said you told her everything and I thought she meant you told her we're getting a divorce."—But Lorrie had been referring to the earlier talk I had with her as I tried to explain why the Markel Electric workers were still striking—"they want to get a decent pay to support their families."

That dramatic scene—Lorrie reacting to the fear that Rhoda and I were going to divorce and separate—changed our home into a depressing morgue. Any time Rhoda or I came near Lorrie and Mindy, Lorrie would protectively grab and tightly hug Mindy, pulling her away from the two adult monsters. Mindy, at age 3, echoing Lorrie's fear and apprehension, was teary, but I don't think she really knew why everything in the house had suddenly become sad.

So let's get back to: "This is the hand that shook the hand of the most dangerous man in Western New York—Manny Fried—he's married to one of the owners of The Park Lane and every dollar you spend there goes to help the Communists."—Father Clancy had actually shaken my hand a few days before he made that fierce denunciation. I had come to listen to the panel of speakers at a public conference at Canisius College—I forget what the subject was—and Father Clancy crossed the room to me, hand extended, and he shook my hand and pleasantly acknowledged my presence. Since I had been a student at Canisius I suspected no sinister intent on his part.

When Rhoda's older brother Howard Lurie—who was actively managing The Park Lane—was told by his insurance agent, a prominent Catholic layman, about Clancy's call for a boycott, he panicked. He phoned Rhoda in her painting studio in The Park Lane and asked her to meet with him immediately in his office. Rhoda told me that Howard had already asked his insurance agent to set up a meeting with Clancy and that to avoid a boycott he was ready to agree to do whatever Clancy asked him to do. He told her that if he had to, he was ready to tell Clancy that she would be cut out of any connection with The Park Lane business—the rest of the family would buy out her part of ownership. Howard had told her he expected her to object to this. So he had offered her an alternative choice.

"It's probably a very difficult choice for you to make. But it should satisfy Clancy and remove the threat of a boycott. You can end your marriage to Manny. File for divorce. And you keep your part ownership of The Park Lane."

In retrospect, it's interesting that although Rhoda had already told me that with all the heat she was taking from her Lurie family and her friends in her Park Lane world because of the bad publicity I was getting about my union work and my politics—and that although she had already told me she had definitely decided that she just had to divorce me—she, surprisingly, was utterly devastated when Howard told her that she had to divorce me in order to placate Clancy and still not be cut out of her part ownership of The Park Lane. I think that Howard made it no longer just a thought in her head, something she might or might not do. Suddenly divorce was for real. While she probably was not consciously thinking about it, I believe she was so deeply distraught because she sensed that if she were cut out of the Park Lane ownership she no longer would be treated in her social set as she had been treated all her life—their crowd looking up to her as Miss Park Lane.

But then a phone call I unexpectedly received from a close friend of my brother Martin changed everything, we thought. Ethel Quinn was prominently recognized in the Catholic community in Buffalo, possibly because her uncle was Cardinal O'Hara, a real power nationally in the Catholic Church.

Her voice was ecstatic. "Manny, I have good news for you. I called my uncle, Cardinal O'Hara, in Baltimore. I told him what's happening here. And he's taking care of everything. Father Clancy is being transferred immediately to Syracuse—and a group of nuns are publicly scheduling their big dinner to be held at The Park Lane. No boycott."

*****

What happens after that is embodied in my one-man autobiographical play *Boilermakers and Martinis*. It's a play that I performed without a script, once in the back room of Rust Belt Books in Buffalo and then five times on the stage of a store front theatre in North Adams, Massachusetts, after which I embodied the material in a script that I used as a sort of a road map—excerpting the order of the beats or scenes from the script when I did one performance, without sticking to the script, at BackLot Theatre in Sarasota, Florida.

Boilermakers and Martinis is a play about my effort—my arrogant and mistaken belief—that I could keep my life running on two separate tracks—the UE union world and The Park Lane world—what I felt at the time was an exciting life, having it all, within each day easily moving back and forth across class lines—sometimes going directly from walking a picket line with striking members of our union to have lunch with Rhoda at The Park Lane—or going directly from The Park Lane to the picket line—or to write and run off leaflets in the union office—and/or to pass out leaflets to workers entering or leaving the factory—or to sit across the table from a management team, negotiating a contract—or arguing on behalf of one or more of our union members who had filed a grievance against the company—and then maybe a stop at a bar for a drink (a boilermaker or its equivalent) with the union guys—and maybe from there back to meet Rhoda for a drink (a martini or its equivalent) at The Park Lane.

*****

What followed the phone call from Ethel Quinn I embody in some detail, telling this directly to the audience, in my performance of *Boilermakers and Martinis*—I go with Rhoda to report the good news to Howard. He's already heard it from his insurance agent friend who says he's talked about it to the bishop and has good advice for Howard.

"With your brother-in-law Manny still married to your sister—we've got a sword hanging over our head—we're still in trouble."

Rhoda is annoyed with Howard:

"You imagine the worst. And you don't fight back."

Howard responds:

"Look, I don't like kissing their ass any more than you do. But if that's what it

195

takes to survive I'm going to smile and I'm going to eat their shit and say it tastes like honey."

A few days later Howard phones Rhoda to meet him downtown in their lawyer's office to sign some papers connected with the business. He tells her it'll take only a few minutes. Rhoda comes back from that meeting, runs upstairs into our bedroom and slams the door shut behind her. I carefully knock on the door. No answer. I knock again.

"Don't come in."

Hours later I come back upstairs to our bedroom door and knock softly.

"I've cooked dinner. The table's all set. The kids are waiting ... C'mon down and eat."

"I'm not hungry."

"Can I come in?"

"No."

I tell the kids their mother doesn't feel well. And after I tuck them into bed and read to Mindy, I knock on our bedroom door and—not waiting to hear from Rhoda—I open the door and quietly step into the blackness of the room. I carefully shut the door behind me.

"Can I turn on the light?"

"No."

My eyes become accustomed to the darkness. I sit on the edge of the bed and reach to touch her. She pushes my hand away.

"What happened?"

It takes a while before she can say anything.

"They said they had plane reservations for me and the kids tomorrow to Miami—and a lawyer ready there to meet me with papers to get a divorce."

She stops and I hear only gulping sounds she can't completely suppress. Then quietly. Not an accusation. A factual statement.

"You won't quit."

I have a hard time saying it, but it's best to get it said and face it.

"If you don't divorce me, they cut you out of the business."

This time it's a pained cry of accusation.

"You won't give an inch."

"Rhoda, anything else—everything else—everything other than that—I'll do anything you want me to do—but I can't— I won't—do that."

The finality with which I intentionally say it so the door is firmly closed—we both know what I mean—breeches the dam, and I can feel the convulsive movement of her body making the bed shiver as she cries in a terribly muffled way that wrenches a spontaneous burst from my gut.

"Rhoda! If it hurts that much, do it! Divorce me!"

That produces an anguished burst from her.

"I don't want to divorce you!"

In the darkness we both fumble to reach and hold each other—tight—our cheeks pressed together—wet.

We stay together, both giving up what The Park Lane means to each of us.

*****

Forced out of the labor movement—blacklisted—hired by a series of employers in western New York—and after each employer is visited by FBI, fired—then finally accepted as a broker to sell life insurance for the U.S. Division of a Canadian company whose top executives refuse the FBI effort to get them to deny me permission to sell their insurance policies—I do well financially, union members I had represented extending themselves to buy life insurance policies from me—do well enough to have time to write about my experience as a UE union organizer married to one of the owners of The Park Lane. And FBI furiously intervenes, trying to prevent production of my plays and publication of my fiction and nonfiction books.

*****

When I was still a union organizer I had been writing a story each week for the CIO's weekly paper in western New York, *The Union Leader*—stories drawn from my union experience at the time—and Hugh Thompson, director of the area's umbrella labor organization, the Congress of Industrial Organizations— told me that, although he did not want to drop my stories from the union's paper, he felt that he had to accede to FBI's insistence that my stories not be published—the same Hugh Thompson who met frequently with heads of the local branch of the Communist Party, asking their help to organize workers in area factories into CIO local unions—the same Hugh Thompson who told me "you're not doing a good job as a union organizer unless you're called a Communist"—the same Hugh Thompson who, when Phil Murray, national head of CIO, acceded to pressure from the Catholic hierarchy and launched a purge of Communists from the CIO, publicly attacked me and urged our UE local unions in Western New York to turn against me and leave our UE organization—the same Hugh Thompson who then, in a private telephone

197

conversation with me, told me he disagreed with the purging ordered by Phil Murray—the same Hugh Thompson who was then fired (that phone conversation obviously overheard by someone tapping into his or my phone)— the same Hugh Thompson who must have gone through hell, backtracking, perhaps having to grovel in some way, and was then reinstated to a position on the CIO staff, but transferred out of western New York where he and his wife had been friendly in a personal way with both Rhoda and me—he was transferred to Boston, Massachusetts.

*****

I'm still trying to figure out why the FBI so vigorously tried to prevent recognition and production of my play *The Dodo Bird* and other plays I wrote after that. *The Dodo Bird* deals with the effort of a working stiff, a blue collar alcoholic, to put his personal life together after his family has been broken up by his going though the experience of being laid off from his job, then enduring a long and difficult strike, followed by permanently losing his job when the factory is closed.

Performed Off-Broadway in New York City in 1967, getting great reviews from the critics, *The Dodo Bird* has been performed regularly since then in cities all over our country, most recently, in 2006, for a 5 week run, here in Buffalo, where it was highly praised by the critics and received support from the entire community—and not a jot of interference from FBI.

The only thing I can come up with as the FBI's reason for trying to kill *The Dodo Bird* back in the '60s—and then for trying to kill the plays and books I wrote during the 30 or so years after that—is that they objected not so much to my plays or my novels and non-fiction stuff, but to me personally, thinking that if I was recognized widely as a worthwhile writer writing about my experience with union and The Park Lane—working class and the rich class—and FBI and all the rest, it might give me a national and possibly even an international platform from which to express my strong leftist views.

I had learned from Angus Cameron, a senior editor at the Knopf publishing firm, that with my writing I was capturing something new, something unique about the change in society in our country and beyond—a drastic change similar in its importance to what playwright Gerhardt Hauptman captured when in the 19th century he wrote *The Weavers*, his play depicting the effect upon society, especially class relationships, caused by the development of the factory with its steam engines replacing the individual craftsmen, the weavers.

"You can count the fingers on one hand and have fingers left over"—Angus Cameron told me—"counting the number of writers who've had the combination of factory and union and theatre and literary and working class and upper class and political and academic experience you've had—who are writing about it."

The FBI apparently thought that this kind of writing by this writer made him dangerous—"the most dangerous man in western New York."

*****

Through all the turmoil in our lives, Rhoda painted every day in her studio—until 3 o'clock in the afternoon—when she rushed to the refrigerator to pour the martinis she beforehand had prepared in a glass pitcher.

Wondering about it now, I can't help thinking that while life with me was often very difficult for Rhoda, it was not dull, not ordinary, not boring. (Half joking, I often said, to Rhoda and to friends, "Boring is grounds for divorce.") Despite all the agony Rhoda endured because of my union involvement, I believe that tied in with that there existed for her, as well as for me, a strong vein of deep and positive love and excitement. Rhoda told me—several times—she believed what I was doing was right, good, worthwhile—though she wished someone else, not me, would be doing it. But then our married life would have been much different, and I'm not sure Rhoda would have enjoyed that different kind of life—a life that, by comparison with the tumultuous life she did lead with me, might have been so ordinary and run-of-the-mill—and yes, boring for her—that she might have sought excitement in more adventurous relationships, playing sexual games with some of the many men who had been chasing after the gorgeous sexy Miss Park Lane.

It would be nice to be able to say at this point that we lived happily ever after that anguished scene in which Rhoda chose to remain married to me, giving up her share of ownership of the elitist apartment house and its restaurant and cocktail lounge—The Park Lane.

Shunned by her friends in that Park Lane world because of me, Rhoda developed close ties with a group of fellow artists—painters—who set aside differences in background and political views to join her once a week in her studio—becoming her good friends—and painted models she provided—not professional models—usually people she did not previously know, people she saw on the street or met with me at meetings or conferences or in theatres—and, thinking they'd be interesting to paint, she'd ask them to sit as models for her group of painters.

Rhoda, by hard work, became a fine painter. Now, at last, long after her death following a stroke in 1989, some of her paintings are drawing public attention. But back then—after I was forced out of the labor movement and was selling life insurance while writing some plays and novels—Rhoda had difficulty selling her paintings. Both of us believed that that was in great part because, in the minds of those who might have bought her paintings, she had chosen to stay married to a "Communist" who refused to publicly repudiate his political and labor activities.

Despite the very difficult bumps in the road, I believe it was a strong loving bond between us that kept us together for 48 years until Rhoda died. ("I'll protect you and you protect me and we'll both be safe.") But the bumps that were there created a constantly recurring melancholy tone beneath the surface of our relationship, prompting us to continually try to sort out our lives together by meeting with a series of therapists, psychologists and psychiatrists, on and on and on over a period of many years, both fumbling for understanding, trying to fight off the heavy burden that kept clouding our relationship. But with each of these therapists we would finally reach that point where Rhoda could no longer hold back her anger and resentment, could no longer completely choke off the tears as she would painfully burst out, "I did nothing wrong and they punished me because of him." And when we'd leave she would tell me she would not continue any further with that particular therapist because "he/she is on your side."

Unfortunately Rhoda died before the political tide shifted and being married to me—getting publicly praised for my writing and for my opposition to the House UnAmerican Activities Committee—might have helped her gain the recognition as an artist that she wished for and deserved, erasing her bitterness, making her life with me something she might be proud of and enjoy.

In many of Rhoda's paintings I see an underlying tone of sadness and depression—connected, I believe, to her difficult life being married to me—a sadness and depression especially evident in her self-portrait hanging on the wall directly above the computer/word processor on which I am now writing, trying to get hold of and convey the dynamics beneath this flickering candle in the wind.

Part Four

"At 95 still asking: 'Why?'"

"If I could, would I do it all over again the same way?"

That question prompted me to write and perform my one character play *Boilermakers and Martinis*, and each time I performed the play, I departed from the script, spontaneously hitting upon and expressing new and deeper understanding of what had happened.

Even now, at 95, I have a light bulb flashing in my head, as I think way back to over fifty years ago, to 1954—the McCarthy era—when I was still an organizer for the UE union, subpoenaed to appear before HUAC—the House Un-American Activities Committee—which led to my receiving a letter from Albert Einstein that contributed, I believe, to Rhoda's resolve to weather the hell that the FBI, to pressure me, deliberately injected into our marriage. (This is detailed in the DVD made of my performance of *Boilermakers and Martinis* before an overflowing audience—added seats inserted in the aisles.)

During the McCarthy era, as part of an effort of the Washington administration to destroy our UE union, in part because of our support for Henry Wallace who ran against Harry Truman for president—Wallace opposed the Cold War, thought we could work things out with the Soviet Union—HUAC staged hearings in Schenectady just prior to an election between the new government-sponsored IUE union and our UE union, involving thousands of General Electric workers. Typically, just prior to the actual voting in these elections, IUE distributed leaflets with a replica of the ballot and an American flag in the box labeled "IUE" and the Soviet hammer and sickle in the box labeled "UE."

Mike Jiminez, next in line above me in our union, told me that Albert Einstein had said that it would be good if someone subpoenaed to appear before HUAC would refuse to recognize the committee's right to exist—not citing any of the constitution's amendments to avoid answering—directly charging that the committee was unconstitutionally created, since no area had been specifically designated for it to investigate; therefore HUAC had no right to ask anybody anything.

I respected Mike. He had fought in Spain, singlehandedly blowing up bridges to slow down the advance of Francisco Franco's forces who were pursuing retreating loyalist troops, Mike becoming the inspiration for Ernest Hemingway's hero in his novel *For Whom The Bell Tolls*. Mike, in World War II, had been O.S.S. General Donovan's favorite, dropping alone by parachute behind enemy lines to contact and coordinate tactics with anti-Nazi partisans, many of them veterans of the battle against Franco's forces in Spain.

Mike had confided to me that General Donovan had told the HUAC guys that if they ever subpoenaed Mike he, Donovan, would blow the whistle on every bit of dirt he had on each one of them. I did not question how Mike got that advice from Albert Einstein, while he went on to say, "I wish I could have the great opportunity you have here to be a real hero."

I remember retorting, "You're so full of shit, Mike—you're damn glad it isn't you."

And Mike laughed his agreement with that.

I followed Einstein's advice, so the courts would decide if I go to jail or if HUAC is dissolved. (All this is detailed in my "autobiographical non-fiction novel *The Un-American*.)

Mike gave me the Princeton University address of Einstein and urged me to write Einstein, telling him what I had done.

Einstein replied.

"Dear Mr. Fried:

I am convinced that you did the right thing and fulfilled your duty as a citizen under difficult circumstances.

My respect,

(Signed) A. Einstein

Albert Einstein"

A Buffalo Evening News writer responded to my press release about the Einstein letter by reporting that he had called Einstein who told him it was wrong of me to have made the letter public that way.

But then my wife's brother George, my brother-in-law, a college librarian at that time, told me he had contacted the Princeton University librarian who checked it out and reported back that it was definitely not Einstein, but someone else at the university whom the Buffalo Evening News writer must have spoken to.

Although HUAC issued a press release stating that they would have Congress indict me, they did not do that—possibly not wishing to risk an adverse court decision ending their existence.

*****

Thinking about it now, that letter from Albert Einstein—a copy posted on my kitchen wall, the original placed in my safe deposit box at the bank—did not slow down the FBI effort to fulfill their objective embodied in the warning that they had had that same newspaper reporter pass on to me—that I am "the symbol of the Left who must be broken."

Just recently, my two daughters, browsing through the thousands of pages in my FBI dossier, estimated that our government had wasted a few million dollars of taxpayers' money to have agents trail me, bug my phone, check through my garbage, talk to my neighbors, my employers, producers, drama critics, publishers, newspaper reporters, other labor guys, and many others—apparently, breaking Manny Fried has become a full industry for the FBI, extending—according to my dossier—over a period of more than seventy years. Yet I've been arrested only once in my entire life, and that was for passing out leaflets to Columbus McKinnon factory workers in Tonawanda, New York, urging them to exercise their right to vote in a state-wide election. I was charged with violating a city ordinance requiring prior approval of the leaflet by the city officials—an ordinance ruled unconstitutional by the city judge who dismissed the charge—after I had spent several hours in jail.

*****

While the FBI continued that effort to tear me down, other individuals and organizations, local and national, even international (BBC—British Broadcasting—and Canadian drama critics, etc.) moved more in more in the opposite direction, granting me honors and awards in recognition of my "lifetime achievement"—often for doing the very things that was prompting the FBI to try to destroy me.

As late as 1993 when I was 79—almost 40 years after the 1954 HUAC and Einstein episode—I received an envelope from the FBI that contained only a photocopy of a column written by a liberal Buffalo News reporter, Donn Esmonde, in which he praised my contribution to defense of civil liberties, after he had written an earlier column in which he had ridiculed new material I'd received (not requested by me) to add to the thousands of pages of my FBI dossier I had already received years earlier under the Freedom of Information Act. I assume it was the FBI's way to let me know they were still keeping tabs on me.

*****

I assume the FBI did not like me writing about what they had done to me and my family over a period of many years. But I believe that as long as the FBI refuses to admit publicly what they have done to me and my family—the immoral, unethical, illegal and just plain rotten things they did—they are preserving their right, their intention, to do those same things to others.

*****

Over a period of several years I gradually shared my experience, my personal stories, with David McDuff, a wealthy local publisher who seemed to enjoy questioning me during the many times we met for lunch. He had registered to join the Western New York Playwrights Workshop that I conducted for over 20 years—to write his play exploring his life, his transition from a North Tonawanda factory worker to a very successful sophisticated businessman publishing magazines and newspapers—and developing his "cash cow"—supplying the classified ads to newspapers all across the country, including The New York Times. Despite his millions, he was unhappy with his marriage—and we spoke about that, eventually about his divorce, and exchanged many other confidences about our lives.

*****

It was David McDuff who at one point suggested that I write this memoir.

I said, "David, who the hell would publish it?"

And he said, "I will."

As I wrote this memoir David read chunks of it. He continually challenged me: "Despite all the difficulties it created for you and your family, why did you stick to what you were doing?" He set aside every answer I gave him, forcing me to dig deeper and deeper.

I've thought about it—and thought about it—and thought about it—and still keep thinking about it, trying to get at a deeper and deeper understanding of the why. I would now tell David that I believed what I was doing was right, and believing that, I could not respect myself if I copped out, if I retreated because of fear—and that in the long run, if I retreated because of fear, I believed that Rhoda and my children, looking back as time went by, would also lose respect for me—that I could not let myself retreat, and I actually consciously decided that even if I faced a firing squad to be shot, I would not deny doing what I believed was right.

But unfortunately I can not tell this to David—he developed cancer in his brain, fought bravely over a period of many months and finally licked the cancer, but died at age 58 just a few months before I am writing this—died because the treatment to kill the cancer, including stem cell experimental treatment to restore full function of his brain, fatally destroyed his internal organs.

*****

I respectfully dedicate this memoir to my generous friend David McDuff.

*****

And I believe David would understand why I also dedicate this memoir to my brother Gerry—we were the two red haired "boys" in our family of nine children—Gerry wanted to be an actor like his older brother but after seeing my poverty-stricken life as an actor took the road to become a very wealthy businessman. However, when he retired he bankrolled the Gerald Fried Theatre Company, heading a partnership between the two of us and my closest friend after Rhoda died, actress Roz Cramer, and my friend, playwright Rebecca Ritchie, who for years was part of my Playwrights Workshop. Gerry died a few months ago at age 90 and we officially dissolved his theatre company.

*****

David and Gerry, wealthy generous men who publicly defied the FBI to defend me.

BOOKS PREVIOUSLY PUBLISHED
BY EMANUEL FRIED

The Dodo Bird

Drop Hammer

Elegy for Stanley Gorski

The Un-American

Big Ben Hood

Meshugah and Other Stories

Made in the USA
Charleston, SC
11 August 2010